W9-CLA-729

ISBN 0-634-04058-8

7777 W. BLUEMOUND RD. P.O. BOX 13819 MILWAUKEE, WI 53213

Visit Hal Leonard Online at
www.halleonard.com

CONTENTS

Barracuda

Words and Music by Roger Fisher, Nancy Wilson, Ann Wilson and Michael Derosier

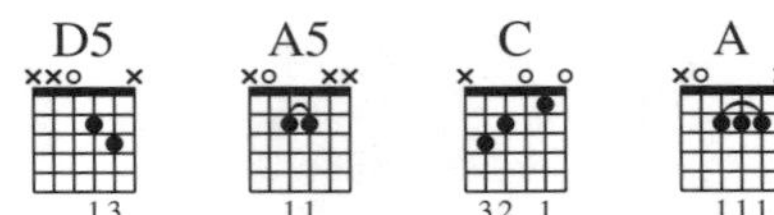

Intro

Moderately fast Rock ♩ = 132

E5 F♯5 G5

Gtr. 1 (elec.)

f

slight P.M.

8va

-1/2 -1/2

Harm.

w/ bar

loco

E5 F♯5 G5 G6 N.C.

Gtr. 2 (elec.) w/ dist. *f*

slight P.M.

Gtr. 1 *divisi*

Harm.

w/ bar

- 1/2 -1 1/2

E5 F♯5 G5

Gtr. 2

slight P.M.

Harm.

w/ bar

-1/2 -1/2 -1/2 -1/2 -1/2

Gtr. 1

slight P.M.

Harm.

E5
F#5 G5
G6
slight P.M.
Harm. w/ bar
Verse
1. So this ain't the end, I saw you a - gain
to - day.
2. Back o - ver time we were all try - ing for free,
I had to turn my heart a - way.
you met the por - poise and me.
C5
C5/B
C5/A
G5
w/ bar
-1/2
-1 1/2

2nd time, Gtr. 2: w/ Rhy. Fill 1
E5
Uh huh.
slight P.M.
slight P.M.
E5
Csus2
Smile like the sun, kiss - es for ev - 'ry one,
No right, no wrong; sell - ing a song, a name.
slight P.M.
slight P.M.
Rhy. Fill 1
Gtr. 2
slight P.M.

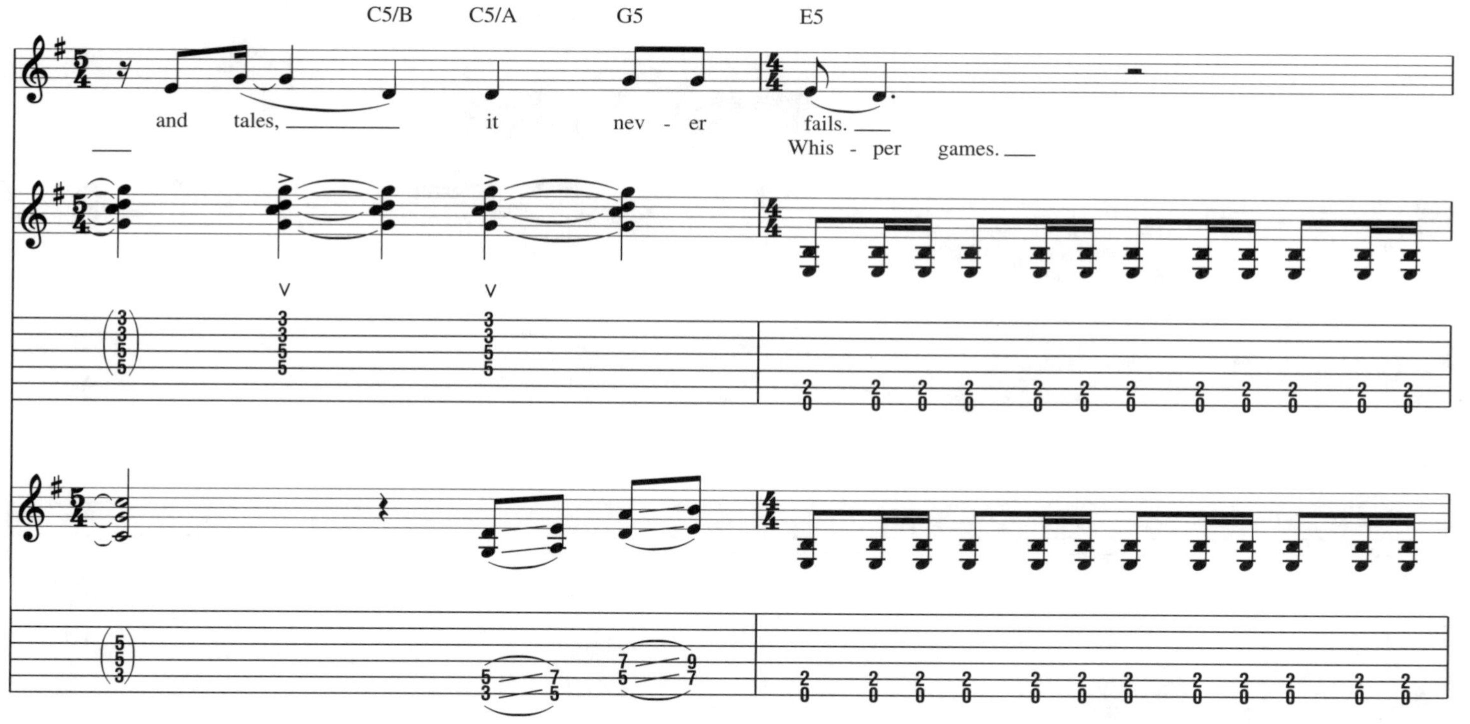
C5/B C5/A G5 E5
and tales, it nev - er fails.
Whis - per games.

Chorus
C5 C5/B A5
2nd time, Gtr. 1: w/ Rhy. Fill 2
E5
You ly - ing so low in the weeds. I
And if the real thing don't do the trick you bet - ter
Rhy. Fig. 1A
Rhy. Fig. 1

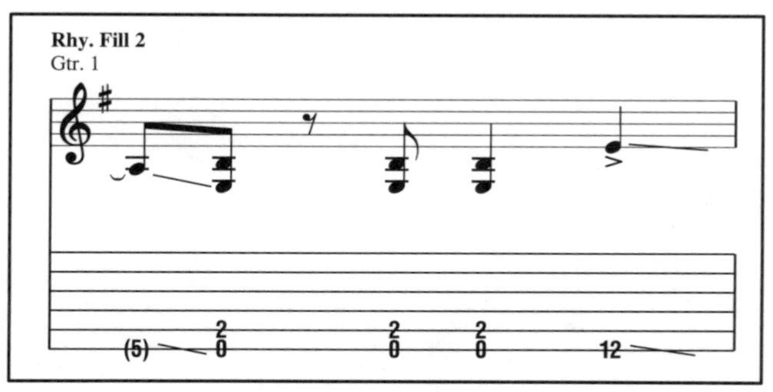
Rhy. Fill 2
Gtr. 1

C
Am
E5
D5
Rhy. Fig. 2
Gtr. 3 (acous.)
mp
bet you gon - na am - bush me.
make up some - thing quick.
You'd have me down, down, down,
You gon - na burn, burn, burn,
To Coda
Gtr. 3 tacet
A5
N.C.
End Rhy. Fig. 2
down on my knees,
burn, burn it to the wick.
now would - n't you, bar - ra - cu -
End Rhy. Fig. 1A
End Rhy. Fig. 1

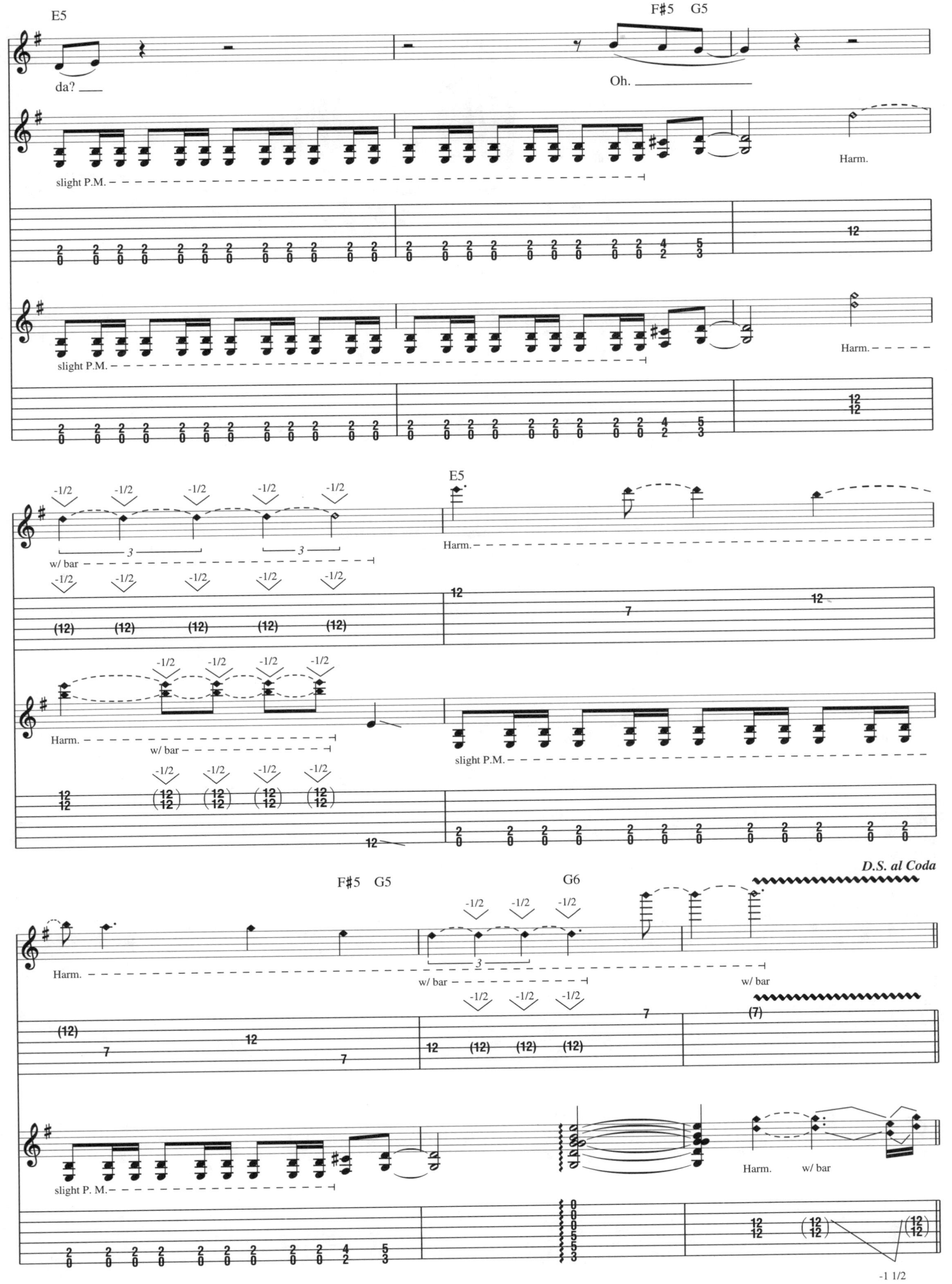
E5
F#5 G5
da?
Oh.
slight P.M.
Harm.
w/ bar
-1/2
E5
F#5 G5
G6
D.S. al Coda
slight P. M.
-1 1/2

Coda
Gtr. 3 tacet
N.C.
E5
G5 A5 D5 E5
Ooh, bar - ra - cu - da.
Oh, yeah.
Gtrs. 1 & 2
Rhy. Fig. 3
slight P.M.
G5 A5 D5 E5
End Rhy. Fig. 3
Bridge
C
A
Rhy. Fig. 4A
Gtr. 3
End Rhy. Fig. 4A
"Sell me, sell you," the por - poise said. Dive down, deep down, save my head. You,
Gtr. 1
Riff A
End Riff A
Gtr. 2
Rhy. Fig. 4
End Rhy. Fig. 4

Gtrs. 1 & 2: w/ Rhy. Fig. 3
Gtr. 3 tacet
E5
G5 A5 D5 E5
I think that you had the blues too.
Gtr. 1: w/ Riff A
Gtrs. 2 & 3: w/ Rhy. Fig. 4 & 4A
G5 A5 D5 E5 C
All that night and all the next
A
swam with - out look - ing back, made for the west - ern
E5
pools.
F#5 G5 A5 E5
Sil - ly, sil - ly fools.
F#5 G5 A5
Gtrs. 1 & 2
Rhy. Fig. 5
End Rhy. Fig. 5
slight P.M.
Guitar Solo
Gtrs. 2 & 3: w/ Rhy. Fig. 4 & 4A
C
Gtr. 1
w/ chorus
A
Gtr. 2: w/ Rhy. Fig. 5 (2 times)
E5
F#5 G5 A5
E5
F#5 G5 A5
Gtrs. 2 & 3: w/ Rhy. Fig. 4 & 4A
C
steady gliss.
w/ bar
A
G5
Gtr. 2: w/ Rhy. Fig. 5 (2 times)
E5

F#5 G5 A5 E5 F#5 G5 A5
The
P.S.
Chorus
Gtrs. 1 & 2: w/ Rhy. Figs. 1 & 1A
C5 C5/B A5 E5 C Am
real thing don't do the trick, no, you bet - ter make up some - thing quick.
E5
Gtr. 3: w/ Rhy. Fig. 2
D5
You gon - na burn, burn, burn, burn, burn it to the
A5 E5
wick. Oh, bar - ra - bar -
Gtr. 2
Harm.
w/ bar
slight P.M.
Gtr. 1
fdbk.
w/ bar
slight P.M.
pitch: F#

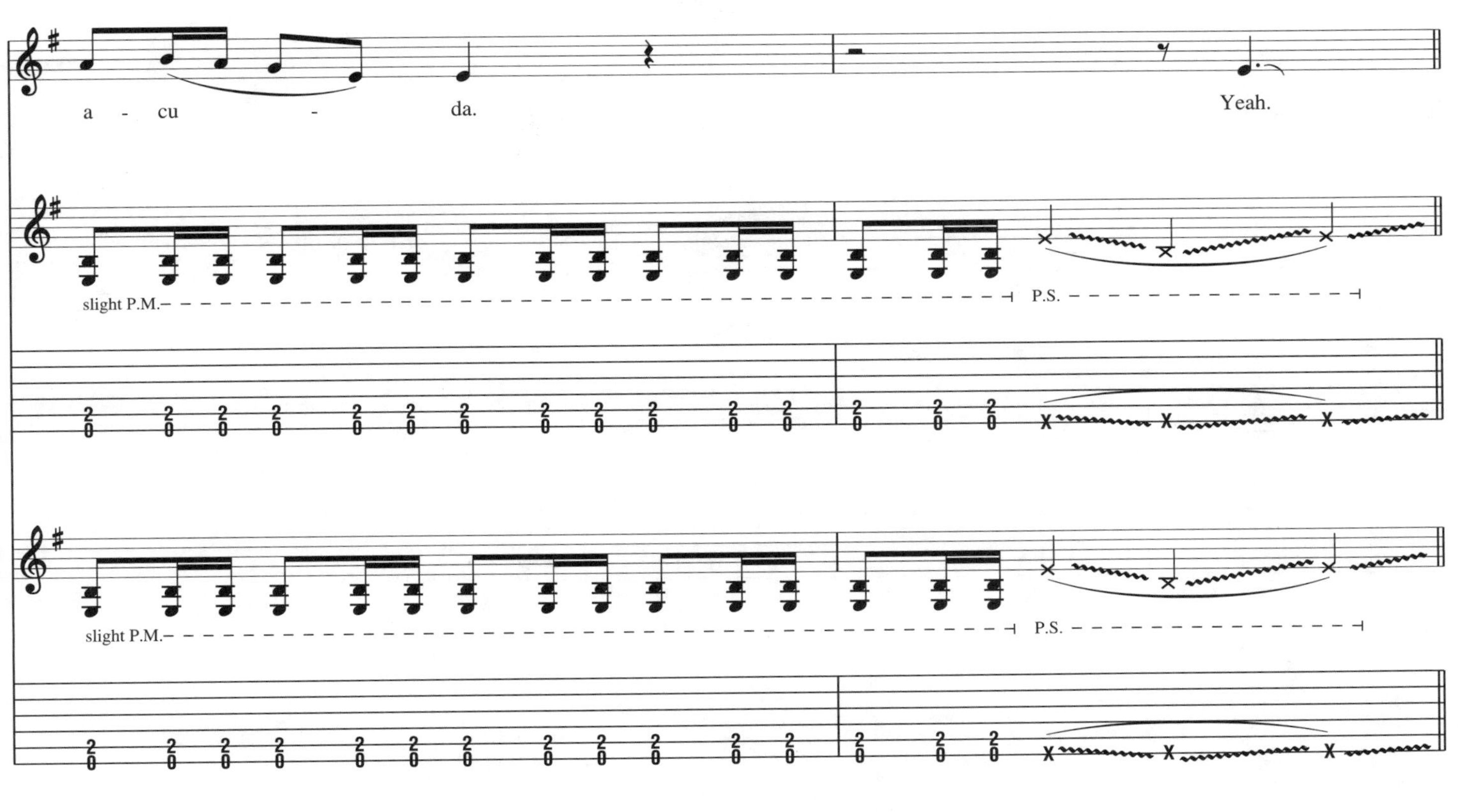
a - cu - da.
Yeah.
slight P.M.
P.S.
slight P.M.
P.S.

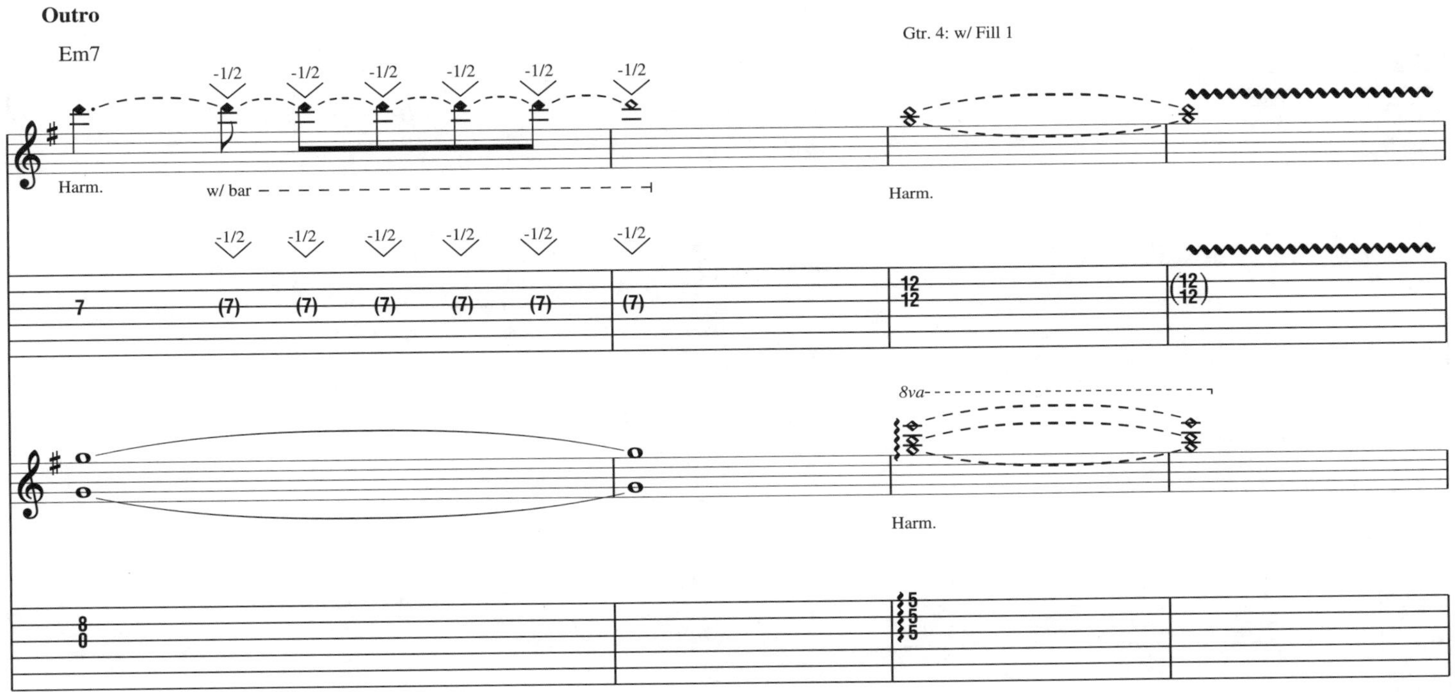
Outro
Em7
Gtr. 4: w/ Fill 1
Harm.
w/ bar
Harm.
8va
Harm.

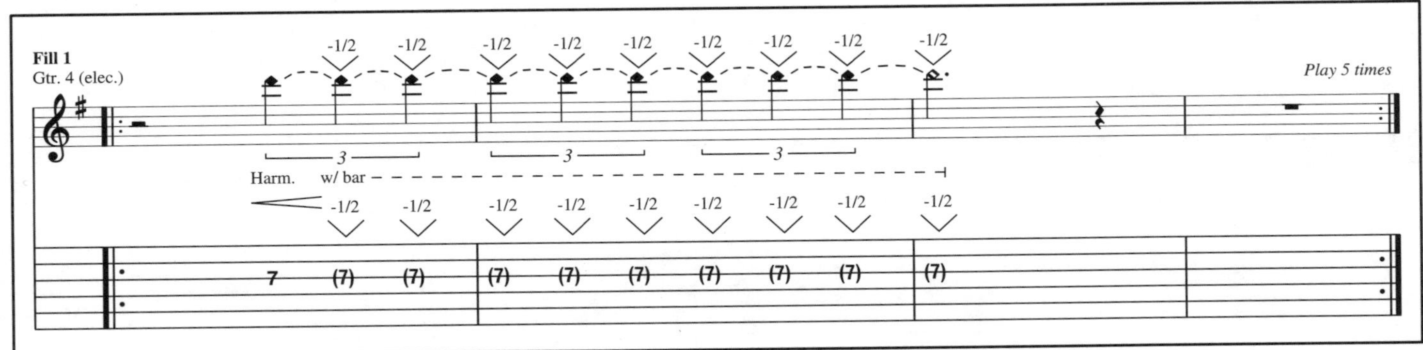
Fill 1
Gtr. 4 (elec.)
Play 5 times
Harm.
w/ bar

-1/2 -1/2 -1/2
Harm.
w/ bar
-1/2 -1/2
Harm.
w/ bar
w/ bar
loco
-1/2 -1/2 -1/2 -1/2 -1/2
Harm.
w/ bar
Harm.
w/ bar
Harm.

Gtr. 2
Gtr. 1 tacet
Harm.
w/ bar
Harm.
w/ bar
Gtr. 1
1.
2.
Ooh,
Harm.
Gtr. 2: w/ Rhy. Fig. 5 (5 times)
E5
1.-4.
5.
F#5
G5
A5
F#5
G5
A5
oh.
* Sing 1st time
Gtr. 1
slight P.M.

Best of My Love

Words and Music by John David Souther, Don Henley and Glenn Frey

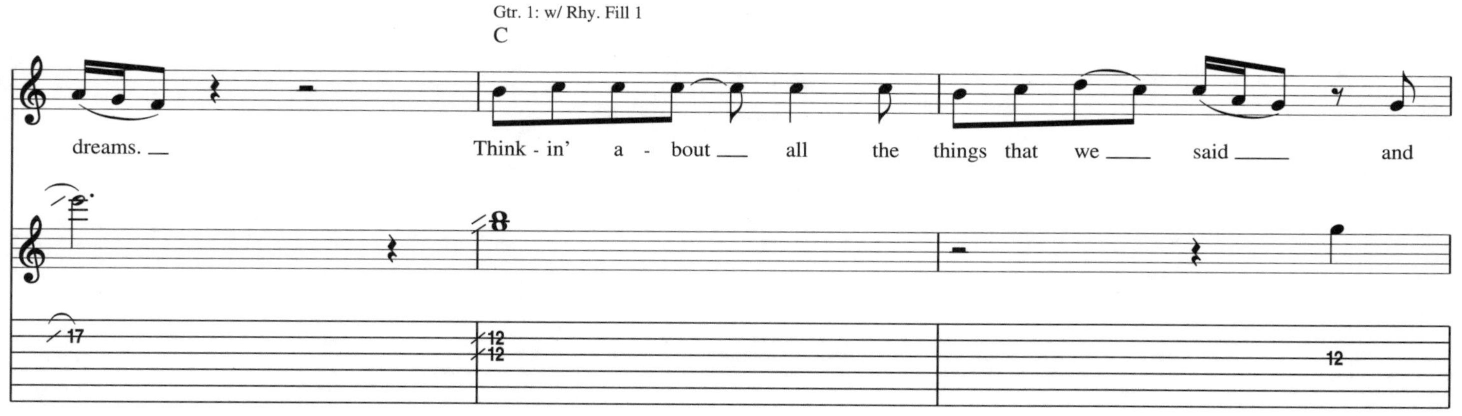
Gtr. 1: w/ Rhy. Fill 1
C
dreams.
Think - in' a - bout all the things that we said and
17
12
12
12

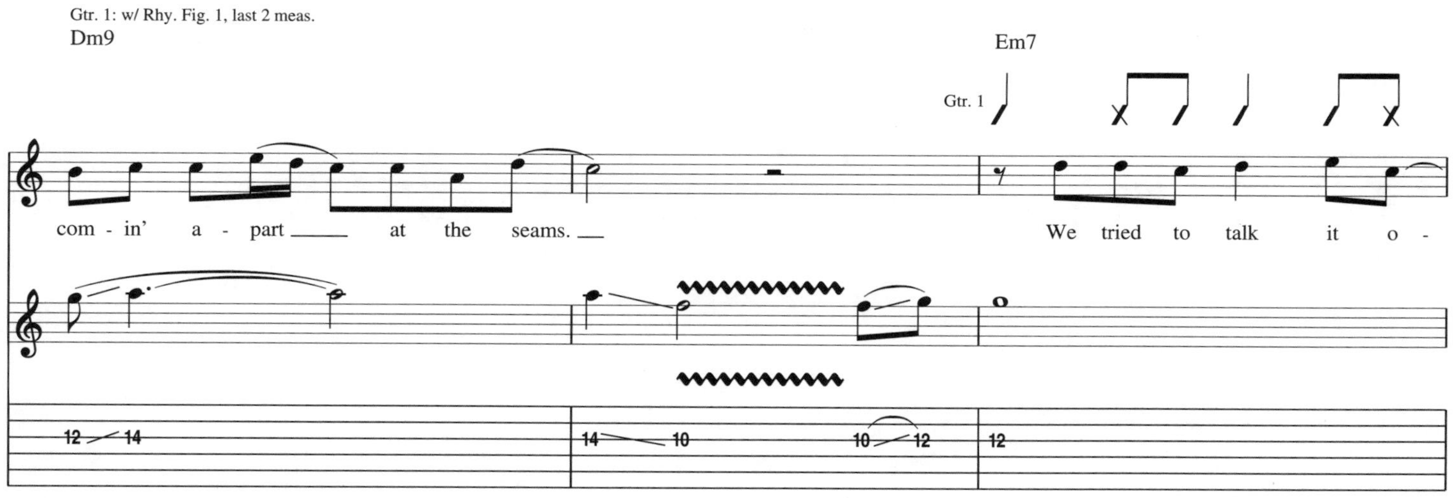
Gtr. 1: w/ Rhy. Fig. 1, last 2 meas.
Dm9
Em7
Gtr. 1
com - in' a - part at the seams.
We tried to talk it o -
12 14
14 10 10 12
12

Dm7
Em7
F/G
(cont. in notation)
- ver but the words come out too rough. I
10 10 10
12 11 12
12 11 12
(12)
(12)
10
10
10 7 8 7

Rhy. Fill 1
Gtr. 1
let ring
T
A
B

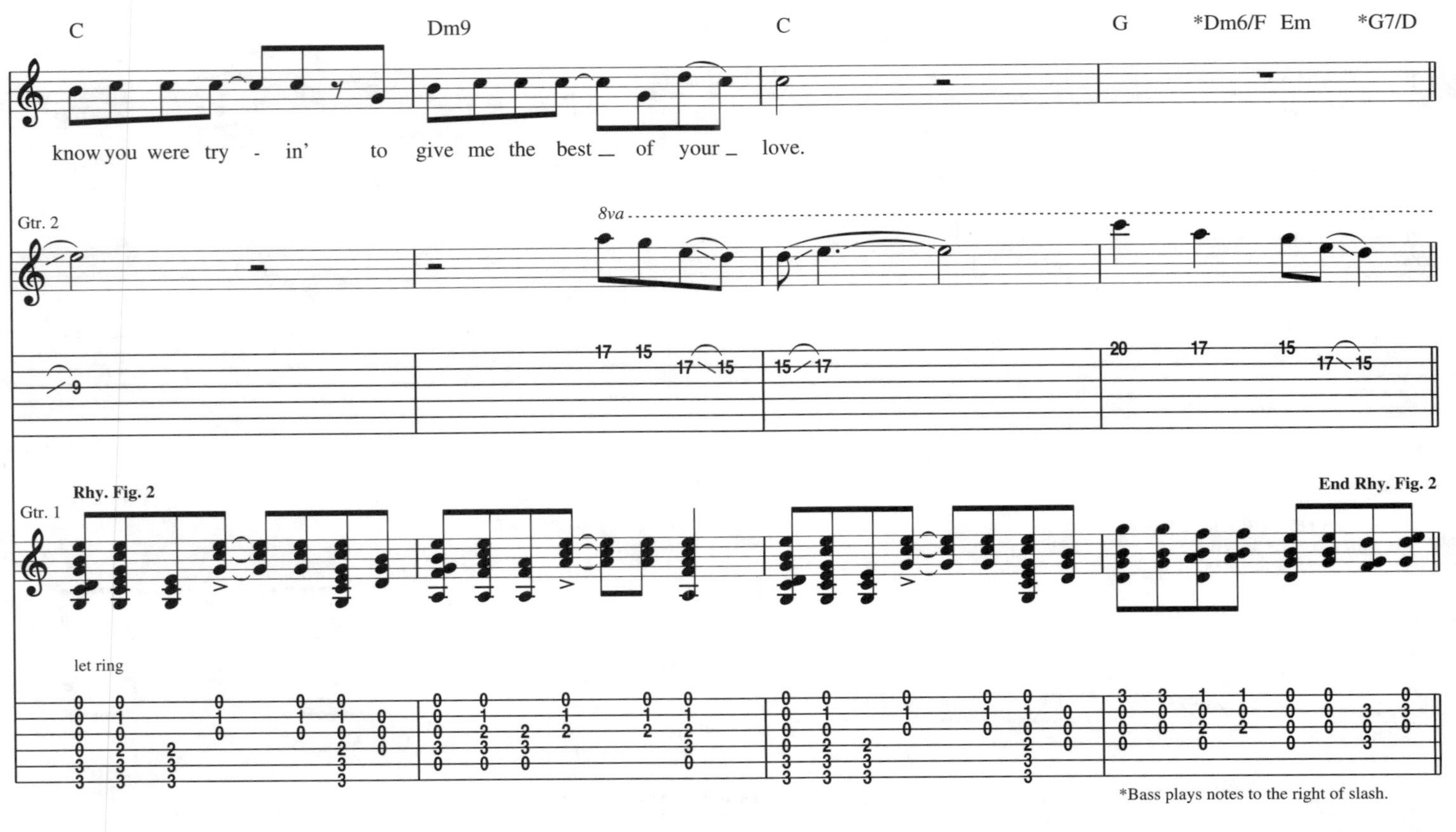
C
Dm9
C
G
*Dm6/F
Em
*G7/D
know you were try - in' to give me the best _ of your _ love.
Gtr. 2
8va
Rhy. Fig. 2
End Rhy. Fig. 2
Gtr. 1
let ring
*Bass plays notes to the right of slash.

Verse

Gtr. 1: w/ Rhy. Fig. 1, 2 times, simile
C
Dm9
2. Beau - ti - ful fac - es and loud emp - ty plac - es, look at the way that we live. _
Gtr. 2
8va
loco

C
Dm9
Wast-in' our time _ on cheap talk and wine _ left us so lit - tle to give. _ That

Em7
Rhy. Fig. 3
Gtr. 1
Em7
same old crowd was like a cold, dark cloud that we could nev - er rise a - bove.
(Oo.
Oo.
Dm7
End Rhy. Fig. 3
Gtr. 1: w/ Rhy. Fill 2
G7
Gtr. 1: w/ Rhy. Fig. 2
C
Dm9
But here in my heart, I give you the best of my
)
C
G
Dm6/F
Em
G7/D
Chorus
C
Rhy. Fig. 4
Gtr. 1
love.
Whoa,
sweet dar - lin',
(You get the best of my
Rhy. Fill 2
Gtr. 1
let ring

*F
Cmaj7
you get the best of my love. Whoa, sweet dar -
love.)
*Bass plays D.
F
End Rhy. Fig. 4
- lin', you get the best of my love.
(You get the best of my love.)
p
mp
Bridge
Fm7
Cmaj7
I'm go - in' back in time and it's a sweet thing. It was a
(Oo.)

Fm7
Dm7
G7
quiet night, and I would be alright if I could go on sleeping 3. But
*Fret higher note w/o slide
Verse
Gtr. 1: w/ Rhy. Fig. 1, 2 times, simile
C
Dm9
ev'ry morning I wake up and worry what's gonna happen today.
C
Dm9
You see it your way and I'll see it mine, but we both see it slippin' away.
Gtr. 1: w/ Rhy. Fig. 3, simile
Em7
Dm7
Em7
You know we always had each other, baby. I guess that wasn't enough.
(Oo. Oo.

Gtr. 1: w/ Rhy. Fill 2
Gtr. 1: w/ Rhy. Fig. 2
Dm7
G7
C
Dm9
Oh, oh, but here in my heart, I give you the best of my
)
Outro-Chorus
Gtr. 1: w/ Rhy. Fig. 4, till end, simile
C
G Dm6/F Em G7/D C
love. Whoa, sweet dar - lin',
F
Cmaj7
*Voc. Fig. 1
End Voc. Fig. 1
you get the best of my love. Whoa, sweet dar-lin',
(The best of my love.)
8va
loco
mp
p
*Refers to downstemmed notes only.
F
C
*Voc. Fig. 1A
End Voc. Fig. 1A
you get the best of my love. Whoa. sweet dar - lin', ev - 'ry night and day,
(The best of my love.)

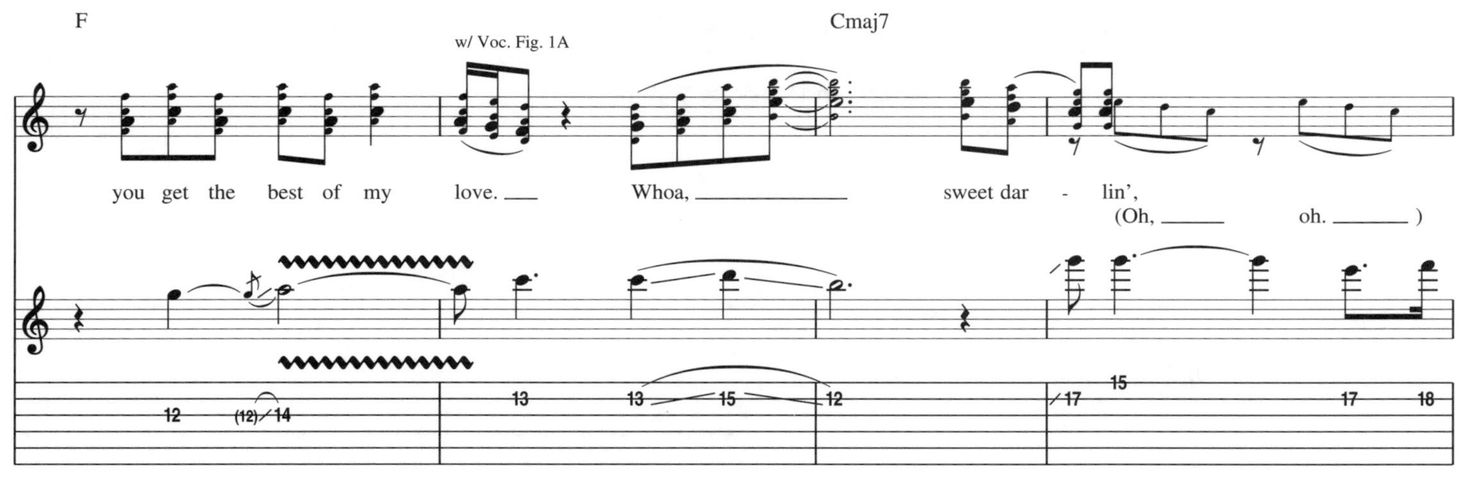
F
w/ Voc. Fig. 1A
Cmaj7
you get the best of my love.
Whoa,
sweet dar - lin',
(Oh, oh.)

Begin Fade

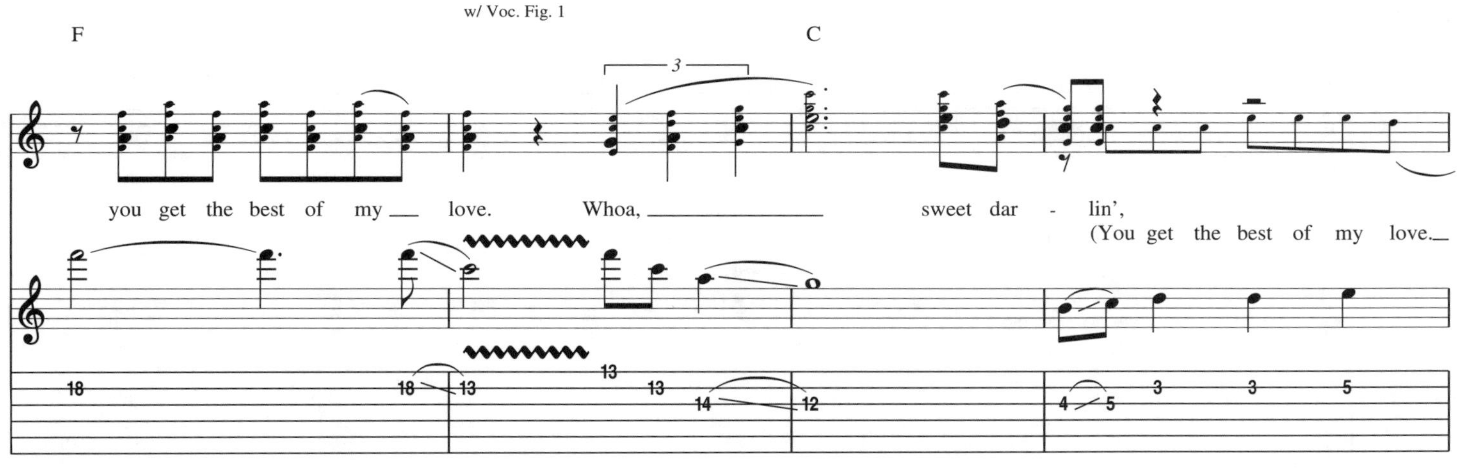
w/ Voc. Fig. 1
F
C
you get the best of my love.
Whoa,
sweet dar - lin',
(You get the best of my love.

w/ Voc. Fig. 1
F
Cmaj7
you get the best of my love.
Whoa,
sweet dar - lin',
)
(Oo.

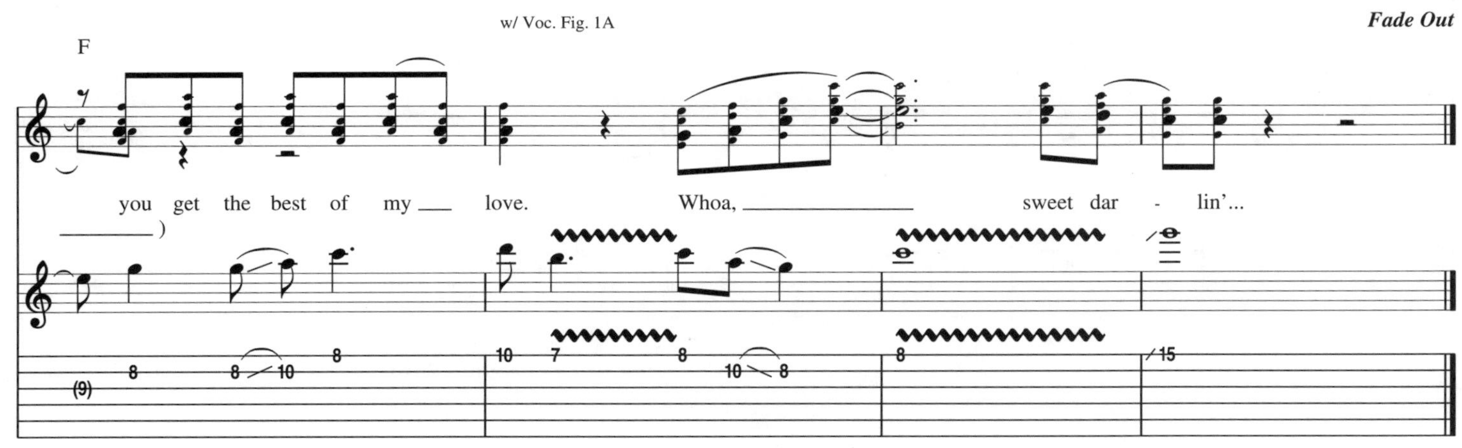
w/ Voc. Fig. 1A
Fade Out
F
you get the best of my love.
Whoa,
sweet dar - lin'...
)

Blue Collar Man (Long Nights)

Words and Music by Tommy Shaw

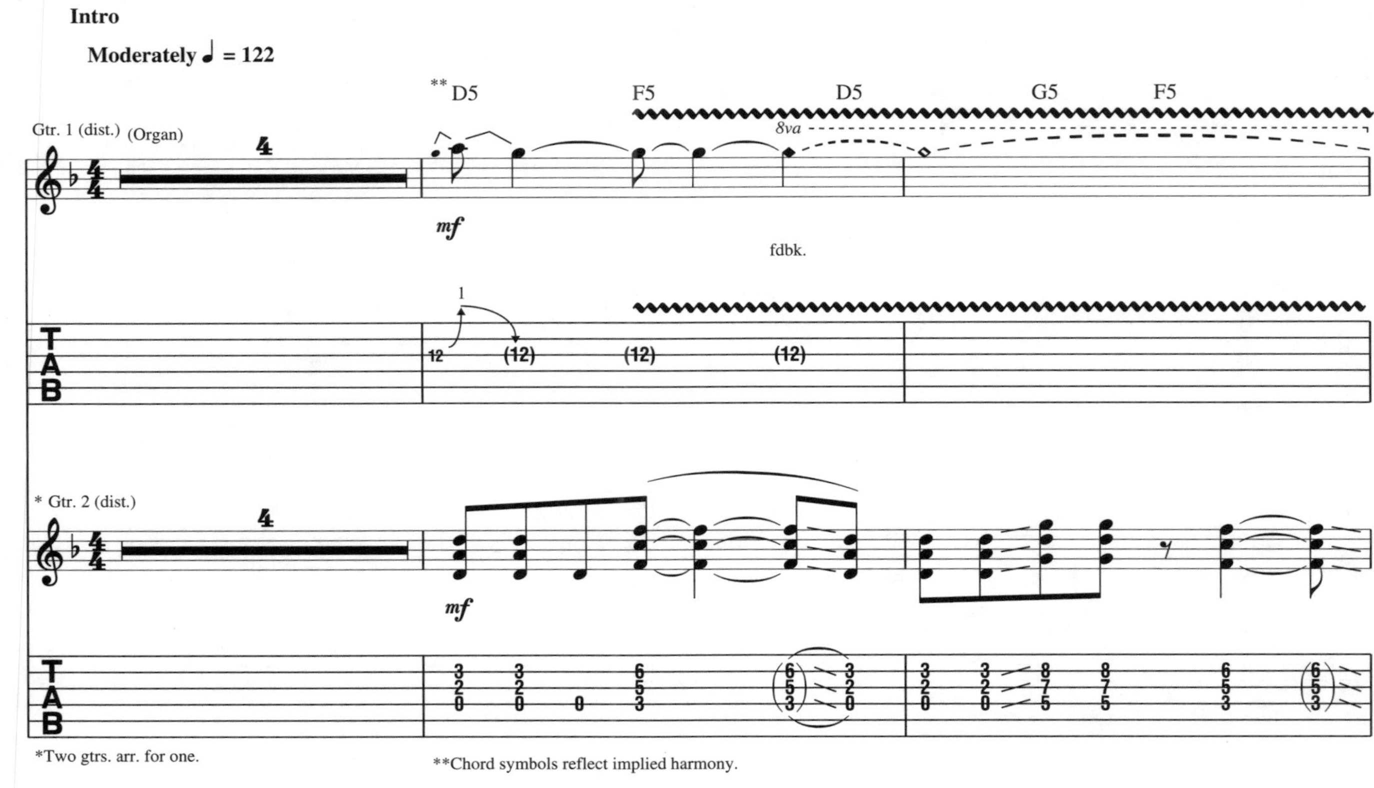

*Two gtrs. arr. for one.

**Chord symbols reflect implied harmony.

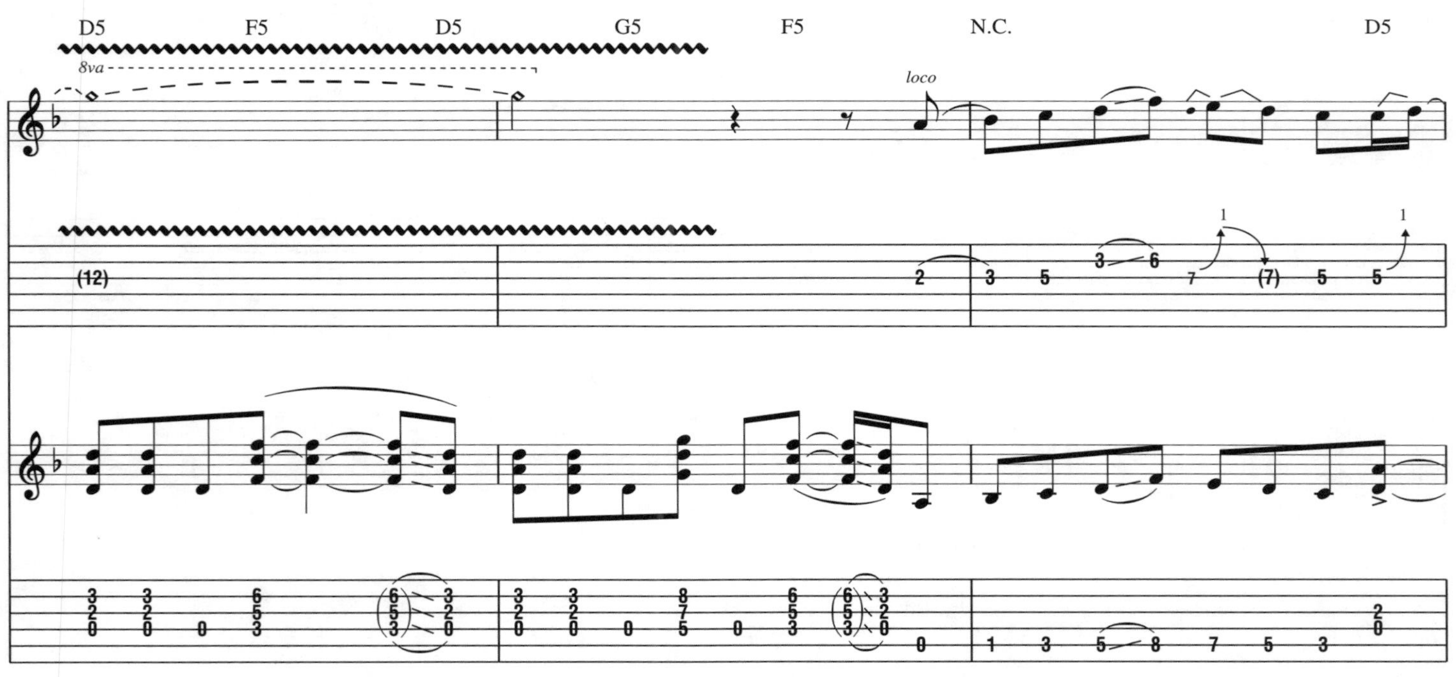

Verse

Gtr. 1 tacet

D5 G5 Gm G5 B♭5 C5

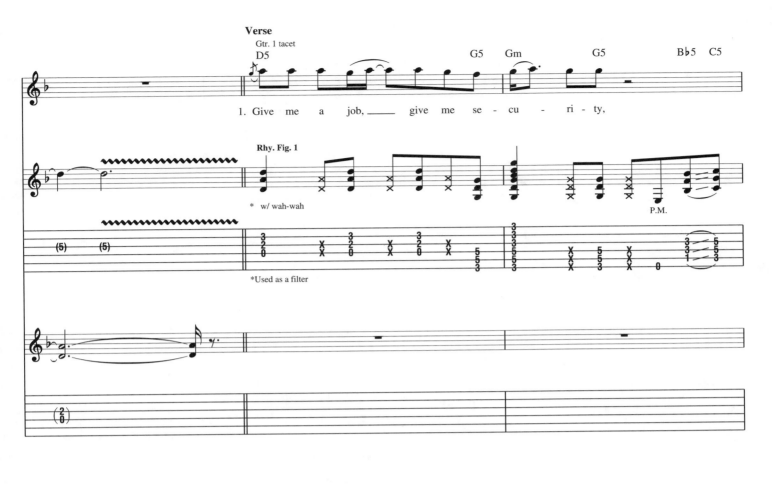

1. Give me a job, give me se - cu - ri - ty,

Rhy. Fig. 1

* w/ wah-wah

P.M.

*Used as a filter

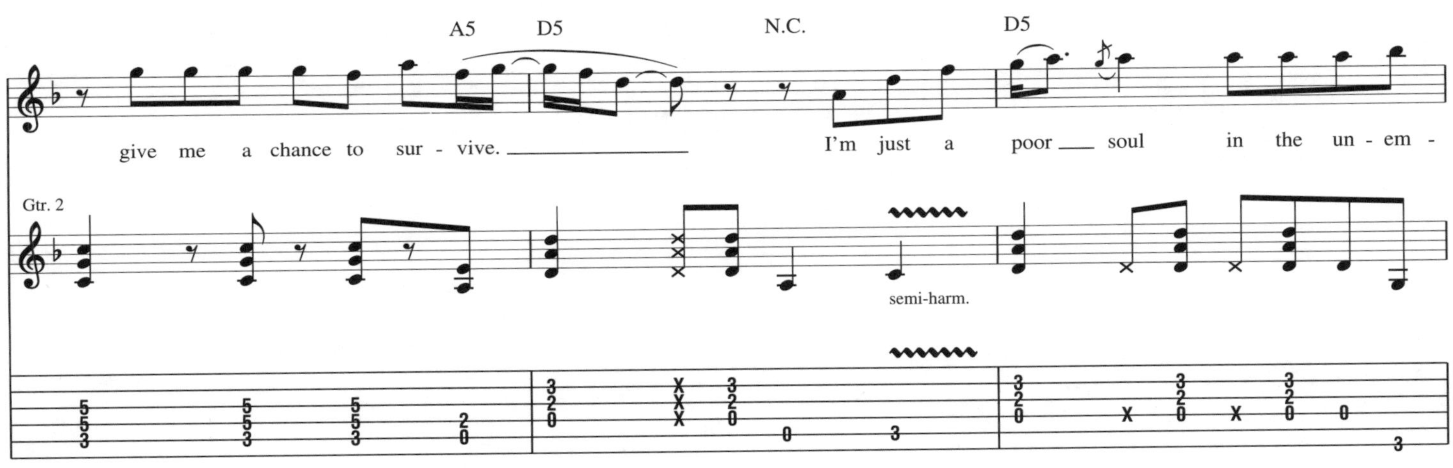

Verse
1st time, Gtr. 2: w/ Rhy. Fig. 1
2nd time, Gtr. 2: w/ Rhy. Fig. 1, 1st 3 meas.
D5
G5
Gm
G5
B♭5
C5
moth - er and fath - er, my wife and my friends,
3. Make me an of - fer that I can't re - fuse.
2nd time, Gtr. 2: w/ Rhy. Fill 1
2nd time, Gtr. 2: w/ Rhy. Fig. 1, last 4 meas.
A5
D5
N.C.
D5
I see them laugh in my face. But I've got the pow - er, and I've
Make me a re - spect - ab - le man. This is my last time in the un - em -
Gm
B♭5 C5
C♭5 B♭5 N.C.
got the will. I'm not a cha - ri - ty case.
ploy - ment line, so like it or not.
I'll take those...
Chorus
3rd time, Gtr. 1; w/ Fill 1
D5
B♭/D
C5/D
D5
B♭
C5
Voc. Fig. 1
End Voc. Fig. 1
(Long nights, im - pos - si - ble odds.)
1. Keep - in' my eye to the key -
2., 3. Keep - in' my back to the
Gtr. 2
Rhy. Fig. 2
P.M.
D5
D5
B♭/D
C5/D
D5
To Coda
Voc. Fig. 2
End Voc. Fig. 2
hole. If it takes...
wall. If it takes...
(All 1., 3. that 2., 4. night to be just what I am.)
Well, I'm
End Rhy. Fig. 2
P.M.
Rhy. Fill 1
Gtr. 2
Fill 1
Gtr. 1

1.
N.C.
D5
N.C.
gon - na be a blue col - lar man.
Gtr. 1
Gtr. 2
D5
2.
N.C.
gon - na be a blue col - lar
Bridge
D5
man.
Keep - in' my mind on
Gtr. 2
Rhy. Fig. 3
P.M.

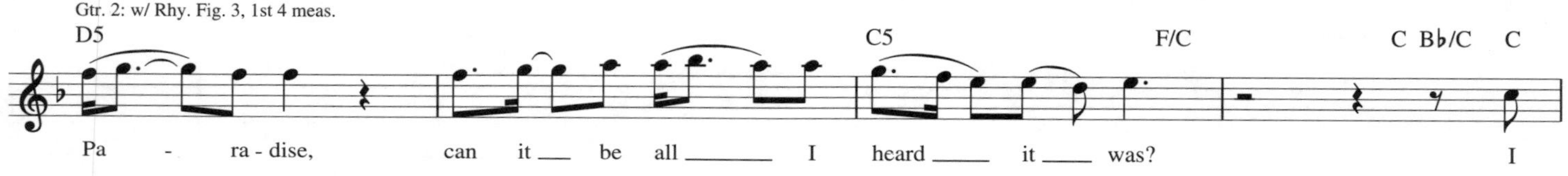

*Harmonic located six-tenths the distance between the 3rd & 4th frets.

Guitar Solo

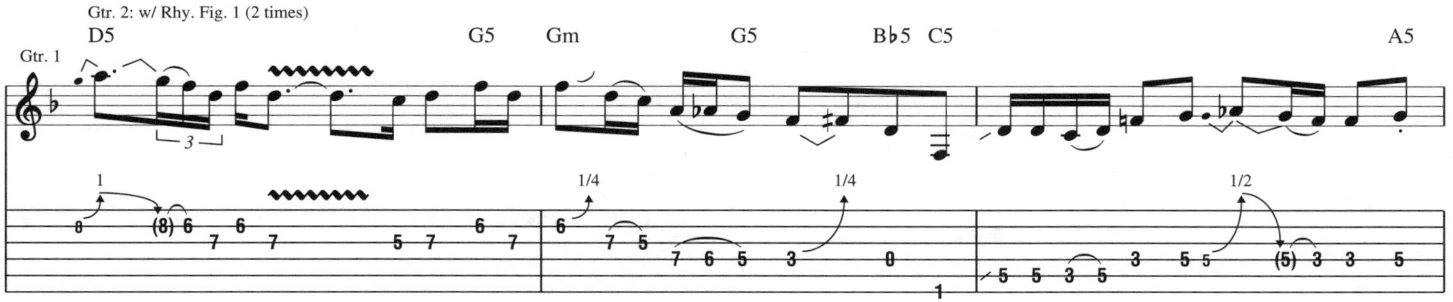
Gtr. 2: w/ Rhy. Fig. 1 (2 times)
D5
G5
Gm
G5
B♭5
C5
A5
Gtr. 1
1
1/4
1/4
1/2

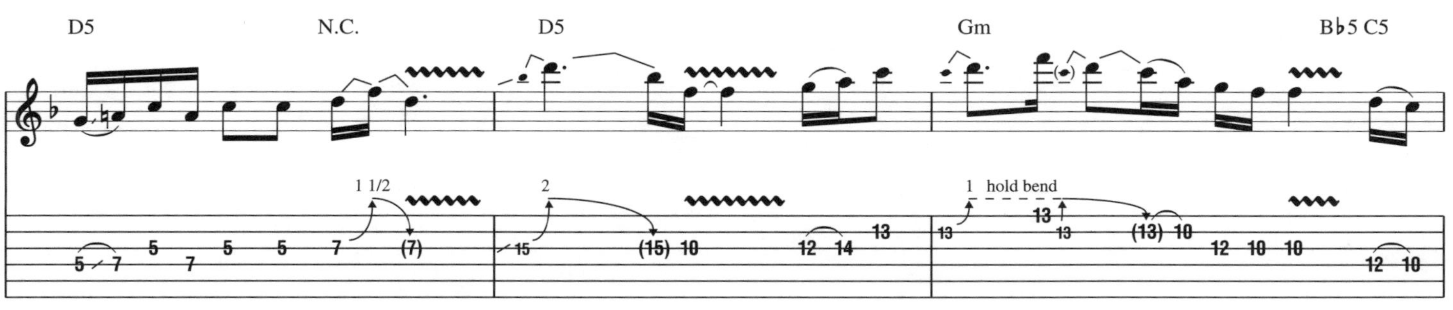
D5
N.C.
D5
Gm
B♭5 C5
1 1/2
2
1 hold bend

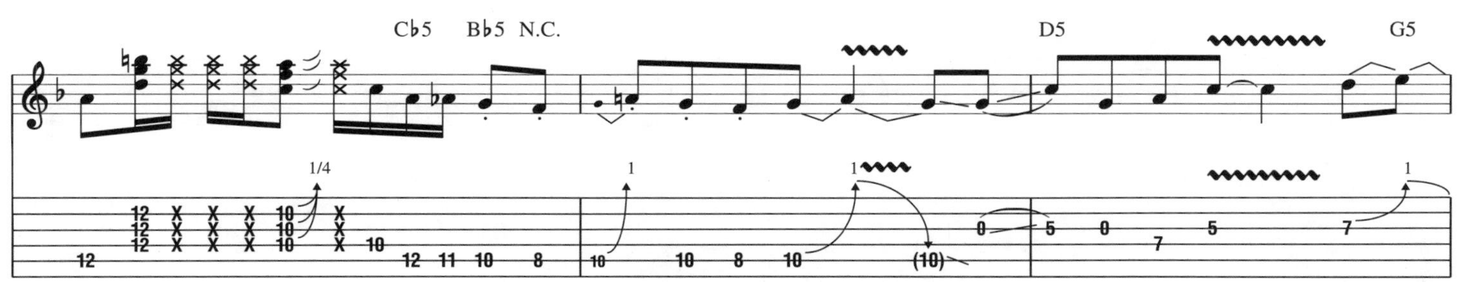
C♭5
B♭5
N.C.
D5
G5
1/4
1
1
1

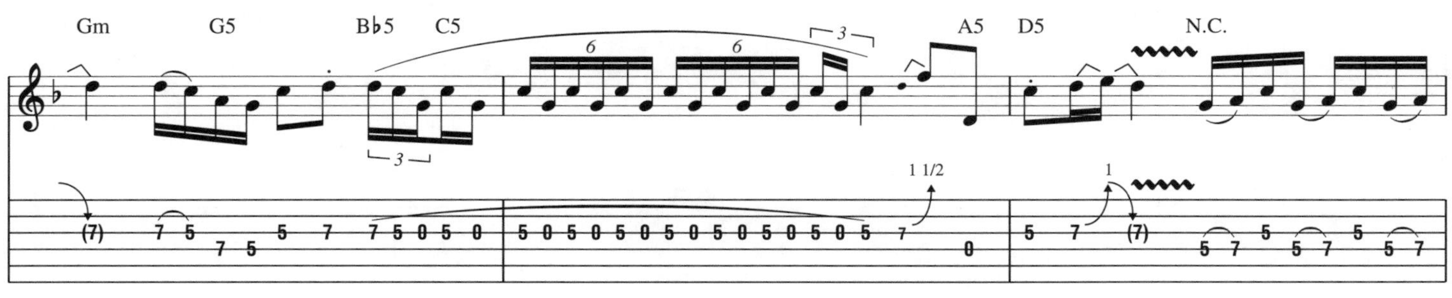
Gm
G5
B♭5
C5
A5
D5
N.C.
1 1/2
1

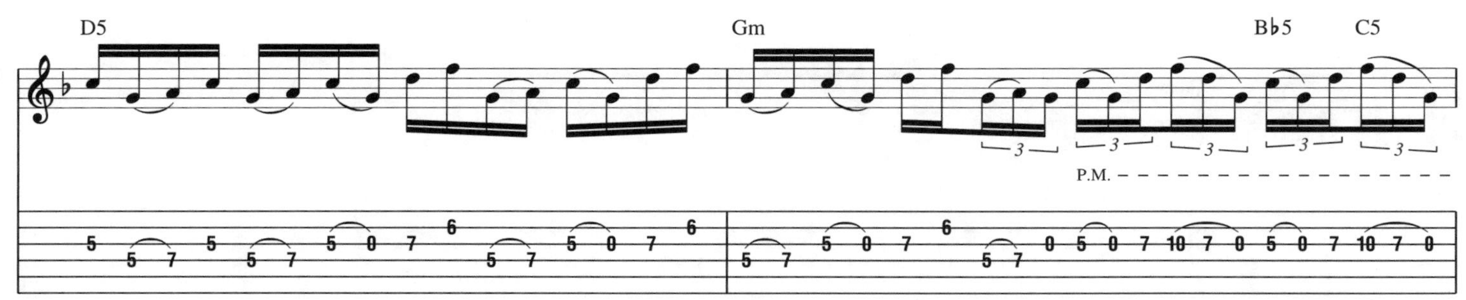
D5
Gm
B♭5
C5
P.M.

D.S. al Coda
Cb5 Bb5 N.C.
I'll take those...
P.M.
1 1/2
1
Coda
Interlude
Bb5
Bb C/Bb Bb
Voc. Fig. 3
gon - na be a blue col - lar man.
(Do, do, do, do, do,
8va
Gtr. 2
fdbk.
pitch: C
Gtr. 2 tacet
Bkdg. Voc.: w/ Voc. Fig. 3 (3 times)
C/Bb Bb C/Bb B C/Bb Bb C/Bb Bb
End Voc. Fig. 3
You don't un-der - stand.
do, do, do.)
Gtr. 1
loco
steady gliss.
P.M.
C/Bb F5 Bb5 C5
I'll take those...
8va loco
steady gliss.
P.H.
pitch: D

Chorus
Bkgd. Voc.: w/ Voc. Fig. 1
Gtr. 2: w/ Rhy. Fig. 2
D5
B♭/D
C5/D
D5
B♭5
C5
Keep - in' my eye to the key -
- hole. If it takes...
Bkgd. Voc.: w/ Voc. Fig. 2
D5
B♭/D
C5/D
D5
N.C.
Well I'd
rath - er be a blue col - lar, rath - er be a blue col - lar, gon - na be a blue col - lar man.
Gtr. 1
Gtr. 2
8va
fdbk.
pitch: A
loco
fdbk.
pitch: A

Outro
D5
F5
D5
F5 G5
F
Al - right.
8va
loco
fdbk.
P.S.
pitch: G
w/ wah-wah
let ring
D5
F5
D5
F5 G5
F5
N.C.
D5
N.C.
rit.
D5
Spoken: Be - lieve it.
8va
fdbk.
rit.
pitch: A
rit.

Breakdown

Words and Music by Tom Petty

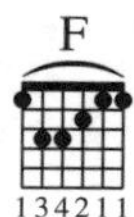

Intro

Moderate Rock ♩ = 110

**A5 G5 A5 G5 A5 Am G N.C.

Gr. 2 (clean)

mf

* Gtr. 1

mf

* Fender Rhodes elec. piano arr. for gtr.

** Chord symbols reflect overall harmony.

Am G Am G Am G Am G

Rhy. Fig. 1

End Rhy. Fig. 1

Gtr. 1: w/ Rhy. Fig. 1 (2 times)

Gtr. 2

Am G Am G Am G Am G

Verse
Gtr. 1: w/ Rhy. Fig. 1 (3 1/2 times)
Gtr. 2 tacet
Am G Am G Am G Am G Am G
1. It's al-right if you love me, it's al-right if you don't. I'm not a-fraid of you
2. There is no sense in pre-tend-ing; your eyes give you a-way. Some-thin' in-side you is
Gtr. 3 (clean)
Rhy. Fig. 2
mf
w/ echo
Am G Am G
run-nin' a-way, hon-ey, I get the feel-ing you won't.
feel-in' like I do. We've said all there is to
1.
Gtr. 3 tacet
F F6 Famj7 F6
Whispered: (I said...)
End Rhy. Fig. 2 Rhy. Fig. 3
Gtr. 1
End Rhy. Fig. 3
2.
Gtr. 1: w/ Rhy. Fig. 3
F F6 Famj7 F6
say. Ba-by.
Chorus
2nd time, Gtr. 5: w/ Fill 1
A5 G5 F5 G5
Break-down, go a-head, give it to me.
Gtr. 4 (fuzz)
Rhy. Fill 1A
End Rhy. Fill 1A Rhy. Fig. 4
Gtrs. 2 & 4
f
End Rhy. Fig. 4
Fill 1
Gtr. 5
w/ bar

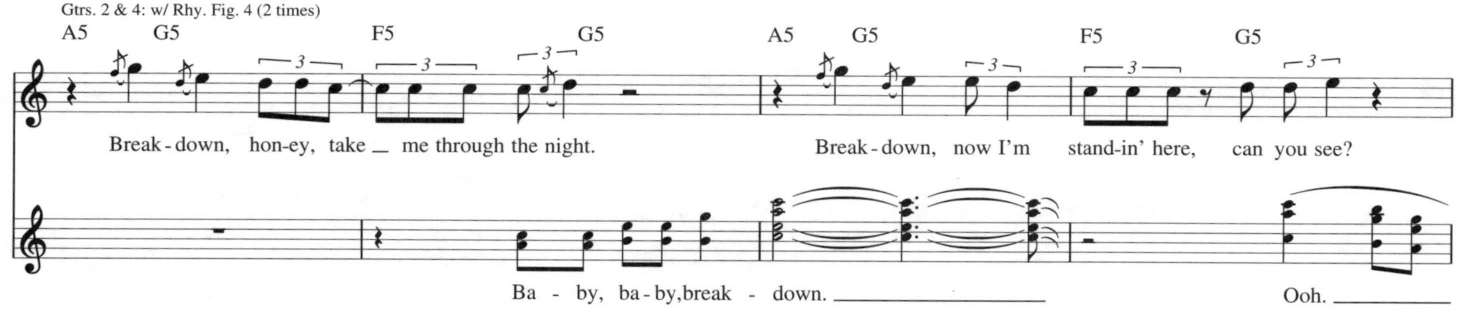
Gtrs. 2 & 4: w/ Rhy. Fig. 4 (2 times)
A5 G5 F5 G5 A5 G5 F5 G5
Break-down, hon-ey, take _ me through the night.
Break-down, now I'm stand-in' here, can you see?
Ba - by, ba-by, break - down.
Ooh.

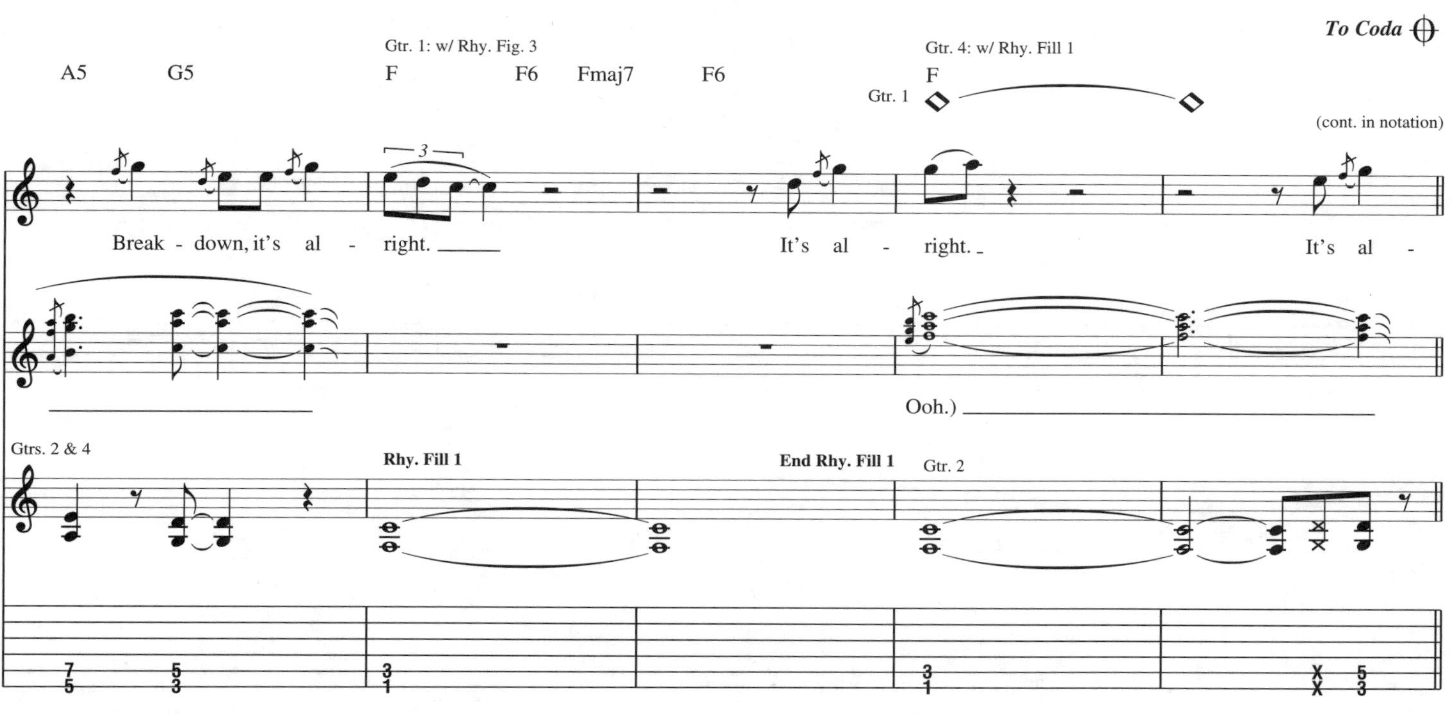
To Coda
A5 G5
Gtr. 1: w/ Rhy. Fig. 3
F F6 Fmaj7 F6
Gtr. 4: w/ Rhy. Fill 1
F
Gtr. 1
(cont. in notation)
Break - down, it's al - right.
It's al - right.
It's al -
Ooh.)
Gtrs. 2 & 4
Rhy. Fill 1
End Rhy. Fill 1
Gtr. 2

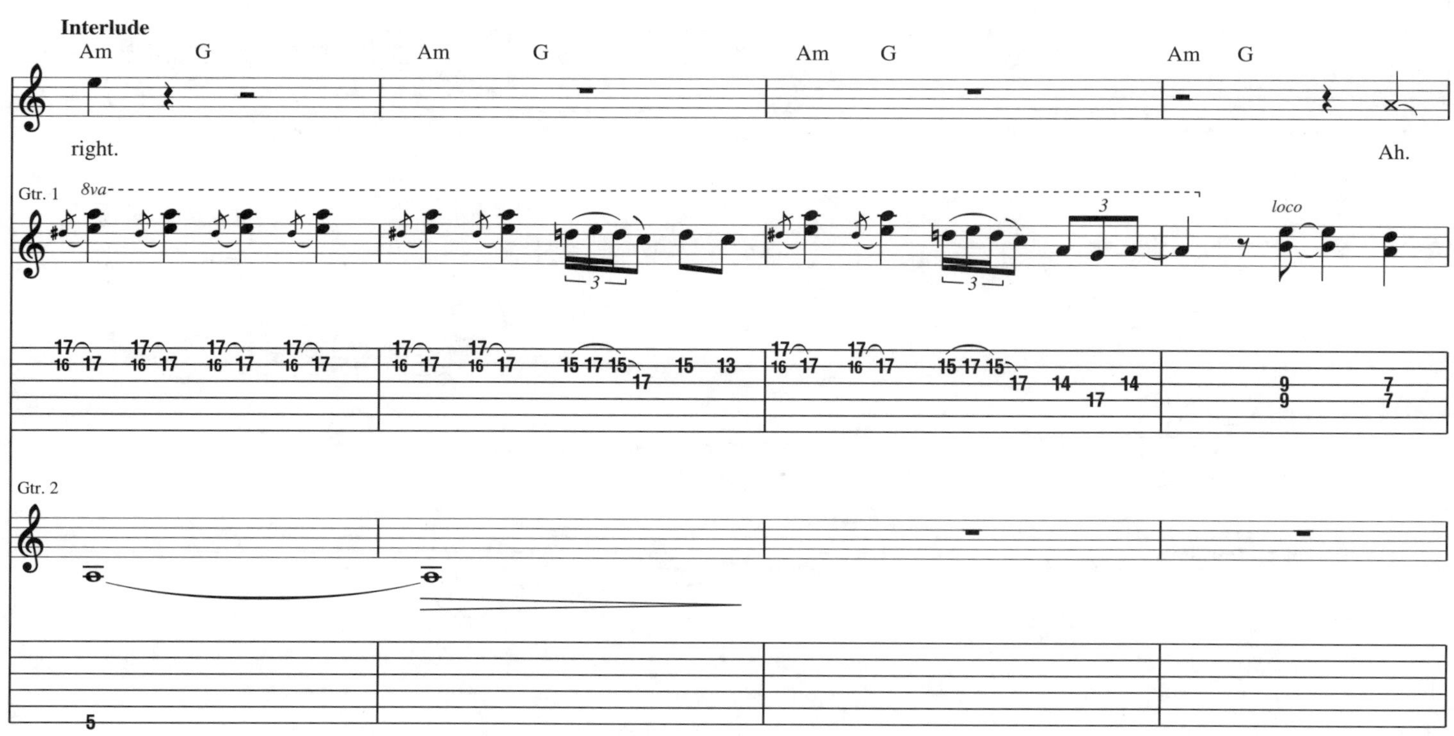
Interlude
Am G Am G Am G Am G
right.
Ah.
Gtr. 1
8va
loco
Gtr. 2

Gtr. 1: w/ Rhy. Fig. 1 (3 1/2 times)
Am
G
(Ah.)
Gtrs. 2 & 4
Gtr. 4
Gtr. 2
divisi
D.S. al Coda
Gtrs. 2 & 4: w/ Rhy. Fill 1A
F
Gtr. 1
Gtr. 5
(fuzz)
let ring
Coda
Outro
Gtr. 1: w/ Rhy. Fig. 1 (till fade)
Gtr. 3: w/ Rhy. Fig. 2 (till fade)
right.
Riff A
End Riff A
Gtr. 2: w/ Riff A (till fade)
Repeat and fade

Burning Love

Words and Music by Dennis Linde

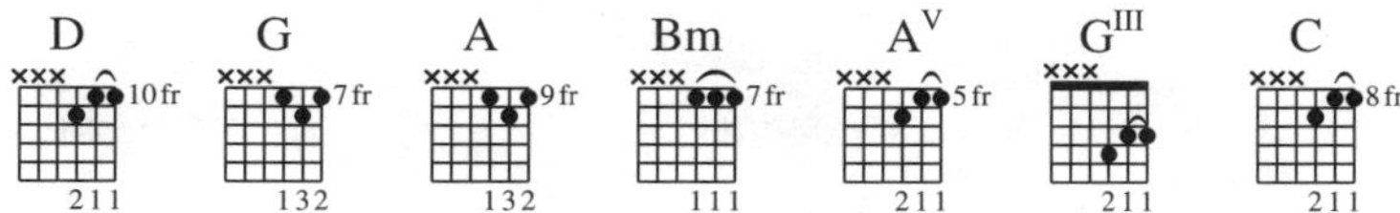

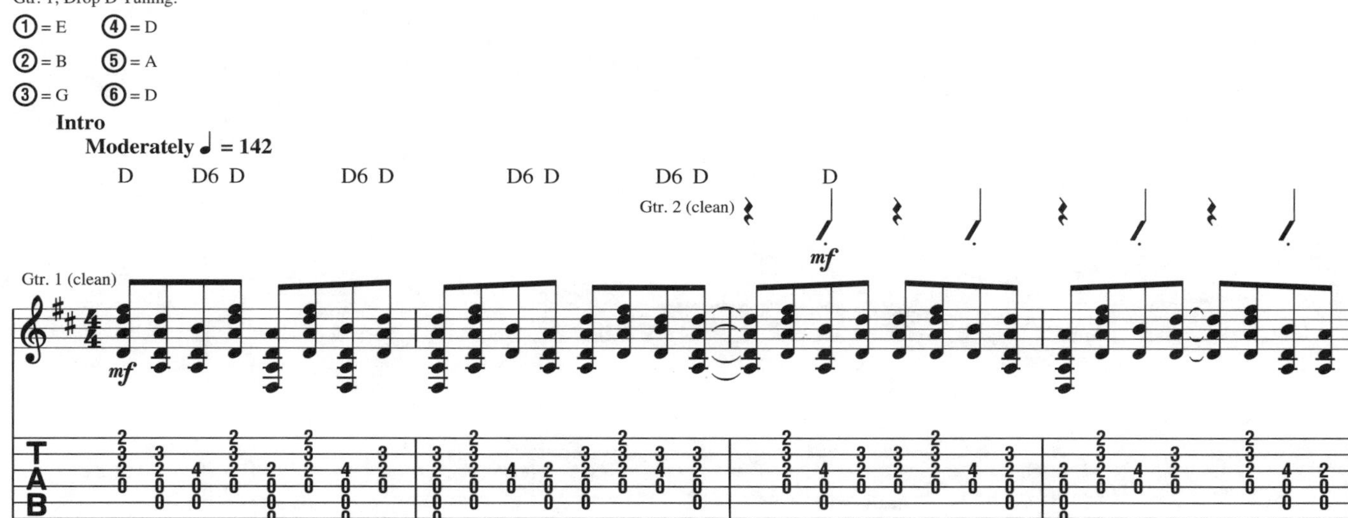

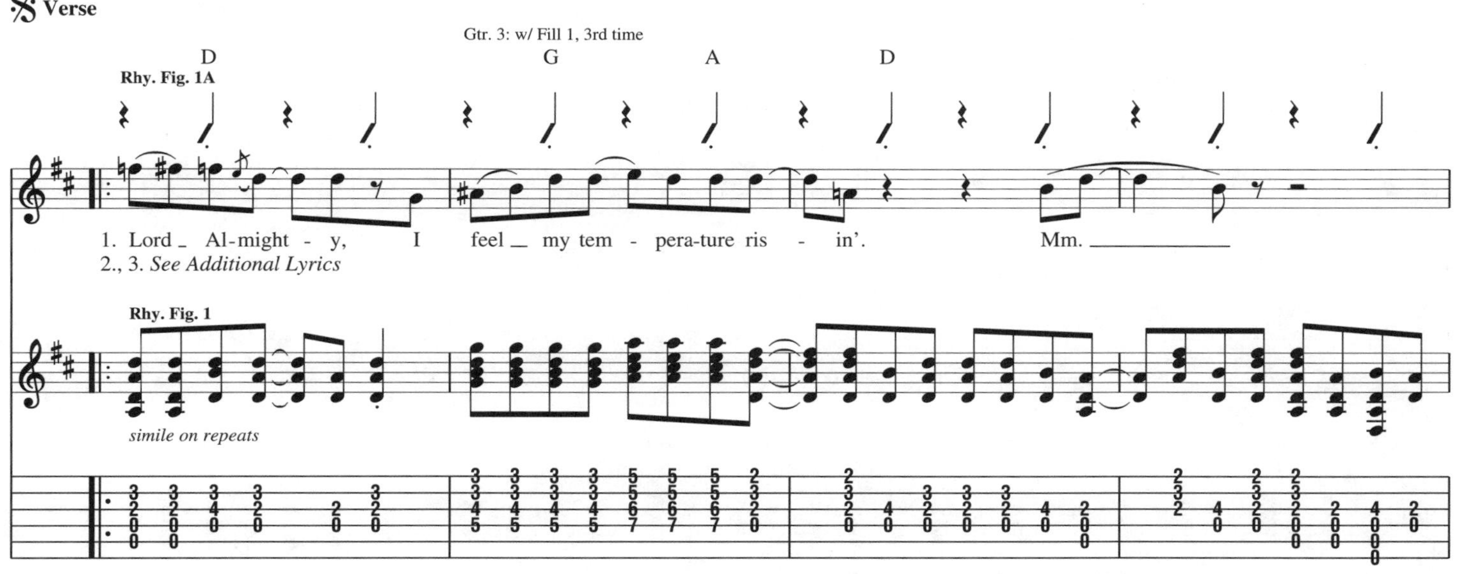

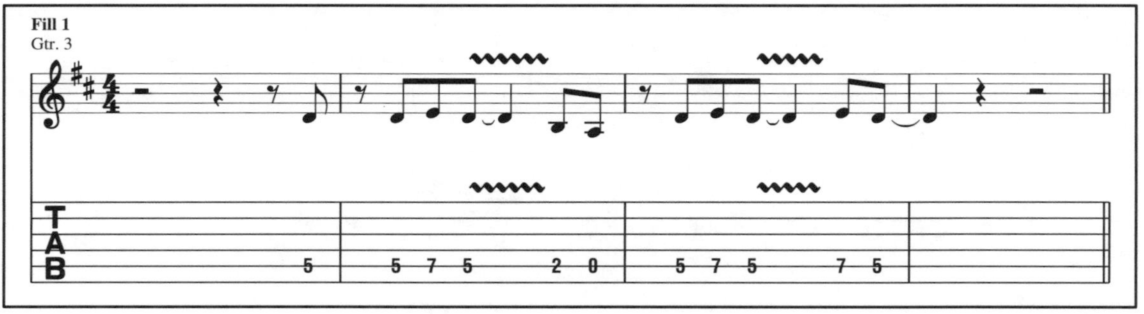

G A D
End Rhy. Fig. 1A
High - er, high - er, it's burn-ing through to my soul. Mm.
End Rhy. Fig. 1
Gtrs. 1 & 2: w/ Rhy. Figs. 1 & 1A, simile
D G A D
Girl, girl, girl, girl, you gone and set me on fire. Mm. My
G A D
To Coda
brain is flam - in', I don't know which way to go. Yeah. Your
Chorus
Bm A V G III Bm A V G III
Rhy. Fig. 2A
Gtr. 2
kiss - es lift me high - er like the sweet song of a choir. You
Voc. Fig. 1
(Ah, ah, ah. Ah, ah, ah,
Gtr. 1
Rhy. Fig. 2
Gtr. 3
(clean)
Rhy. Fig. 2B
mp

End Rhy. Fig. 2A

Bm A G^III D

light my morn - ing sky, burn - in' love. Mm.

End Voc. Fig. 1

Ah, ah, ah. Burn - in' love.)

End Rhy. Fig. 2

End Rhy. Fig. 2B

Interlude

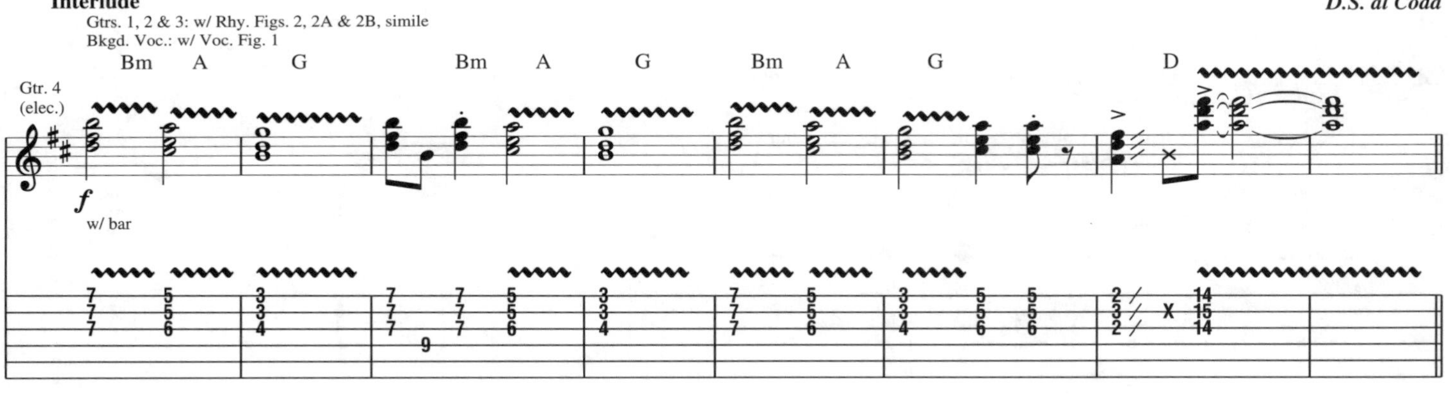

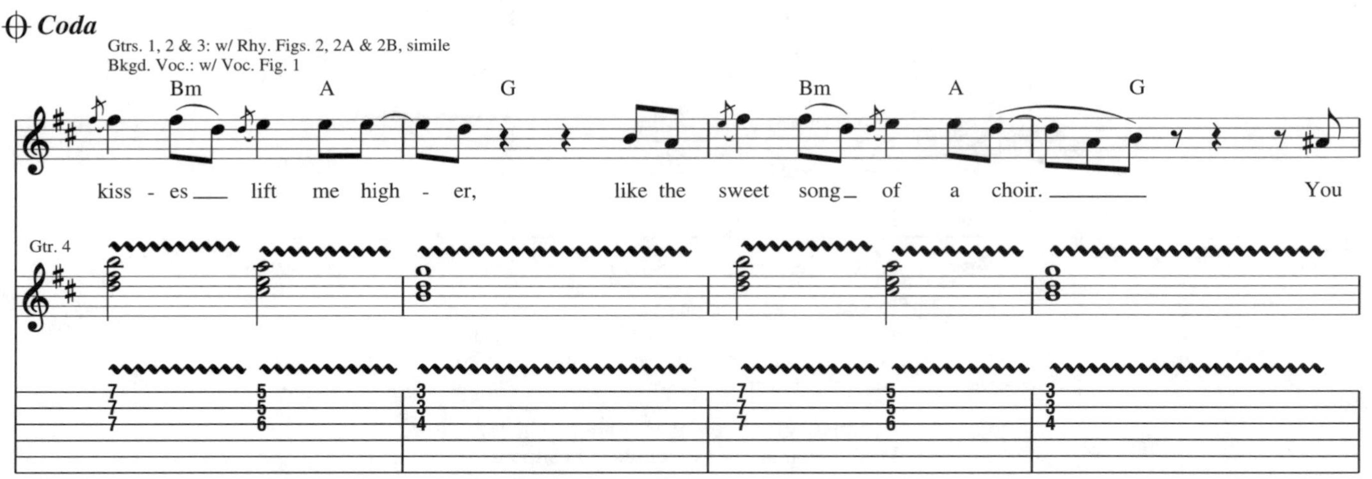

Additional Lyrics

2. Hoo, hoo, hoo. I feel my temperature risin', mm.
Help me I'm flamin', I must be a hundred and nine, mm.
Burnin', burnin', burnin', and nothin' can cool me, yeah.
I just might turn to smoke, but I feel fine.

3. It's comin' closer, the flames are now lickin' my body, mm.
Won't you help me? I feel like I'm slippin' away, yeah.
It's hard to breathe, my chest is heaving, mm, mm.
Lord have mercy, I'm burnin' a hole where I lay, yeah.

Dust in the Wind

Words and Music by Kerry Livgren

C G/B Am G Dm7
All my dreams pass be - fore my eyes, a cu - ri - os - i - ty.
All we do crum-bles to the ground though we re - fuse to see.
slips a - way and all your mon - ey won't an - oth - er min - ute buy.
Chorus
To Coda
D/F# G Am Am/G
Dust in the wind
1.
D/F# G Am G/B
All they are is dust in the wind.
(we)
2.
Am(add9)
wind.
G/A F(#11)/A F6(#11)/A
Oh, ho, ho.

Instrumental Bridge
Am(add9)
G/A
F(♯11)/A
F6(♯11)/A
D.C. al Coda
Coda
D/F♯
G
Am
Am/G
All we are is dust in the wind.
(All we are is dust in the wind.
Dust in the wind.
Ev - 'ry-thing is dust in the wind.)
Ev - 'ry-thing is dust in the
Outro
*Play 4 Times and Fade
Asus2
Asus4(♭13)
wind.
The wind.
*ad lib. voc. on repeat

Evil Woman

Words and Music by Jeff Lynne

Verse

Gtrs. 2 & 3: w/ Rhy. Figs. 1 & 1A (3 times)
Em7
Dm7
Em7
Am
Em7
Dm7
1. Hey wom - an, you got the blues. Guess you ain't got no one else

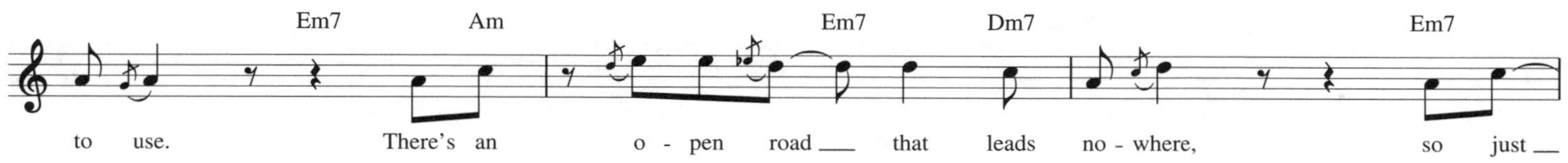
Em7
Am
Em7
Dm7
Em7
to use. There's an o - pen road that leads no - where, so just

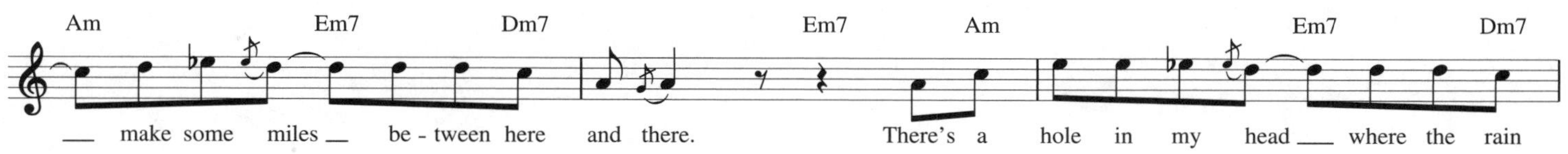
Am
Em7
Dm7
Em7
Am
Em7
Dm7
make some miles be - tween here and there. There's a hole in my head where the rain

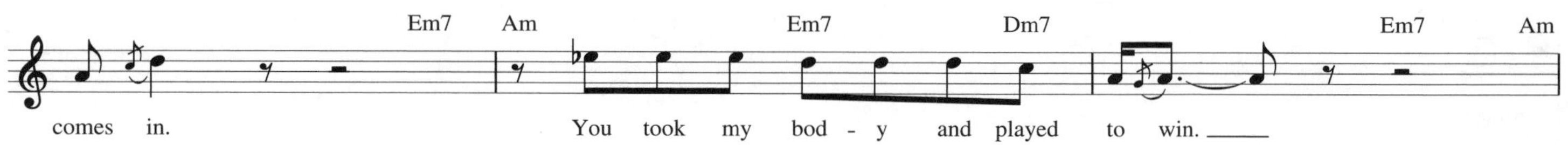
Em7
Am
Em7
Dm7
Em7
Am
comes in. You took my bod - y and played to win.

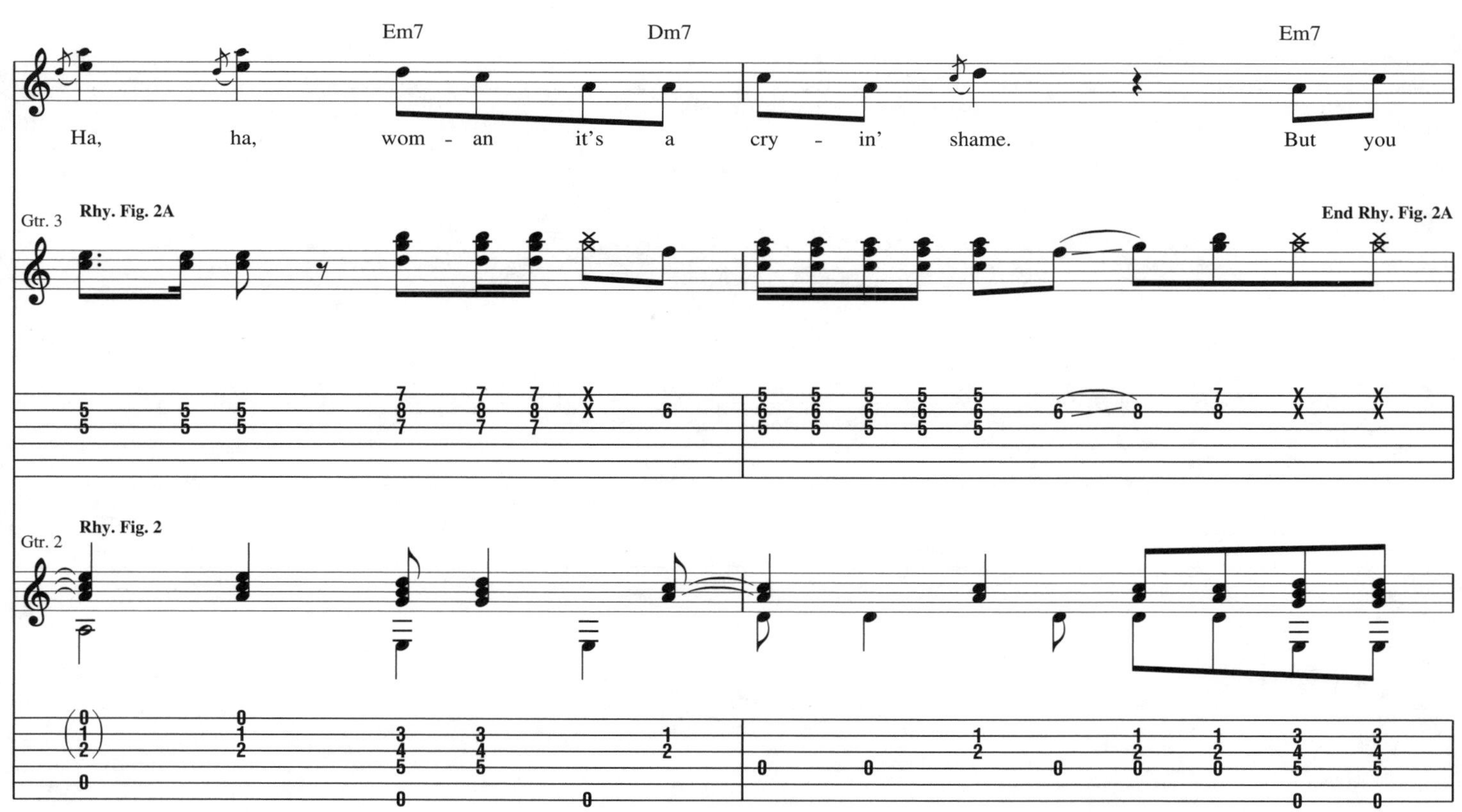
Em7
Dm7
Em7
Ha, ha, wom - an it's a cry - in' shame. But you
Gtr. 3
Rhy. Fig. 2A
End Rhy. Fig. 2A
Gtr. 2
Rhy. Fig. 2

Gtr. 3 tacet
Fmaj7
G
C
ain't got no - bod - y else to blame.
End Rhy. Fig. 2
Gtr. 2
Chorus
Gtr. 2: w/ Rhy. Fig. 1 (2 times)
2nd time, Gtr. 3: w/ Rhy. Fig. 4 (2 times)
Am Em7 Dm7 Em7 Am Em7 Dm7 Em7 Am
E - vil wom - an, e - vil wom - an.
Gtr. 3
Gtr. 4 (fuzz)
Riff A
f
* w/ octave pedal
*Set one octave lower & one octave higher.
To Coda
Em7 Dm7 Em7 Am Em7 Dm7 Em7 Am
E - vil wom - an, e - vil wom - an.
Rhy. Fig. 3
End Rhy. Fig. 3

Verse
Gtrs. 2 & 3: w/ Rhy. Figs. 1 & 1A (3 times)
Am
Em7
Dm7
Gtr. 4 tacet
Em7
2. Rolled in from an - oth - er town, hit some
Gtr. 1
Gtr. 4
End Riff A
Am
Em7
Dm7
Em7
Am
Em7
Dm7
gold too hot to set - tle down. But a fool and his mon - ey soon go
Gtr. 1
Riff B
Em7
Am
Em7
Dm7
Em7
Am
sep - 'rate ways. You found a fool ly - in' in a daze.
End Riff B
Gtr. 1: w/ Riff B
Em7
Dm7
Em7
Am
Em7
Dm7
Ha, ha, wom - an what you gon - na do? You de - stroyed all the vir - tues that the Lord

Gtr. 2: w/ Rhy. Fig. 2
Gtr. 3: w/ Rhy. Fig. 2A
Em7 Am Em7 Dm7 Em7
gave you. It's so good that you're feel-in' pain, but you
Gtr. 1
Fmaj7 G C
Gtr. 1 tacet
bet - ter get your face on board the ver - y next train.
(Train.)
Chorus
Gtrs. 2 & 3: w/ Rhy. Figs. 1 & 3 (2 times)
Gtr. 4: w/ Riff A
Am Em7 Dm7 Em7 Am Em7 Dm7 Em7 Am
E - vil wom - an, e - vil wom - an.
Em7 Dm7 Em7 Am Em7 Dm7 Em7 Am
E - vil wom - an, e - vil wom - an.
(You're an e - vil wom - an.)
String Solo
Gtr. 3: w/ Rhy. Fig. 1A (3 1/2 times)
Em7 Dm7 Em7 Am Em7 Dm7 Em7 Am Em7 Dm7 Em7
(Hey, hey, hey, hey!)
Gtr. 1

Am
Em7
Dm7
Em7
Am
Em7
Dm7
Em7
Am
Em7 Dm7
Em7
Am
Em7
Dm7
Em7
(Hey, hey, hey, hey!)
Chorus
Gtr. 1 tacet
Gtr. 2: w/ Rhy. Fig. 1 (2 times)
Gtr. 4: w/ Riff A
Fmaj7
G
Dm7
Em9
Am
Em7
Dm7
(Hey, hey, hey.)
E - vil wom -
Gtr. 1
w/ heavy flanger
Gtr. 3
8va
loco
w/ heavy flanger
Em7
Am
Em7
Dm7
Em7
Am
Em7
Dm7
an,
e - vil wom - an.
E - vil wom -
Gtr. 3
8va
loco
Rhy. Fig. 4
8va
loco

Em7
Am
Em7
Dm7
Em7
Am
an,
(You're an e - vil wom - an.)
E - vil wom - an.
8va
loco
End Rhy. Fig. 4
Verse
Gtrs. 2 & 3: w/ Rhy. Figs. 1 & 1A (3 times)
Em7
Dm7
Em7
Am
Em7
Dm7
3. E - vil wom - an, how you done me wrong,
but now you try to wail a dif -
Gtr. 1
Em7
Am
Em7
Dm7
Em7
- 'rent song.
Ha, ha, fun - ny how you broke me up.
Am
Em7
Dm7
Em7
Am
Em7
Dm7
You made the wine, now you drink the cup.
I came a run - nin' ev - 'ry -

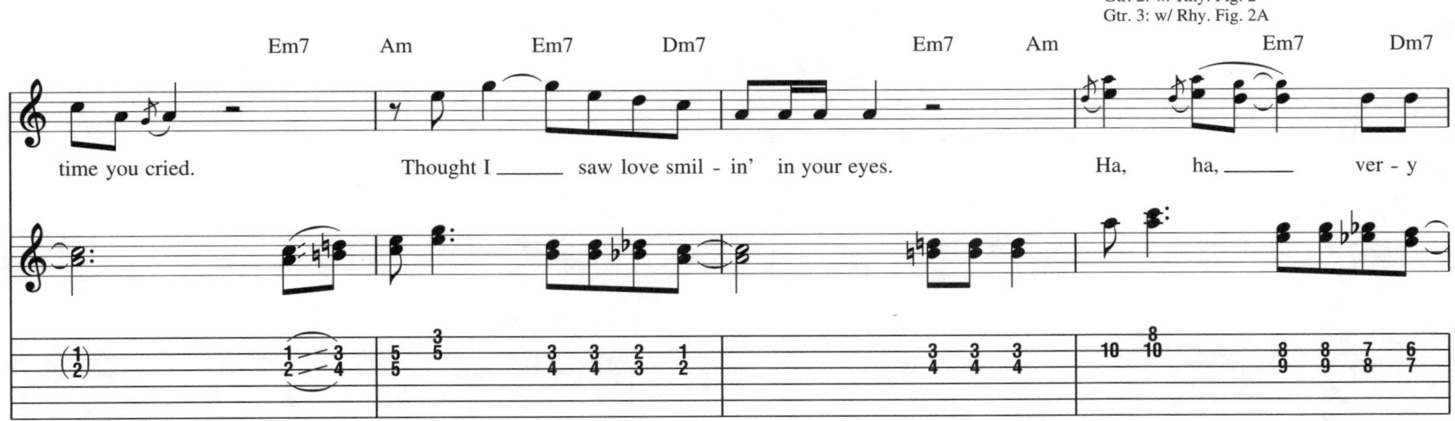
Gtr. 2: w/ Rhy. Fig. 2
Gtr. 3: w/ Rhy. Fig. 2A
Em7 Am Em7 Dm7 Em7 Am Em7 Dm7
time you cried. Thought I ___ saw love smil - in' in your eyes. Ha, ha, ___ ver - y

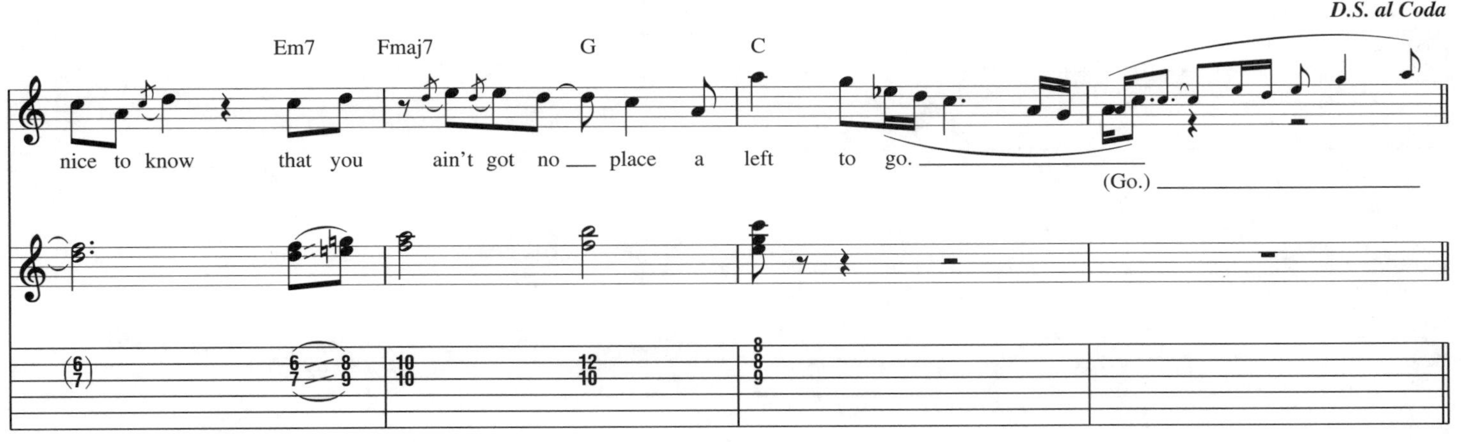
D.S. al Coda
Em7 Fmaj7 G C
nice to know that you ain't got no ___ place a left to go. ___
(Go.) ___

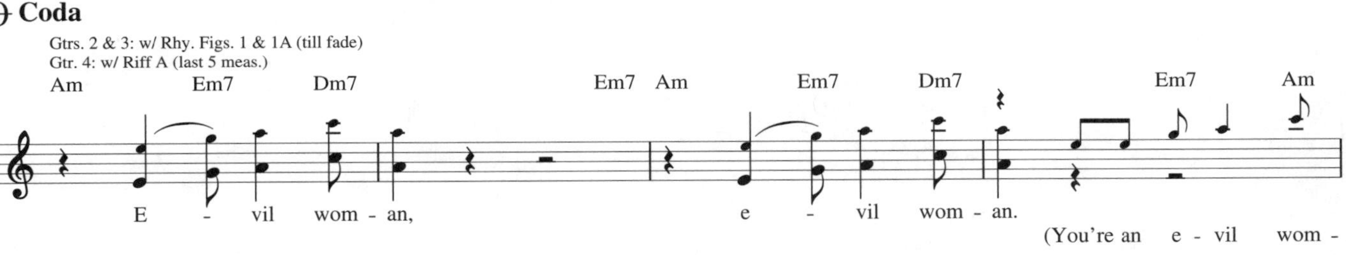
Coda
Gtrs. 2 & 3: w/ Rhy. Figs. 1 & 1A (till fade)
Gtr. 4: w/ Riff A (last 5 meas.)
Am Em7 Dm7 Em7 Am Em7 Dm7 Em7 Am
E - vil wom - an, e - vil wom - an.
(You're an e - vil wom -

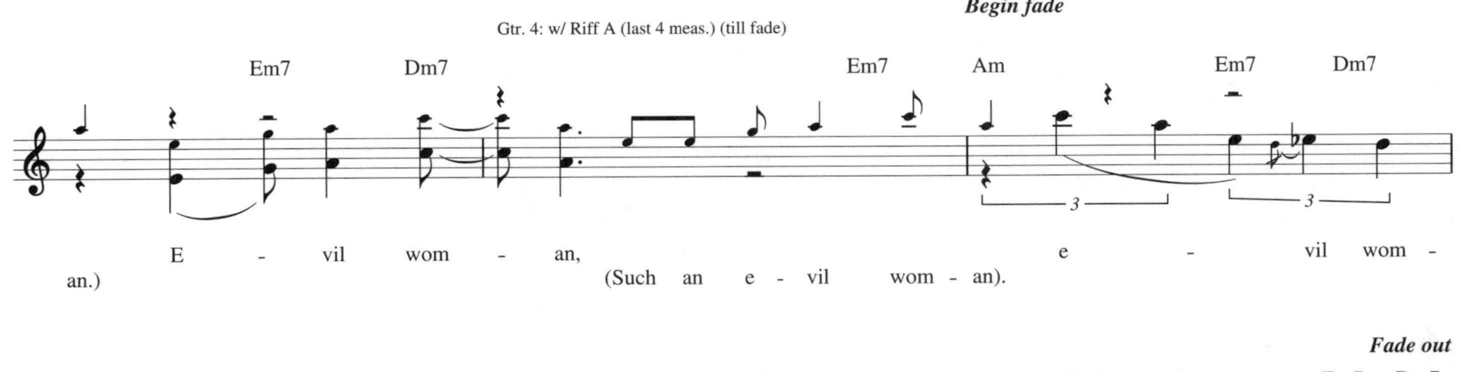
Begin fade
Gtr. 4: w/ Riff A (last 4 meas.) (till fade)
Em7 Dm7 Em7 Am Em7 Dm7
E - vil wom - an, e - vil wom -
an.) (Such an e - vil wom - an).

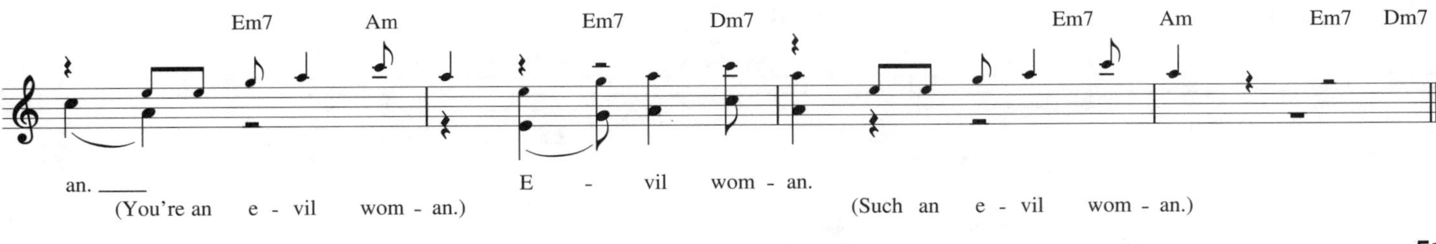
Fade out
Em7 Am Em7 Dm7 Em7 Am Em7 Dm7
an. ___ E - vil wom - an.
(You're an e - vil wom - an.) (Such an e - vil wom - an.)

Freeway Jam

By Max Middleton

C
Gtr. 2 tacet
Gtr. 1
G7
string noise
w/ bar
string noise
w/ bar
string noise
w/ bar
string noise
*
mf
Harm.
string noise
w/ bar
* ③ is sounded sympathetically.
D
G
F/G
Riff A
Gtrs. 1 & 2

G
F/G
w/ bar
Gtr. 2: w/ Riff A (1 1/2 times)
End Riff A
Gtr. 1
1/2
-1
Gtr. 1
Gtr. 2
-1 1/2

E
Gtr. 2 tacet
F/G
F7sus2
D/G
*15ma
Gtr. 1
* P.H.
*Applies to harmonic pitches only.
F/G
F7sus2
Amaj7
15ma
loco
P.H.
slight P.H.
Gadd9/A
F/G
B♭7
A♭7
G7
slight P.H.
w/ bar
** T
**T = Thumb on ⑥
F
G
F/G
G
F/G
G
F/G

*Applies to harmonic pitch only.

G
Gtr. 2: w/ Riff A (1st 7 meas. only)
Gtr. 1
w/ bar
slight P.H.
Gtrs. 1 & 2
H
Gtr. 2 tacet
F7sus2
D/G
Amaj7

Gadd9/A
F/G
B♭7
A♭7
G7sus4
G7
Begin fade
let ring
Segue into "Diamond Dust"
Gtr. 1 tacet
Fade out

Godzilla

Words and Music by Donald Roeser

F#5 B5 C#5 G#5 A5 D#5 E5 B5^VII E5 open E7sus4 F#7sus4

Intro

Moderately ♩ = 90

Gtr. 1: w/ Rhy. Fig. 1, 2 times, simile

F#5 B5 C#5 G#5 A5 D#5 E5 B5^VII F#5 B5 C#5 G#5 A5 D#5 E5 B5^VII

Rhy. Fig. 1 End Rhy. Fig. 1

*Gtr. 1 (dist.)

w/ panned delay

mf

Gtr. 2 (dist.)

Riff A

mf

full full

Gtr. 3 (dist.)

Riff A1

mf

full full

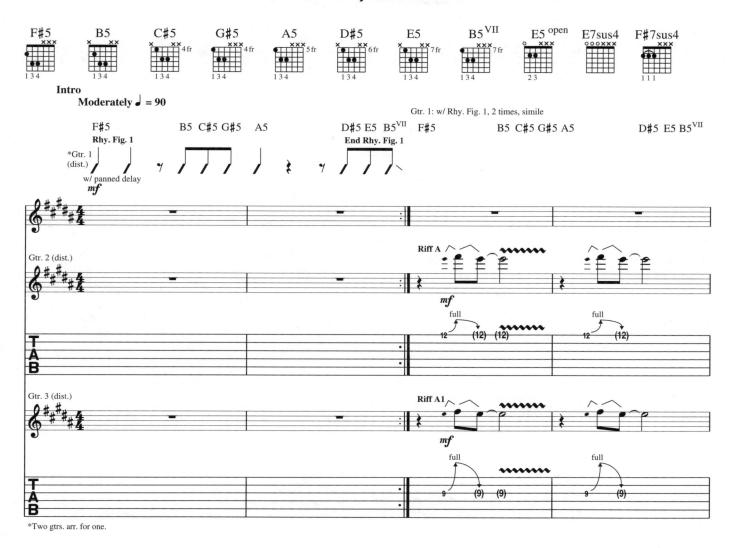

*Two gtrs. arr. for one.

A5 D♯5 E5 B5[VII] F♯5 B5 C♯5 G♯5 A5 D♯5 E5 B5[VII]

pulls the spin-ning, high ten - sion wires ___ down.

f

w/ slide

F♯5 B5 C♯5 G♯5 A5 D♯5 E5 B5[VII] F♯5 B5 C♯5 G♯5

Help-less peo-ple on sub-way trains scream bug-eyed _ as he looks in on them.

w/ o slide

full

full

hold bend

A5 D♯5 E5 B5[VII] F♯5 B5 C♯5 G♯5 A5 D♯5 E5 B5[VII]

He picks up a bus and he throws it back down, as he wades through the build-ings toward the cen - ter of town. _

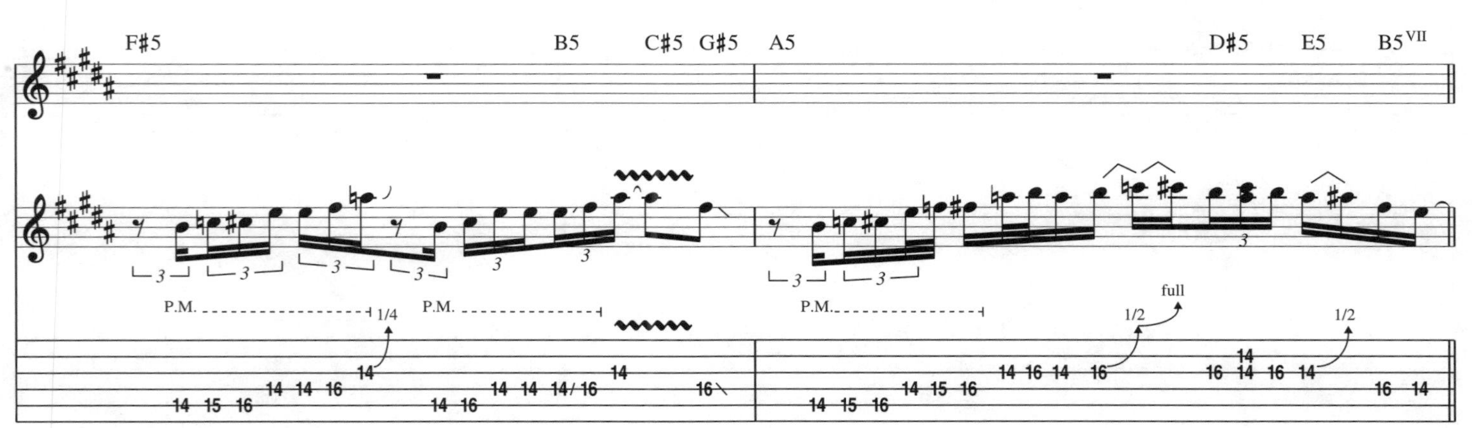

Chorus
E5 open
E7sus4
F#5
F#7sus4
Gtr. 1
Oh, no, they say he's got to go. Go, go God - zil-la.
Whoo.
full
hold bend
P.M.
1/2
Oh, no there goes To-kyo. Go, go God -
zil - la.
Whoo.
Guitar Solo
Gtr. 1: w/ Rhy. Fig. 1, 4 times
B5
C#5
G#5
A5
D#5
E5
B5 VII
8va
loco

F#5
B5
C#5
G#5
A5
D#5
E5
B5VII
full
Chorus
E5 open
E7sus4
F#5
F#7sus4
Gtr. 1
Oh no, they say he's got to go. Go, go God - zil-la. Whoo.
8va
loco
1 1/2
P.M.
Oh no, there goes To-kyo. Go, go God -

F♯5
F♯7sus4 F♯5
F♯7sus4 F♯5
F♯7sus4 F♯5
E
2fr
Interlude
F♯
4fr
zil - la.
Whoo.
full
1/2
Gtrs. 1 & 4 tacet
w/ Vocal ad Lib.
N.C. (F♯7)
8
Gtr. 1
E5
Oh
1/2
1/4
(cont. in slash)
Chorus
E5open
E7sus4 E5open
E7sus4
E5open
E7sus4 E5open
E7sus4
F♯5
F♯7sus4 F♯5
F♯7sus4
Gtr. 1
no,
they
say
he's got
to go.
Go,
go God
-
zil-la.
Whoo.
Gtr. 4
full
full
full
full
full
full
F♯5
F♯7sus4
F♯5
F♯7sus4
E5open
E7sus4
E5open
E7sus4
Oh
no,
full
full

E5open E7sus4 E5open E7sus4 F#5 F#7sus4 F#5 F#7sus4 F#5 F#7sus4 F#5 F#7sus4
there goes To-kyo. Go, go God - zil-la. Whoo.
full
1/2
P.M.
full
full
Outro
Gtr. 1: w/ Rhy. Fig. 1, 9 times, simile
Gtrs. 2 & 3: w/ Riffs A & A1
Gtr. 4 tacet
F#5 B5 C#5 G#5 F#5 B5 C#5 G#5
His - to - ry shows, a - gain and a - gain, how
Gtr. 4
A5 D#5 E5 B5VII F#5 B5 C#5 G#5 A5 D#5 E5 B5VII
play 3 times
na-ture points out the fol - ly of man. God - zil - la.
Gtr. 4
w/ octaver effect
w/ bar
+ 1/2
P.H.
Gtr. 4 tacet
F#5 B5 C#5 G#5 A5 D#5 E5 B5VII F#5
Gtr. 1
His-to - ry shows, a - gain and a - gain, how na-ture points out the fol - ly of man. God - zil - la.

Happy

Words and Music by Mick Jagger and Keith Richards

Gtrs. 1 & 2: Open G Tuning, Capo IV
① = D ④ = D
② = B ⑤ = G
③ = G ⑥ = D

Gtr. 3; Open D Tuning
① = D ④ = D
② = A ⑤ = A
③ = F♯ ⑥ = D

Intro

♩ = 130

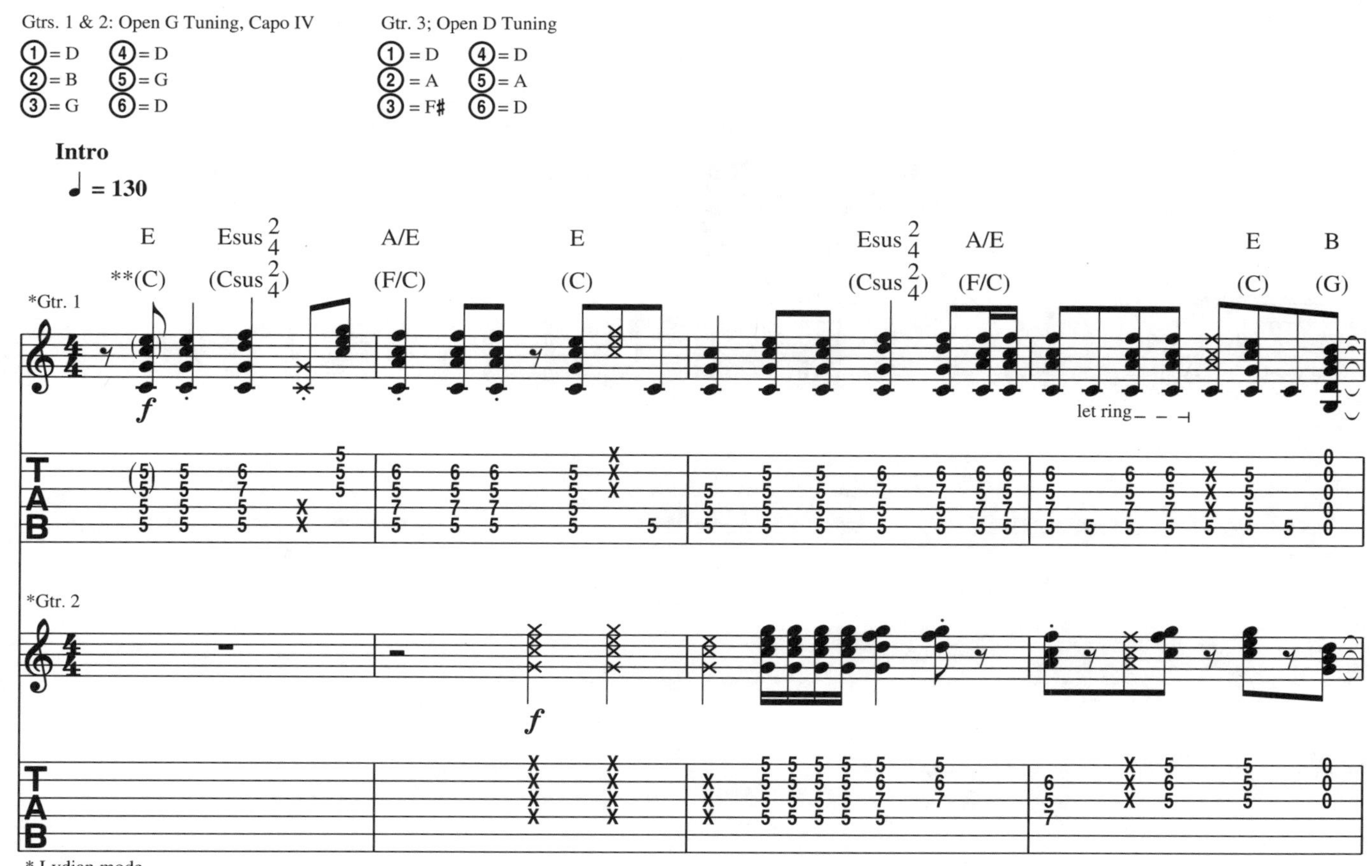

* Lydian mode

** Symbols in parenthesis represent chord names respective to capoed guitar. Symbols above reflect actual sounding of chord.

* Two gtrs. arr. for one.

Verse

E/B (C/G) B (G) E/B (C/G) B (G) E/B (C/G) B (G) E/B (C/G) B (G)

- er kept a dol-lar past sun - set; al - ways burned a hole in my pants. Nev -

Rhy. Fig. 2

w/o slide

w/ slide

E/B (C/G) B (G) E/B (C/G) B (G) E/B (C/G) B (G) E/B (C/G) B (G) E/B (C/G) B (G) E/B (C/G) B (G) E (C)

- er made a school ma-ma hap - py; nev - er blew a sec-ond chance on love.

End Rhy. Fig. 2

w/o slide

let ring

w/ slide

Pre-Chorus
Esus2/4 (Csus2/4) E (C) A/E (F/C) E (C) Esus2/4 (Csus2/4) E (C) A/E (F/C) E (C) B (G)
1., 3. I need a love _ to keep me hap - py, I need a love _ to keep me hap - py.
2. I need a love _ to keep me hap - py. I need a love, _ ba - by won't ya keep me
Rhy. Fig. 3
End Rhy. Fig. 3
2nd & 3rd times simile
2nd & 3rd times simile
Chorus
Gtrs. 1 & 2: w/ Rhy. Figs. 1 & 1A, simile
To Coda 1
To Coda 2
E/B (C/G) B (G) E/B (C/G) B (G) E/B (C/G) B (G) E/B (C/G) B (G)
Ba - by, ba - by keep me hap-py. Ba - by, ba - by keep me hap-py. _ 2. Al -
hap - py? Ba - by won't ya keep me hap - py? Ba
Verse
E/B (C/G) B (G) E/B (C/G) B (G) E/B B (C/G)(G) E/B B (C/G)(G) B6 (G6) B5 (G5) E/B (C/G) B (G) B6 (G6) B5 (G5) B (G)
- ways took can-dy from stran - gers; did - n't wan-na get me no trade. _ Nev -
Gtr. 1
let ring
Gtr. 2
w/o slide
w/ slide

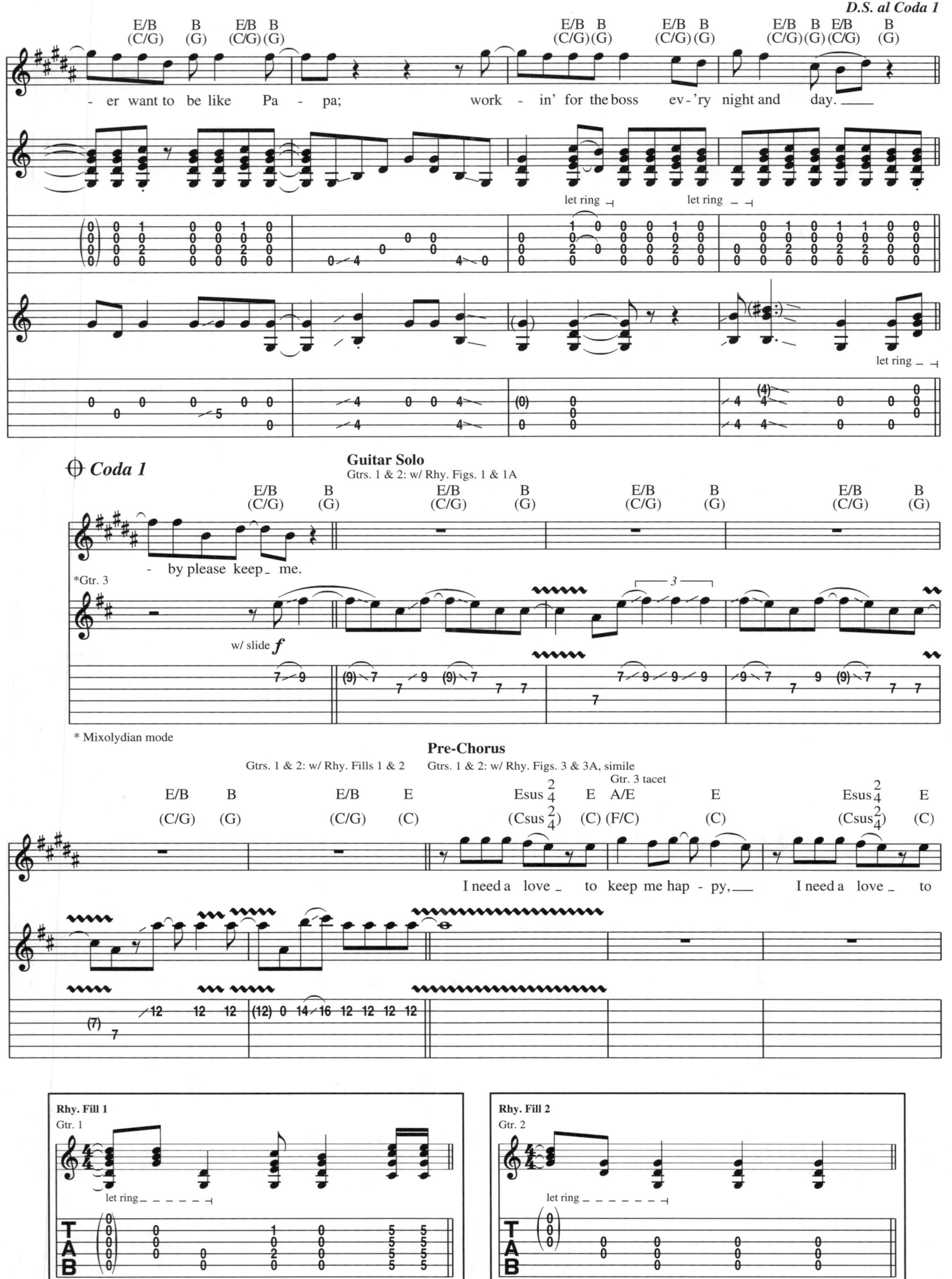
D.S. al Coda 1
E/B (C/G) B (G)
- er want to be like Pa - pa; work - in' for the boss ev - 'ry night and day.
let ring
Coda 1
Guitar Solo
Gtrs. 1 & 2: w/ Rhy. Figs. 1 & 1A
- by please keep me.
*Gtr. 3
w/ slide
* Mixolydian mode
Pre-Chorus
Gtrs. 1 & 2: w/ Rhy. Fills 1 & 2
Gtrs. 1 & 2: w/ Rhy. Figs. 3 & 3A, simile
Gtr. 3 tacet
Esus 2 4 (Csus 2 4) E (C) A/E (F/C)
I need a love to keep me hap - py, I need a love to
Rhy. Fill 1
Gtr. 1
Rhy. Fill 2
Gtr. 2

Chorus
Gtrs. 1 & 2: w/ Rhy. Figs. 1 & 1A, simile
A/E (F/C) E (C) B (G) E/B (C/G) B (G) E/B (C/G) B (G) E/B (C/G) B (G) E/B (C/G) B (G)
keep ma hap - py. Ba - by, ba - by keep me hap-py. Ba - by. 3. Nev-

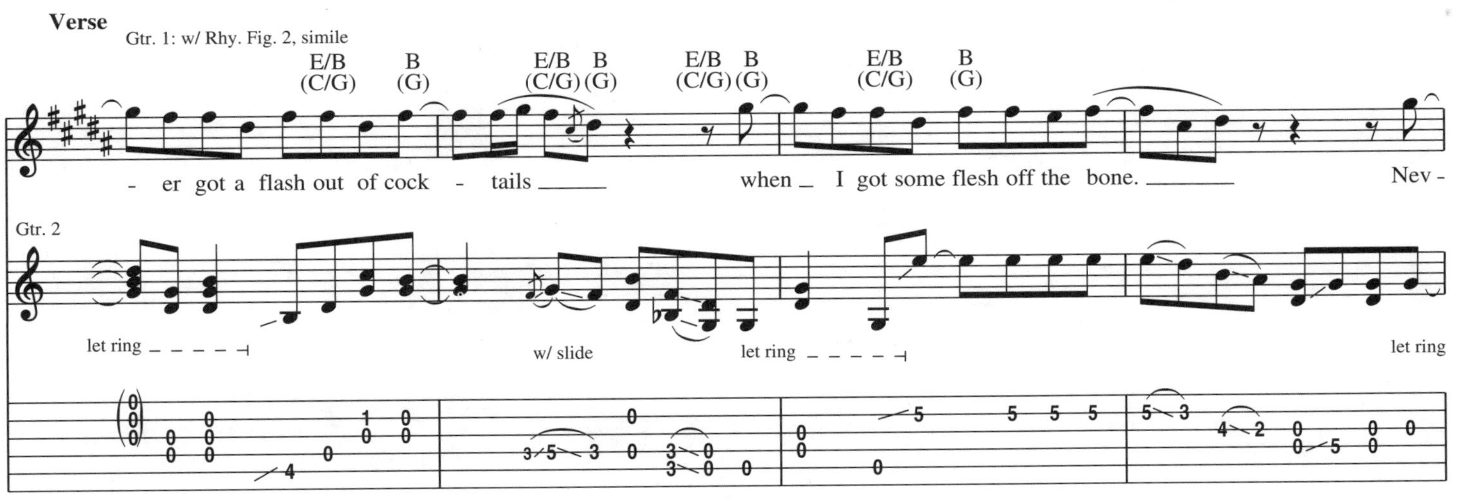
Verse
Gtr. 1: w/ Rhy. Fig. 2, simile
E/B (C/G) B (G) E/B (C/G) B (G) E/B (C/G) B (G) E/B (C/G) B (G)
- er got a flash out of cock - tails when I got some flesh off the bone. Nev -
Gtr. 2
let ring
w/ slide
let ring
let ring

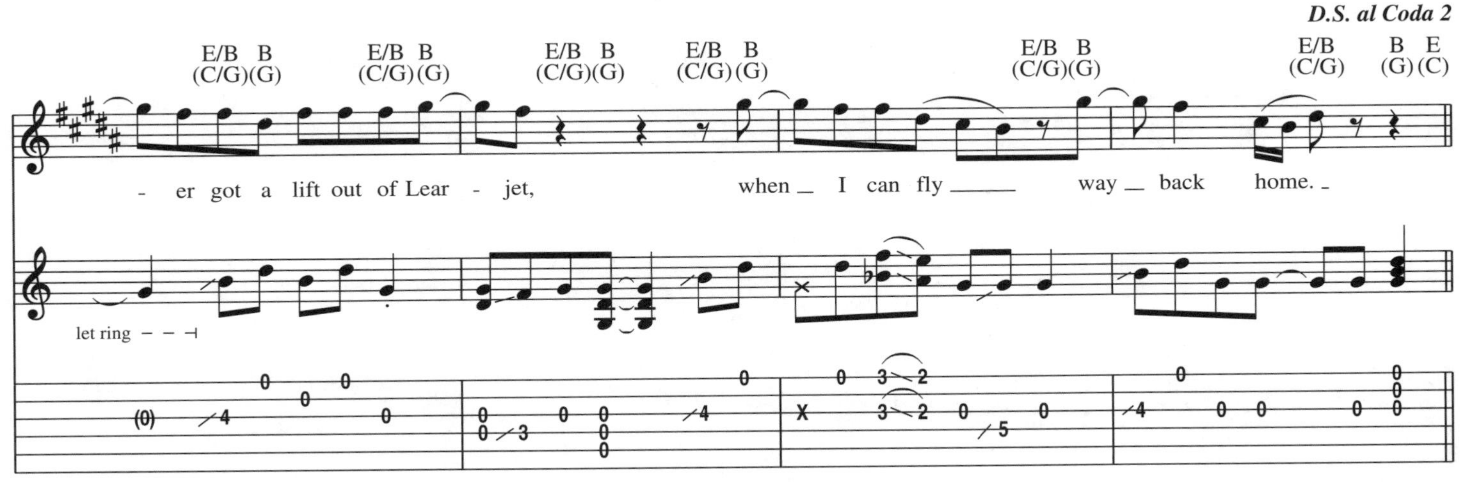
D.S. al Coda 2
E/B (C/G) B (G) E/B (C/G) B (G) E/B (C/G) B (G) E/B (C/G) B (G) E/B (C/G) B (G) E/B (C/G) B (G) E (C)
- er got a lift out of Lear - jet, when I can fly way back home.
let ring

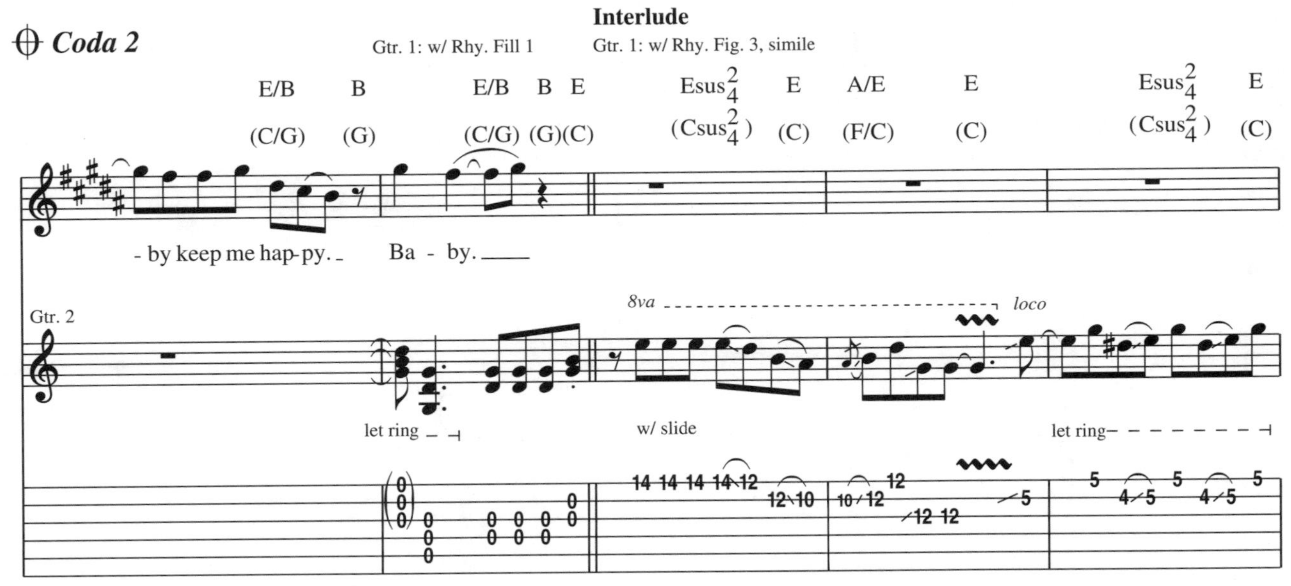
Coda 2
Gtr. 1: w/ Rhy. Fill 1
Interlude
Gtr. 1: w/ Rhy. Fig. 3, simile
E/B (C/G) B (G) E/B (C/G) B (G) E (C) Esus2/4 (Csus2/4) E (C) A/E (F/C) E (C) Esus2/4 (Csus2/4) E (C)
- by keep me hap-py. Ba - by.
Gtr. 2
8va
loco
let ring
w/ slide
let ring

Out-Chorus
Gtr. 1: w/ Rhy. Fig. 1
A/E (F/C)
E (C)
B (G)
E/B (C/G)
Hap - py, ba - by won't ya' keep me hap - py? Ba - by won't ya keep me
8va
let ring
Gtr. 1: w/ Rhy. Fill 3, 4 times
Gtr. 1: w/ Rhy. Fig. 1, 1 1/4 times
Voc. Fig. 1
End Voc. Fig. 1
hap - py? Ba - by won't you keep me hap-py? Ba - by won't keep me me hap - py? Ba -
loco
* Slide positioned half way between 3rd & 4th frets.
w/ Voc. Fig. 1, 8 1/2 times
Gtr. 1: w/ Rhy. Fill 4, 4 times
Begin Fade
Gtr. 1: w/ Rhy. Fig. 1, 2 1/4 times
Fade Out
Rhy. Fill 3
Gtr. 1
Rhy. Fill 4
Gtr. 1

Landslide

Words and Music by Stevie Nicks

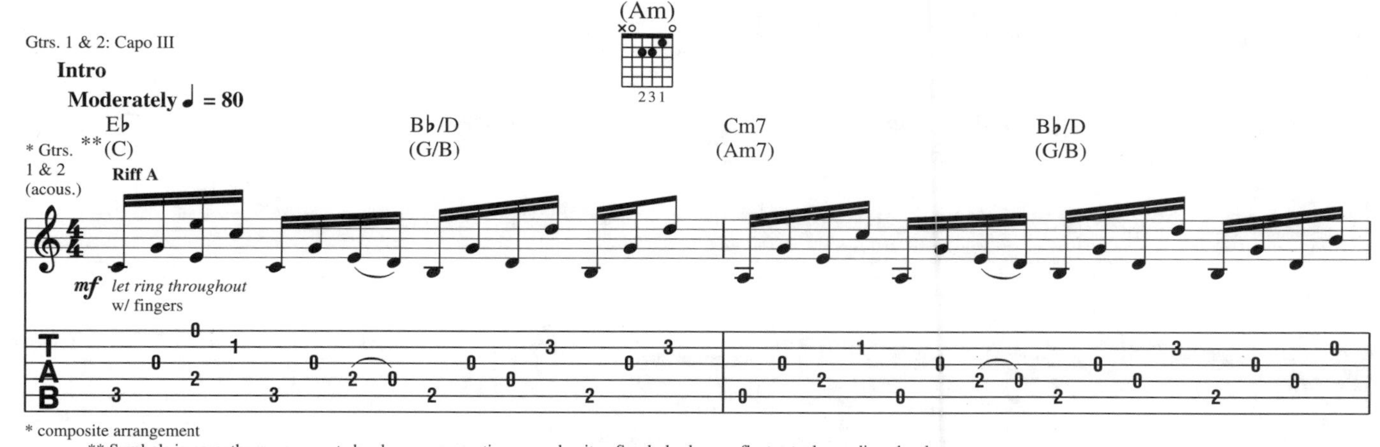

* composite arrangement

** Symbols in parentheses represent chord names respective capoed guitar. Symbols above reflect actual sounding chords. Capoed fret is "0" in tab. Chord symbols reflect implied harmony.

Eb (C) | Bb/D (G/B) | Cm7 (Am7) | Bb/D (G/B)

End Riff A

Verse

Gtrs. 1 & 2: w/ Riff A (1 1/2 times)

Eb (C) | Bb/D (G/B) | Cm7 (Am7) | Bb/D (G/B)

1. I took my love, took it down.
mir - ror in the sky, what is love? Can the child

Eb (C) | Bb/D (G/B) | Cm7 (Am7) | Bb/D (G/B)

Climbed a moun - tain and I turned a - round. And I saw
with - in my heart rise a - bove? Can I sail

Eb (C) | Bb/D (G/B | Cm7 (Am7) | Bb/D (G/B)

my re - flec - tion in the snow - cov - ered hills till the
through the chang - ing o - cean tides? Can I

1.

Eb (C) | Bb/D (G/B) | Cm7 (Am7) | Bb/D (G/B)

land - slide brought me down.
han - dle the sea - sons of
2. Oh,

Gtrs. 1 & 2

2.
Cm7
(Am7)
Bb/D
(G/B)
Eb
(C)
Bb/D
(G/B)
my
life?
Gtr. 1
* Gtr. 2
* Two gtrs. arr. for one.
Mm.
Chorus
Cm7
(Am7
F7/A
(D7/F#)
Bb
(G)
F/A
(D/F#)
Well, I've been a - fraid of chang -
Riff B
Riff B1

Gm
(Em)
Eb
(C)
Bb/D
(G/B)
- in' 'cause I've built my life a - round you.
Cm7
(Am7)
F7/A
(D7/F#)
Bb
(G)
F7/A
(D7/F#)
But time makes you bold - er. E - ven

Gm
(Em)
E♭
(C)
B♭/D
(G/B)
chil - dren get old - er and I'm get-tin' old - er too.
End Riff B
End Riff B1
Guitar Solo
Gtrs. 1 & 2: w/ Riff A (1 3/4 times)
Cm7
(Am7)
B♭/D
(G/B)
E♭
(C)
B♭/D
(G/B)
Cm7
(Am7)
B♭/D
(G/B)
Gtr. 3 (elec.)
mf
w/ clean tone
Gtr. 1
Gtr. 2

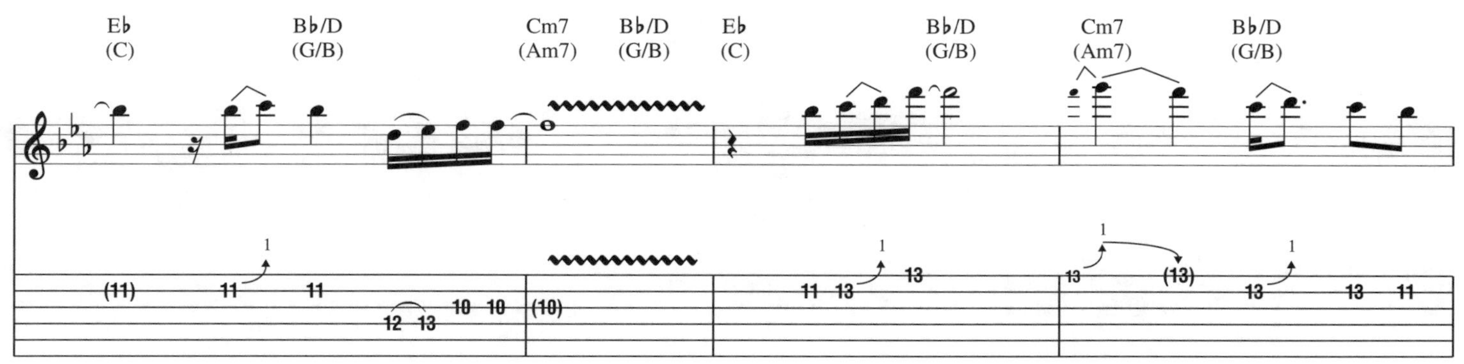
Eb (C)
Bb/D (G/B)
Cm7 (Am7)
Bb/D (G/B)
Eb (C)
Bb/D (G/B)
Cm7 (Am7)
Bb/D (G/B)

Gtr. 1: w/ Fill 1
Gtr. 2: w/ Fill 1A
Eb (C)
Bb/D (G/B)
Cm7 (Am7)
F7/A (D7/F#)
Well, I've
hold bend
p

Chorus

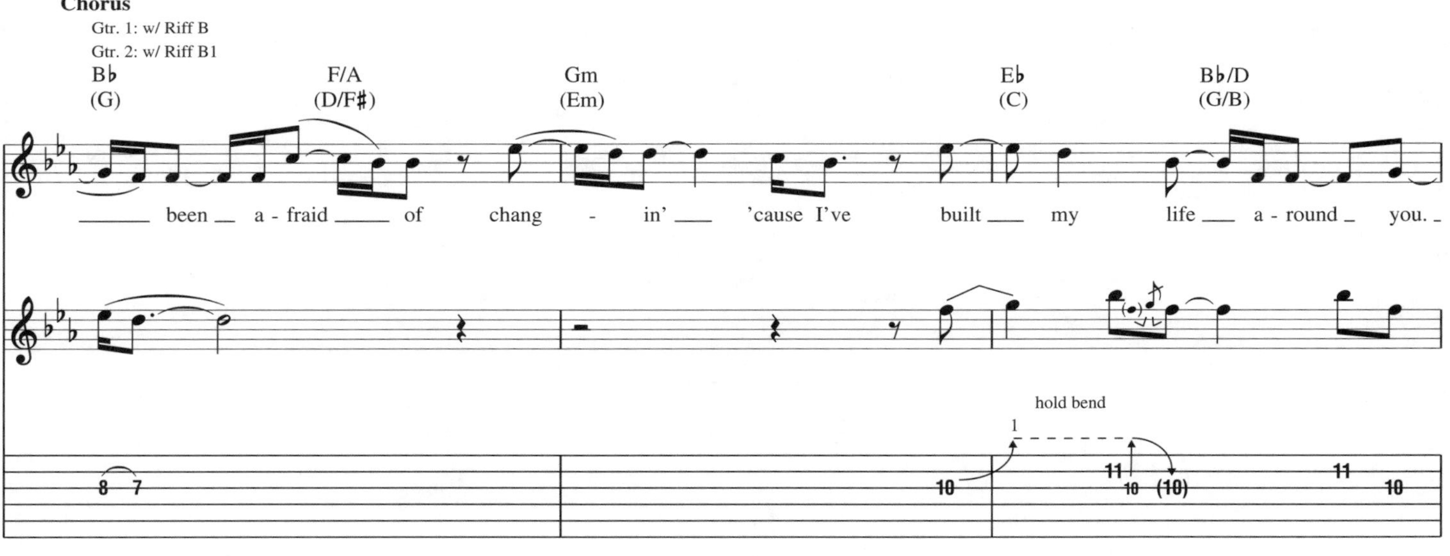
Gtr. 1: w/ Riff B
Gtr. 2: w/ Riff B1
Bb (G)
F/A (D/F#)
Gm (Em)
Eb (C)
Bb/D (G/B)
been a - fraid of chang - in' 'cause I've built my life a - round you.
hold bend

Fill 1
Gtr. 1

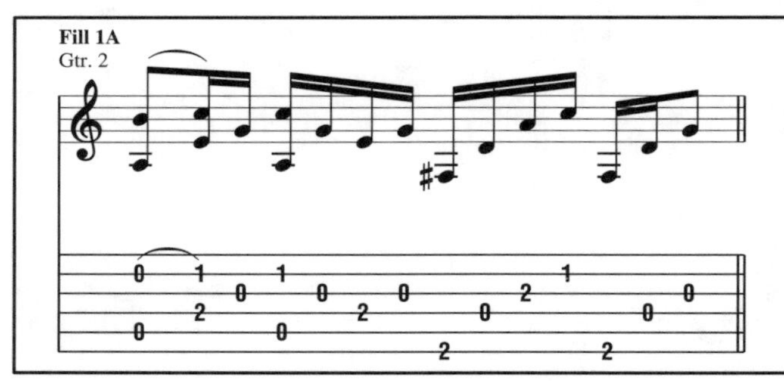
Fill 1A
Gtr. 2

Gtr. 3 tacet
Cm7 (Am7) F7/A (D7/F#) B♭ (G) F7/A (D7/F#) Gm (Em)
But time makes you bold - er. E-ven chil - dren get old - er and I'm
Gtr. 2: w/ Riff A (3 times)
E♭ (C) B♭/D (G/B) Cm7 (Am7) B♭/D (G/B)
get - tin' old - er too. Oh, I'm
Gtr. 1
E♭ (C) B♭/D (G/B) Cm7 (Am7) B♭/D (G/B)
get - tin' old - er too. Ah,
p
Gtr. 1: w/ Riff A (2 times)
E♭ (C) B♭/D (G/B) Cm7 (Am7) B♭/D (G/B) E♭ (C) B♭/D (G/B)
take my love, take it down. Ah, climbed a moun - tain and turned a - round.
Cm7 (Am7) B♭/D (G/B) Cm7 (C) B♭/D (G/B)
And if you see my re - flec - tion in the snow -

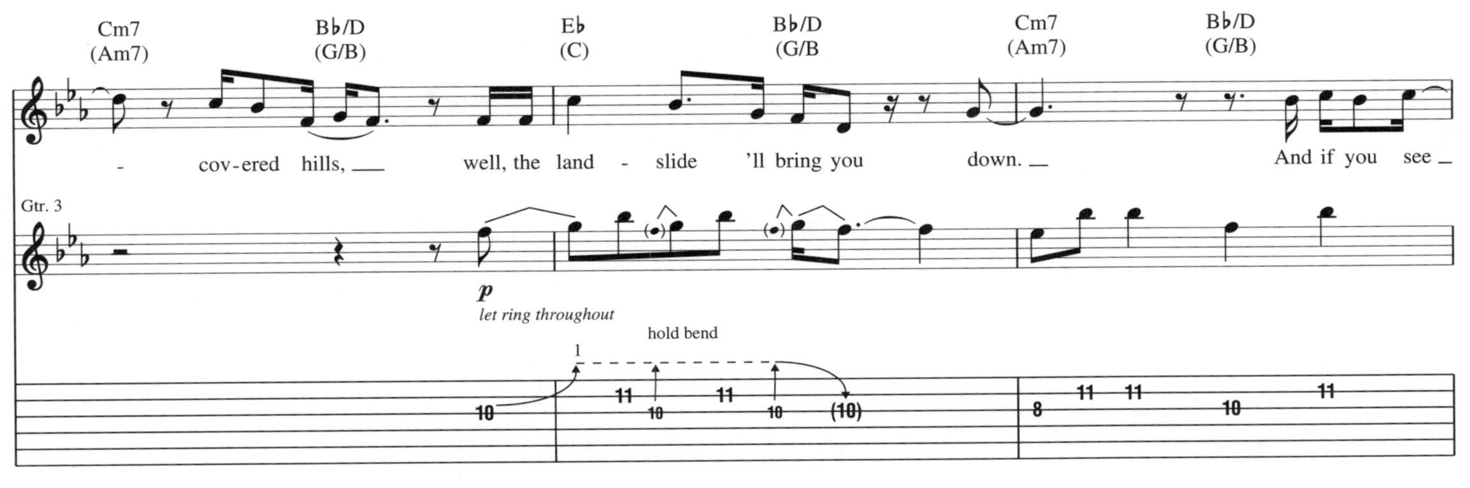
Cm7
(Am7)
Bb/D
(G/B)
Eb
(C)
Bb/D
(G/B
Cm7
(Am7)
Bb/D
(G/B)
- cov-ered hills, well, the land - slide 'll bring you down. And if you see
Gtr. 3
p
let ring throughout
hold bend

Gtrs. 1 & 2: w/ Riff A (1st meas.)
Eb
(C)
Bb/D
(G/B)
Gtrs. 1 & 2: w/ Fill 2
Cm7
(Am7)
Bb/D
(G/B)
Gtrs. 1 & 2: w/ Riff A (1st 3 meas.)
Eb
(C)
Bb/D
(G/B)
my re-flec - tion in the snow - cov-ered hills, well the land - slide 'll bring you down.
hold bend

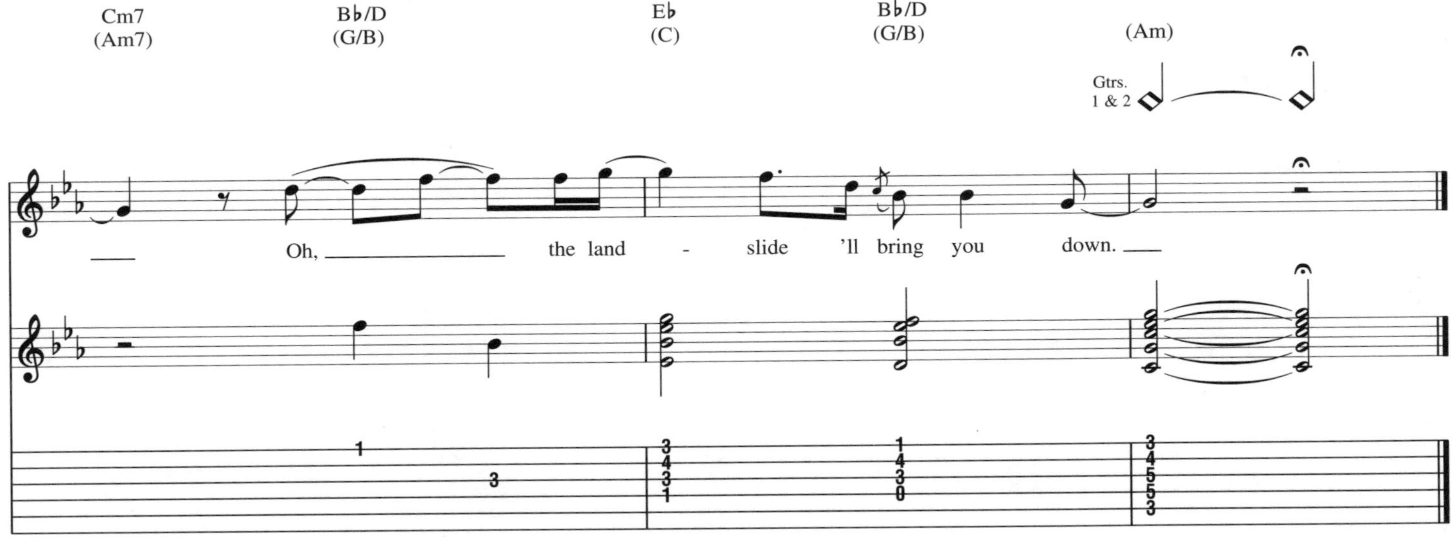
Cm7
(Am7)
Bb/D
(G/B)
Eb
(C)
Bb/D
(G/B)
(Am)
Gtrs. 1 & 2
Oh, the land - slide 'll bring you down.

Fill 2
* Gtrs. 1 & 2

Lay Down Sally

Words and Music by Eric Clapton, Marcy Levy and George Terry

𝄋 Verse

A

1. There's no rea - son that is wrong for want - ing you to stay here with
(2.) sun ain't near - ly on the rise an' we still got the moon and stars a -
(3.) long to see the morn - ing sun col - or - ing your face so dream - i - ly.

Gtr. 1

simile on repeat

Gtr. 2

simile on repeat

D A

me. I know you've got some - where to go, but
bove. Un - der - neath the vel - vet skies,
*mumbles:

let ring

1/2

*Clapton forgets lyrics.

D

won't you make _ your - self ___ at home _ and stay with me? _ 'N' don't you
love us all ___ that mat - ters. Won't _ you stay _ with me? _ 'N' don't you
If you wave _ your trou - bles down _ and stay with me? _ 'N' don't you

Chorus

E5 E6 E5 A

ev - er leave. _
ev - er leave. _
ev - er leave. _

Lay _ down _ Sal - ly, 'n'

Rhy. Fig. 2

D5 D6 D5 D6 D5 D6 D5 D6 E5 E6 E5 E6 E5 E6 E5

rest here in __ my __ arms. __ Don't you think __ you want __ some - one __ to talk __

A

__ to? Lay __ down __ Sal - ly, there's no

let ring

1.

A

talk to you.

let ring

End Rhy. Fig. 2

1/2

1/4

2. The
let ring
1/2
full

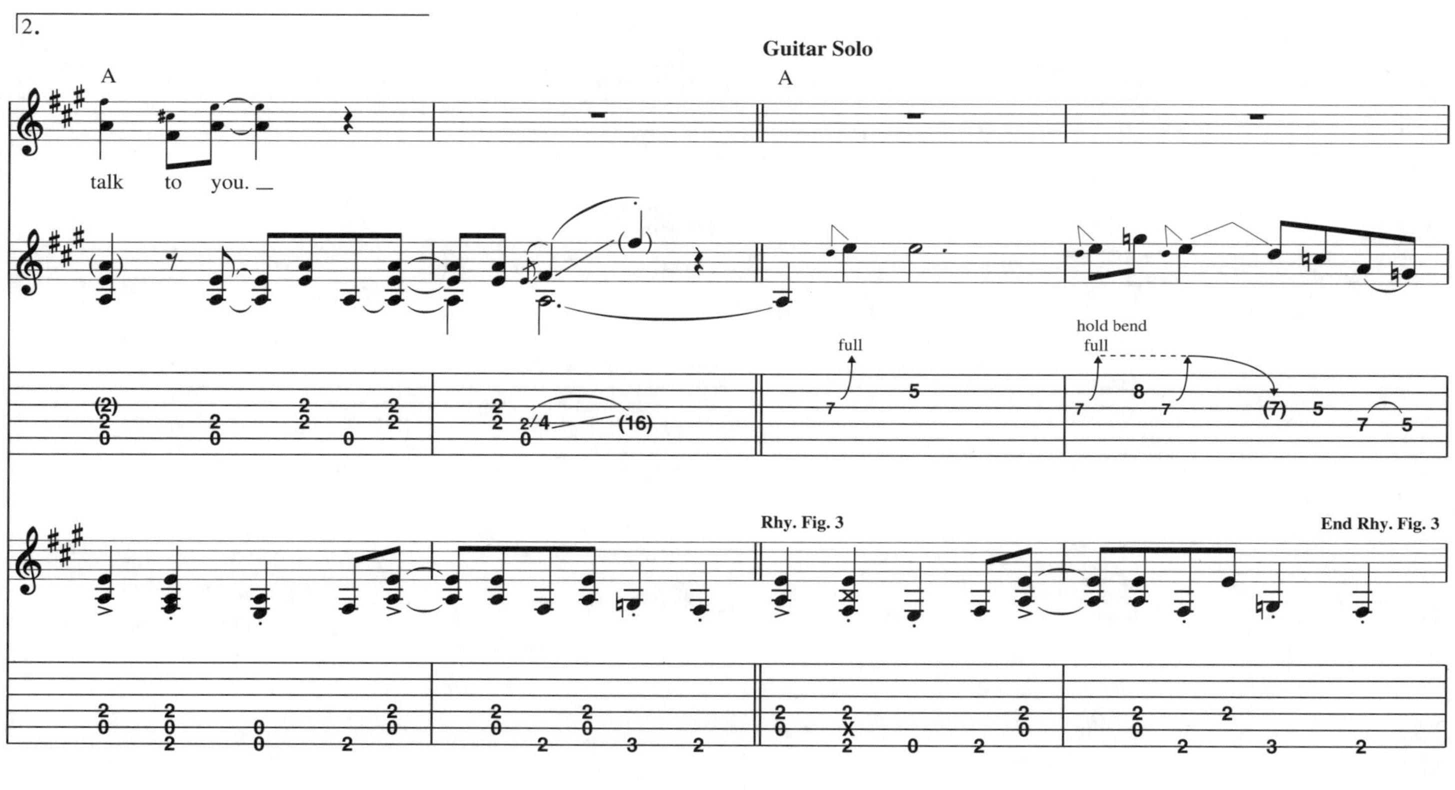
2.
Guitar Solo
A
A
talk to you.
full
hold bend
full
Rhy. Fig. 3
End Rhy. Fig. 3

Gtr. 1: w/ Rhy. Fig. 3, 23 times, simile
1/2
1/4
1/4
1/4
full
1/2
full
1/4

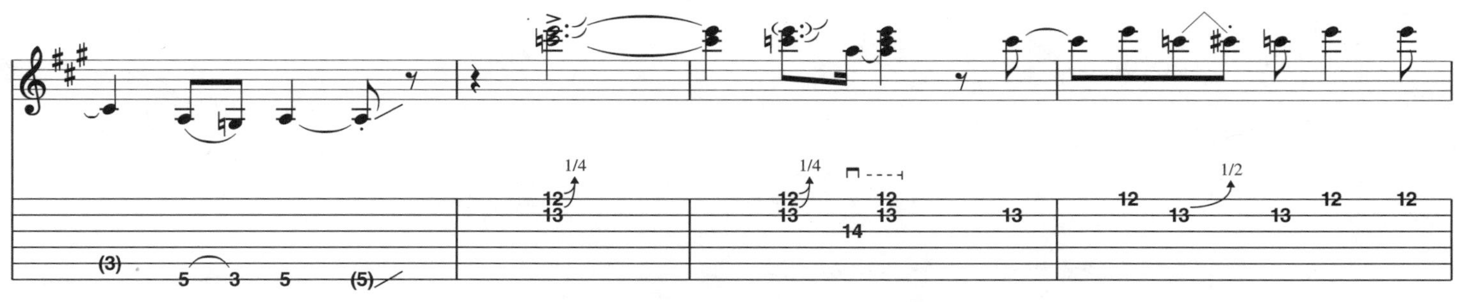

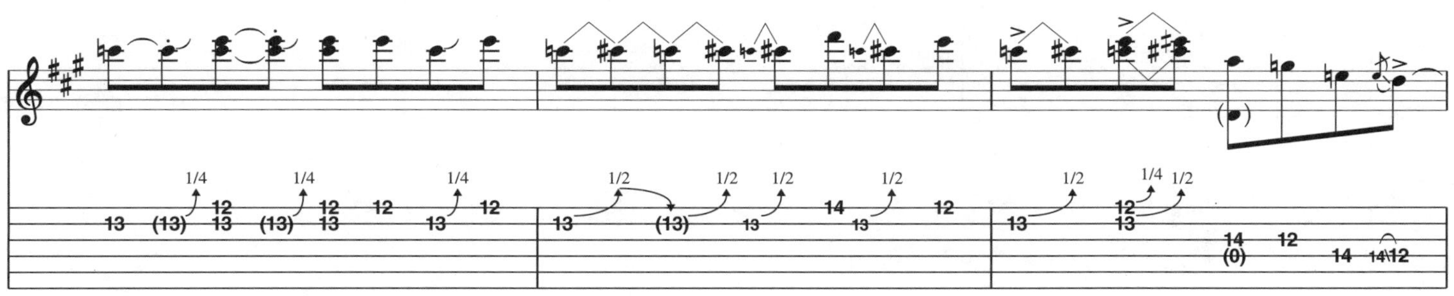

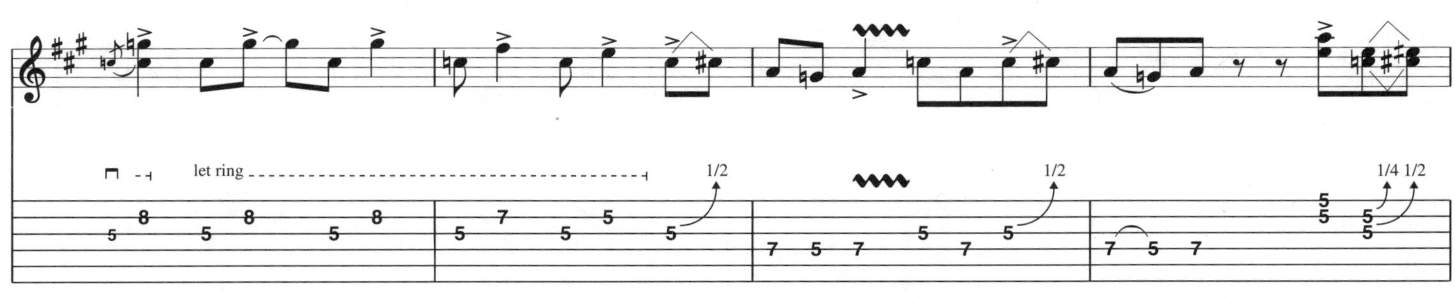
let ring

D.S. al Coda
3. I
let ring

Coda
Chorus
Gtr. 1: w/ Rhy. Fig. 2
A5 A6 A5
A5 A6 A5 A6
talk to you. Lay down Sal - ly,
let ring

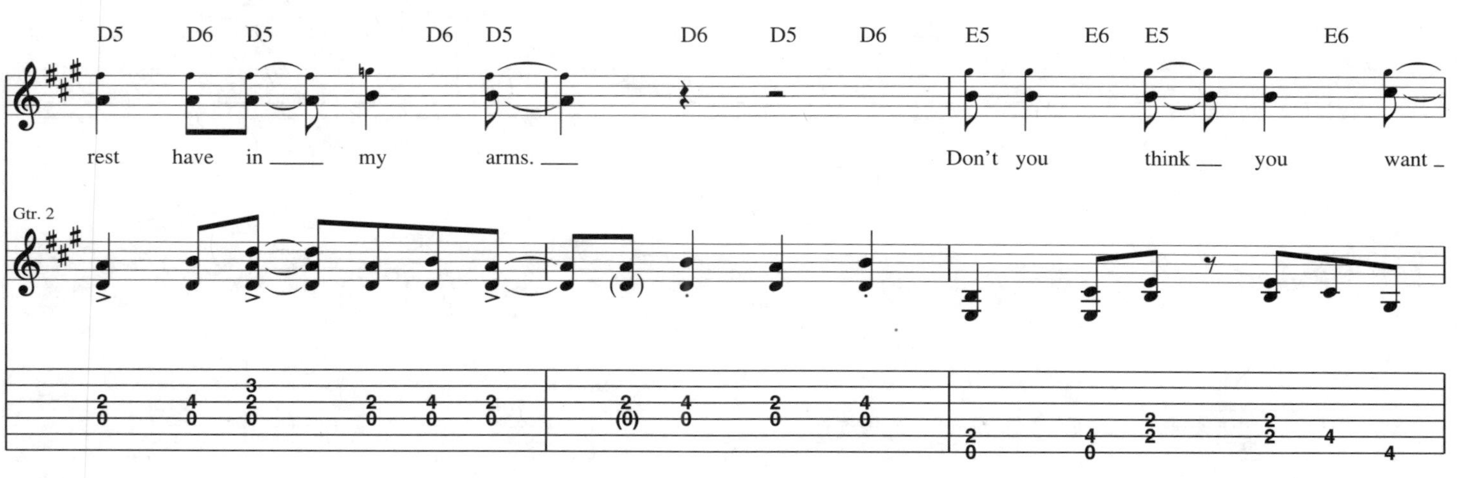
D5 D6 D5 D6 D5 D6 D5 D6 E5 E6 E5 E6
rest have in my arms. Don't you think you want
Gtr. 2

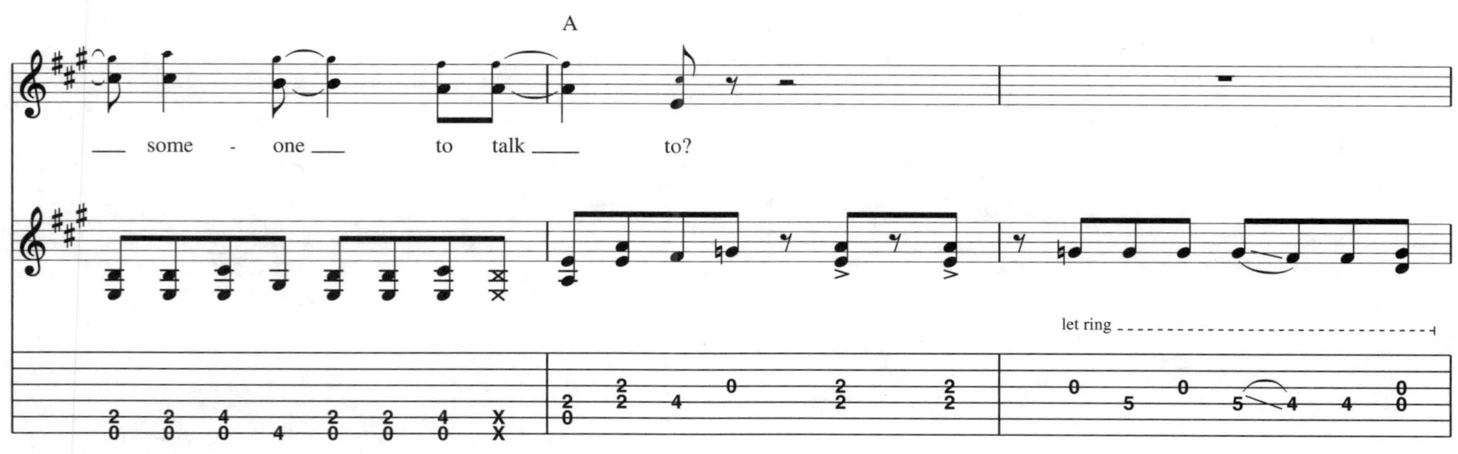
A
some - one to talk to?
let ring

D5
D6
D5
D6
D5
Lay down Sally, no need to leave so soon.
D6
D5
D6
E5
E6
E5
E6
E5
E6
E5
E6
I been tryin' all night long just to
A5
A6
A5
talk to you.
Outro
Gtr. 1: w/ Rhy. Fig. 3, 22 times, simile
A
mf
let ring
1/2
full
let ring
1/2
full

let ring
1/2
full
let ring
1/2
full
full
let ring
P.M.
Harm.
1/2
full
let ring
1/2
full
let ring
1/2
full

let ring
P.M.
1/4
1/2
full
1., 2., 3., 4.
5.
on cue:
A
Gtr. 1
Gtr. 2
simile on repeats
steady gliss.
*slow trill

Let It Be

Words and Music by John Lennon and Paul McCartney

Chorus
Gtr. 1 tacet
Am G6 Fmaj7 C G
let it be. Ah, let it be, let it be. Whis-per words of wis-dom, let it
(Oo, oo, oo, oo. Oo, oo,
F C Verse G Am Fmaj7 F6
be. 2. And when the bro - ken heart - ed peo-ple liv-ing in the world a - gree,
oo, oo.) 4. And when the night is cloud - y, there is still a light that shines on me,
Gtr. 1: w/ Fill 1, 2nd time
C G F C G
there will be an an - swer, let it be. For though they may be part - ed, there is
shine un-til to-mor - row, let it be. I wake up to the sound of mu-sic,
Am Fmaj7 F6 C G F C
still a chance that they will see. There will be an an-swer, let it be.
Moth-er Mar - y comes to me, speak - ing words of wis-dom, let it be.
Let it be,
Chorus
Gtr. 1: w/ Fill 2, 2nd time
To Coda
Am G6 Fmaj7 C G
let it be. Ah, let it be, let it be. Yeah, there will be an an - swer, let it
(Oo, oo, oo, oo. Oo, oo,
F C Am G6 Fmaj7 C
be. Let it be, let it be. Ah, let it be, let it be.
oo, oo. Oo, oo, oo, oo.
Fill 1
Gtr. 1
Fill 2
Gtr. 1
full

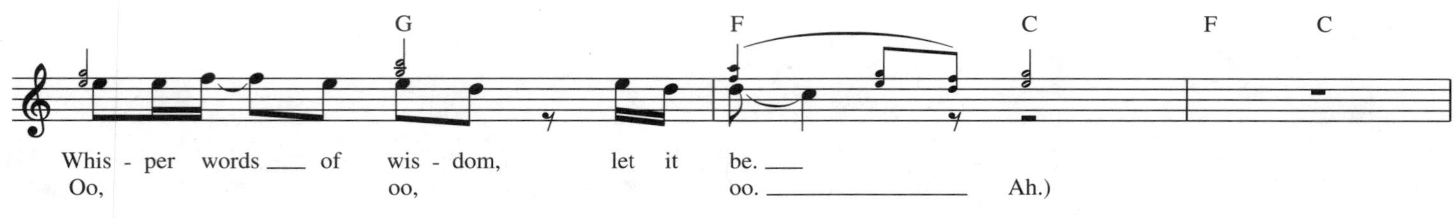
G
F
C
F
C
Whis - per words of wis - dom, let it be.
Oo, oo, oo. Ah.)

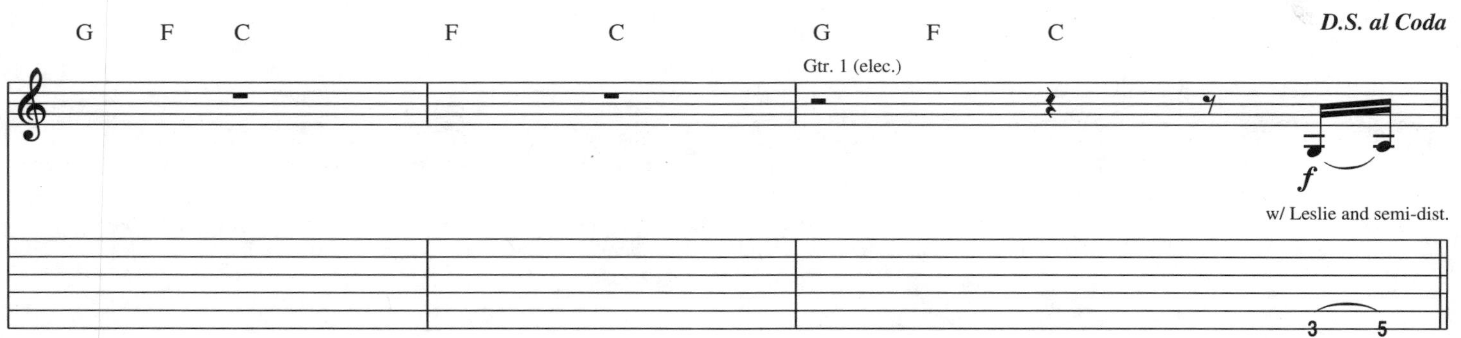
D.S. al Coda
G F C
F C
G F C
Gtr. 1 (elec.)
w/ Leslie and semi-dist.

Coda
F C Am G6 Fmaj7 C
be, hee, ah. Let it be, let it be. Ah, let it be, yeah, let it be.
oo, oo. Oo, oo, oo, oo.)
Gtr. 1
1/4
1/4
full
full
full

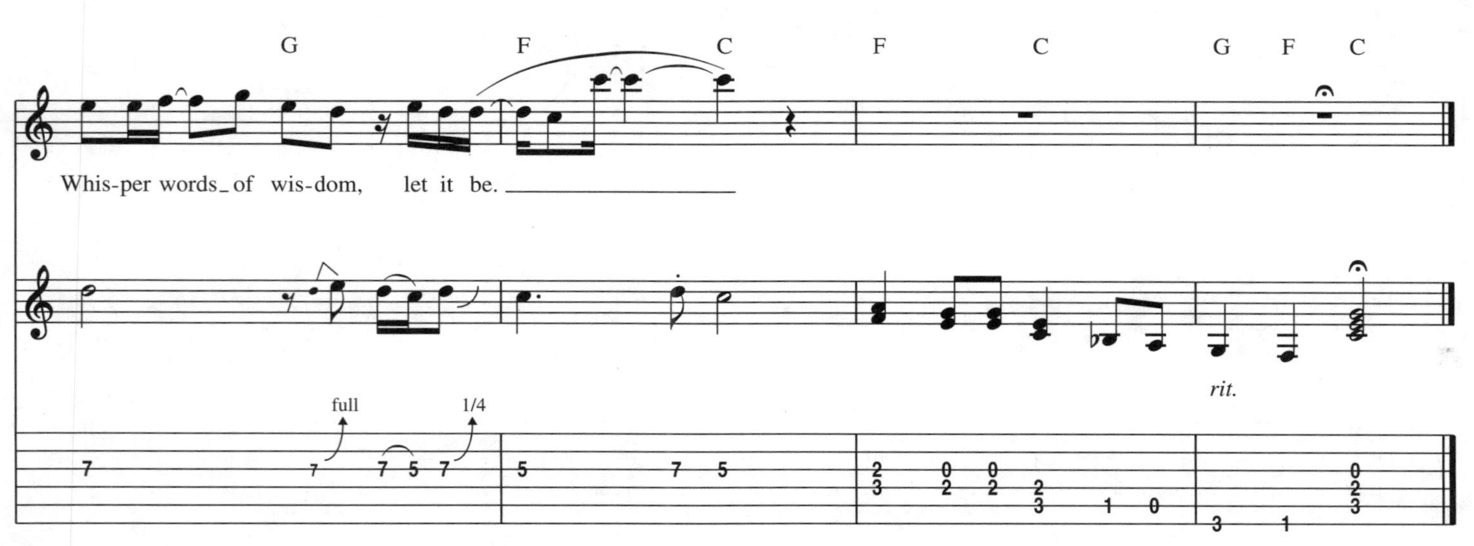
G F C F C G F C
Whis-per words of wis-dom, let it be.
full
1/4
rit.

Maggie May

Words and Music by Rod Stewart and Martin Quittenton

Verse
Gtr. 3 tacet
A
G5/D
D
1. Wake up, Mag - gie, I think I got some - thin' to say to you.
2. morn - in' sun, when it's in your face, real - ly shows your age.
3. All I need - ed was a friend to lend a guid - ing hand.
4. See Additional Lyrics
Gtr. 2
simile on repeats
A
G5/D
It's late Sep - tem - ber and I real - ly should be back
But that don't wor - ry me none; in my eyes, you're ev -
But you turned in - to a lov - er, and moth - er what a lov - er; you wore
D
G5
D
at school. I know I keep you a - mused, but I
'ry - thing. I laughed at all of your jokes. My love
me out. All you did was wreck my bed, and in the
G5
A
Em
F#m7
feel I'm be - ing used.
you did - n't need to coax.
morn - in' kick me in the head.
Oh Mag - gie, I could - n't have tried an - y

Chorus

Gtr. 2: w/ Rhy. Fill 2, 2nd, 3rd & 4th times, simile

Em Dadd9/F# Em A

more. ___ 1., 2. You led me a - way from home just to
3. You led me a - way from home 'cause you

Em A Em

save you from be - ing a - lone. (1.) You stole my heart, ___ and that's ___
(2.) You stole my soul, and that's a
did - n't wan - na be a - lone. 3. You stole my heart; ___ I could - n't

To Coda 𝄌

Gtr. 2: w/ Rhy. Fill 3, 2nd, 3rd & 4th times

A D

play 3 times

___ what real - ly hurts. ___ 2. The
pain I can do ___ with - out. ___
leave you if ___ I tried. ___

Rhy. Fill 2
Gtr. 2

Rhy. Fill 3
Gtr. 2

Guitar Solo
Em
A
D
G
6
3fr
G5
Rhy. Fig. 1
Gtr. 2
Gtr. 4 (elec.)
mf
w/ slight dist.
1/2
Em
D
G5
D
D.S. al Coda
End Rhy. Fig. 1
1/2
1/2
full
Coda
Guitar Solo
Gtr. 2: w/ Rhy. Fig. 1, 1 1/2 times, simile
Gtr. 4
Em
A
D
1/2
G5
Em
D
G5
1/2
1/2
1/2
D
Em
1/2
1/2

A
D
G5
1/2
1/2
(9)
Em
Gtr. 2
G5
1/2
1/2
Mandolin Solo
D
Dsus4
Gtr. 4 tacet
G5/D
*Gtr. 3
8va
*Two mandolins arr. for one gtr.
Gtr. 4
let ring
1/2
D
D
Rhy. Fig. 2
*Dsus4/E
Gtr. 3
8va
*Bass plays E.

Gtr. 2: w/ Rhy. Fig. 2, 3 times, simile
G5/D
D
Em7/D
End Rhy. Fig. 2
Dsus4/E
G5/D
D
Em7/D
D
Dsus4/E
G5/D
D
Em7/D
D
Dsus4/E
G5/D
Outro
D
Em7/D
D
Rhy. Fig. 3
*Dsus4/E
Gtr. 2
Mag - gie, I wished I'd nev -
Gtr. 3
*Bass plays E.

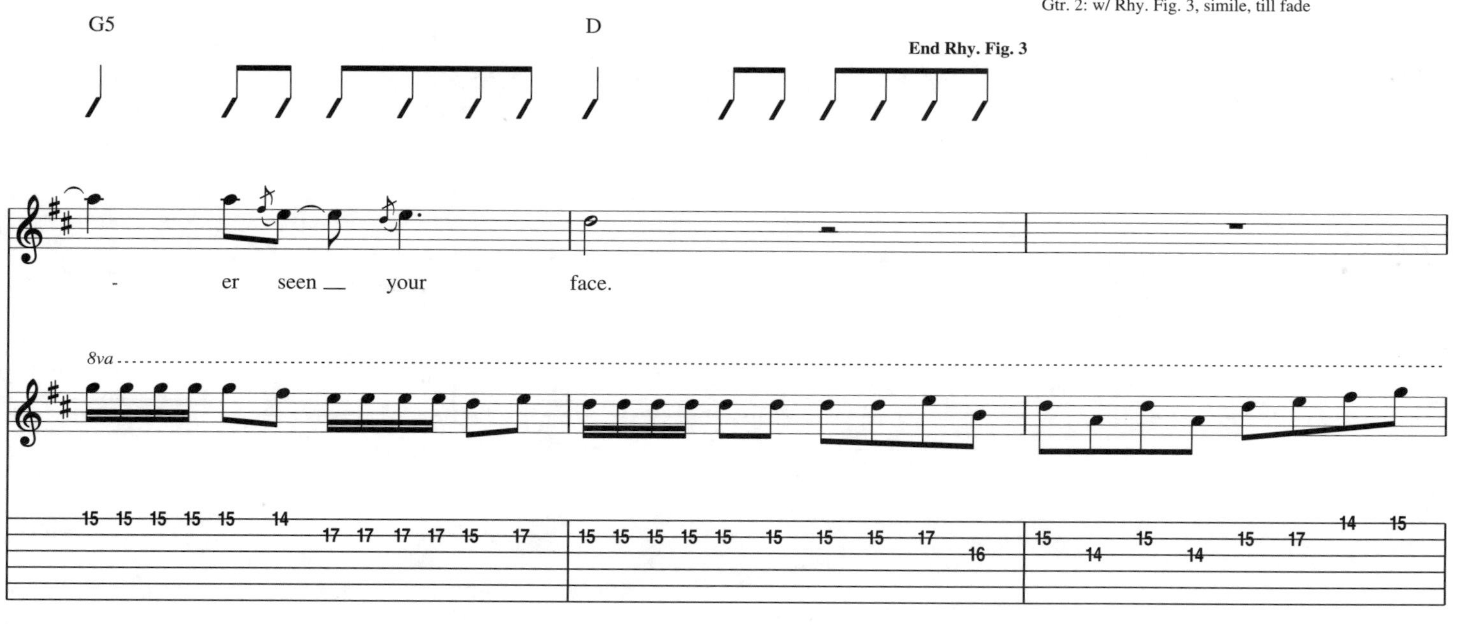
Gtr. 2: w/ Rhy. Fig. 3, simile, till fade
G5
D
End Rhy. Fig. 3
- er seen your face.
8va
15 15 15 15 15 14 17 17 17 17 15 17
15 15 15 15 15 15 15 15 17 16
15 14 15 14 15 17 14 15

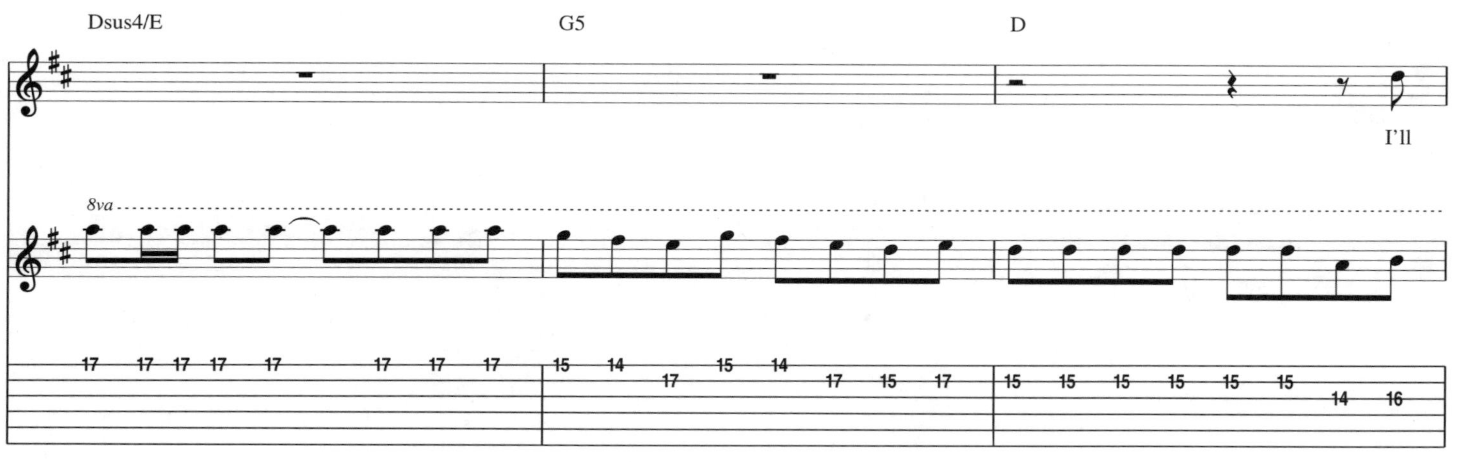
Dsus4/E
G5
D
I'll
8va
17 17 17 17 17 17 17 17
15 14 17 15 14 17 15 17
15 15 15 15 15 15 14 16

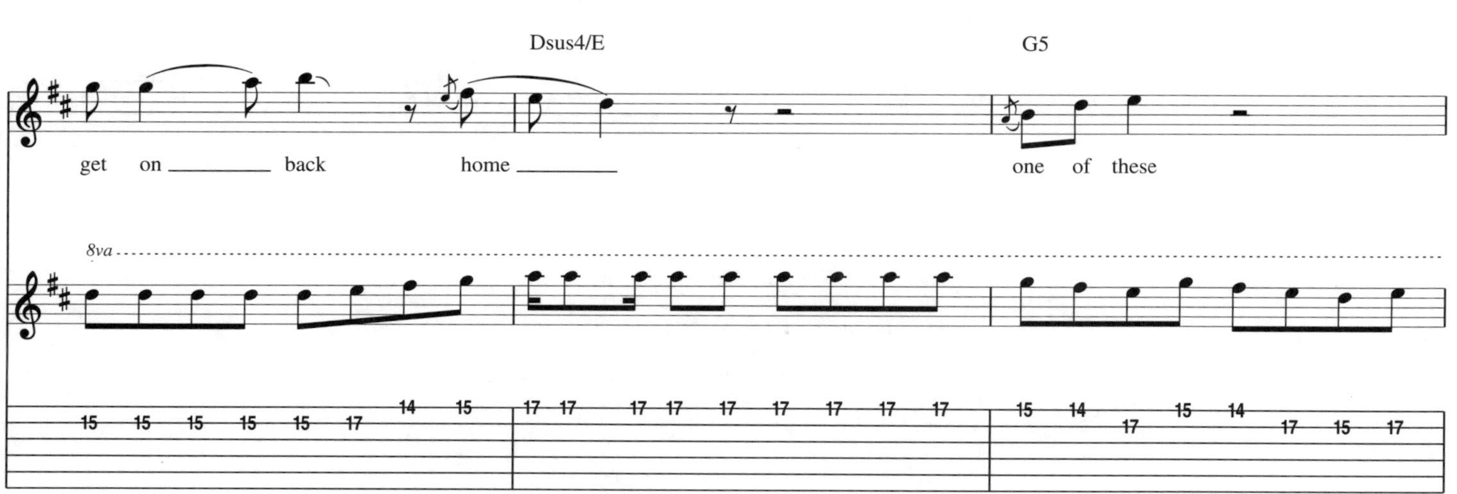
Dsus4/E
G5
get on back home
one of these
8va
15 15 15 15 15 17 14 15
17 17 17 17 17 17 17 17 17
15 14 17 15 14 17 15 17

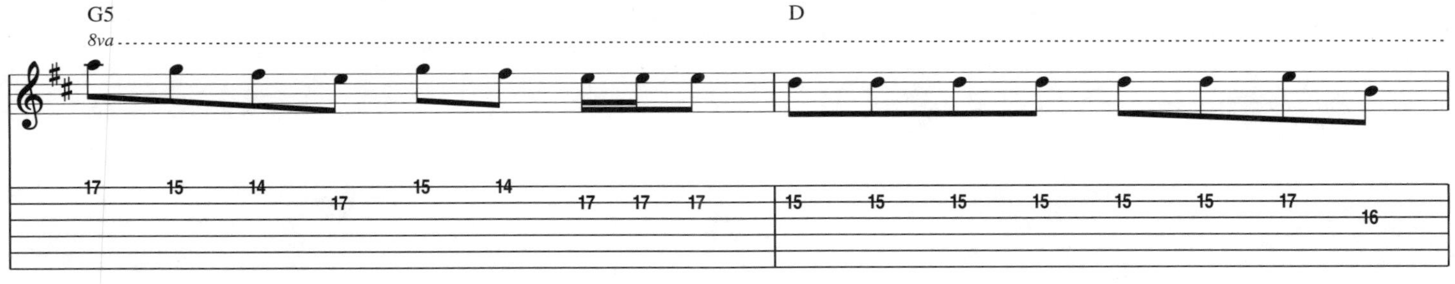

Begin Fade

Fade Out

Additional Lyrics

4. I suppose I could collect by books and get back to school,
   Or steal my daddy's cue and make a living out of playing pool,
   Or find myself a rock and roll band that needs a helping hand.
   Oh Maggie, I wished I'd never seen your face.
   You made a first class fool out of me,
   But I was blind as a fool can be.
   You stole my heart, but I love you anyway.

No Woman No Cry

Words and Music by Vincent Ford

Verse
Gtr. 1: w/ Riff A, 7 times, simile
Gtr. 2: w/ Rhy. Fig. 2, 7 times, simile
C C/B Am F C C/B
1. Said, I re - mem - ber when we used to sit in the gov-ern-ment's yard in
2.,3. Said I re-mem - ber when we used to sit in the gov-ern-ment's yard in
Gtr. 1
Riff A
End Riff A
Gtr. 2
(clean)
Rhy. Fig. 2
End Rhy. Fig. 2
let ring
mf
Am F C C/B Am F
Trench - town. O - ba, o - ba, serv - ing the hyp - o - crites as they
Trench - town. And then Georg - ie would make a fire light, as it was
C C/B Am F C C/B
would min - gle with the good peo - ple we met. Good friends we had, oh
log-wood burn - in' through the night. Then we would cook corn - meal
Am F C C/B Am F
good friends we've lost a - long the way. (Yeah.)
por - ridge, of which I'll share with you. (Ooh.)
C C/B Am F
In this bright fu - ture you can't for - get your past.
My feet is my on - ly car - riage.
To Coda
1.
2.
C C/B Am F Am F
So dry your tears I say. And
So I've got to push on through. But while I'm gone, I'm mean - a...

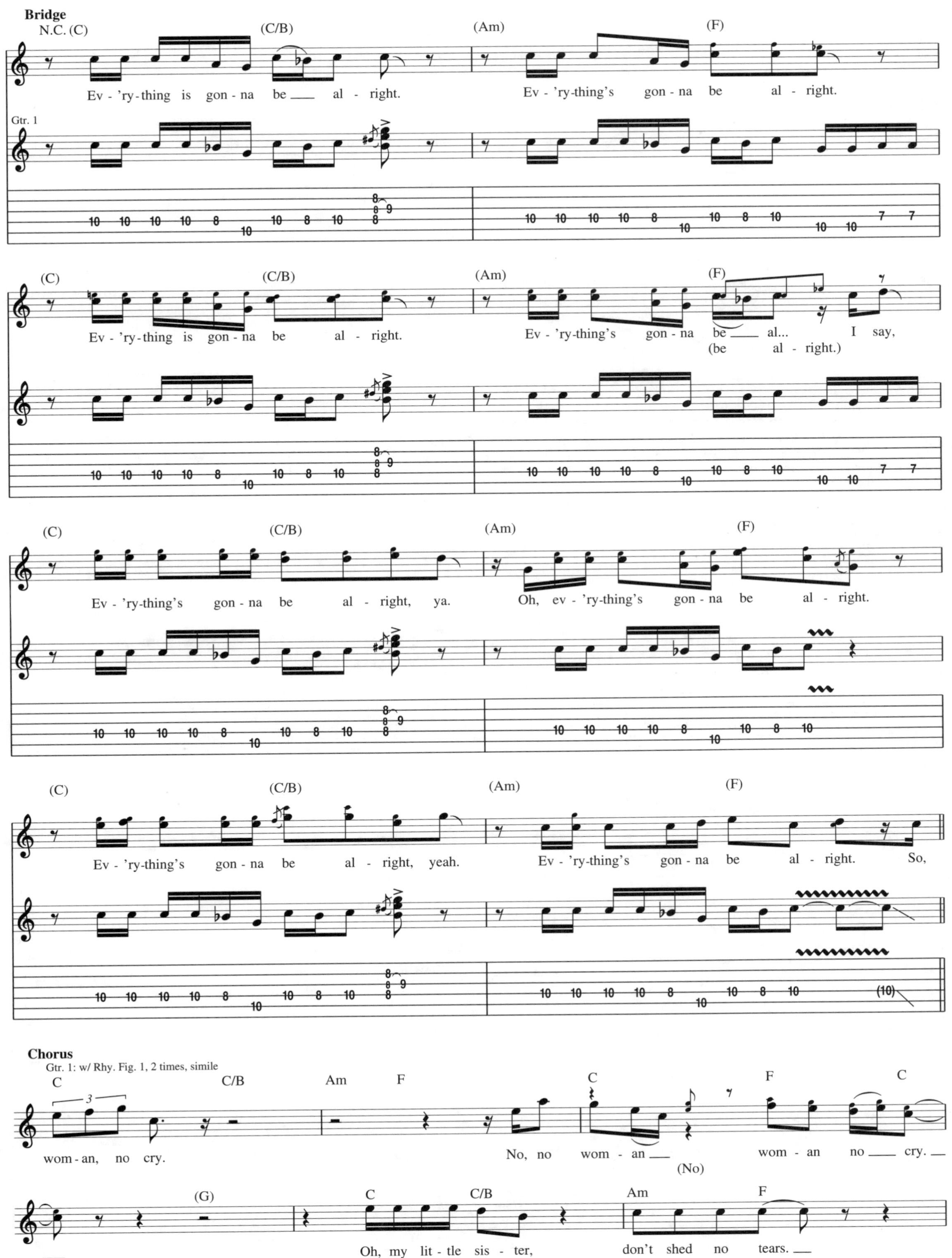
Bridge
N.C. (C)
(C/B)
(Am)
(F)
Ev - 'ry-thing is gon - na be al - right.
Ev - 'ry-thing's gon - na be al - right.
Gtr. 1
(C)
(C/B)
(Am)
(F)
Ev - 'ry-thing is gon - na be al - right.
Ev - 'ry-thing's gon - na be al... I say,
(be al - right.)
(C)
(C/B)
(Am)
(F)
Ev - 'ry-thing's gon - na be al - right, ya.
Oh, ev - 'ry-thing's gon - na be al - right.
(C)
(C/B)
(Am)
(F)
Ev - 'ry-thing's gon - na be al - right, yeah.
Ev - 'ry-thing's gon - na be al - right. So,
Chorus
Gtr. 1: w/ Rhy. Fig. 1, 2 times, simile
C
C/B
Am
F
C
F
C
wom - an, no cry.
No, no wom - an
(No)
wom - an no cry.
(G)
C
C/B
Am
F
Oh, my lit - tle sis - ter,
don't shed no tears.

C
F
C
(G)
No, wom - an, no cry.
Gtr. 2
Guitar Solo
C
C/B
Am
F
C
F
C
Gtr. 2
full
full
Gtr. 1
Rhy. Fig. 3
let ring throughout
(G)
Gtr. 1: w/ Rhy. Fig. 3, 3 times, simile
C
C/B
Am
F
let ring
End Rhy. Fig. 3
C
F
C
(G)
full
1/4
full
1/2
full
1/2
1/2
full
C
C/B
Am
F
full
full

C
F
C
(G)
full

C
C/B
Am
F
let ring

D.S. al Coda

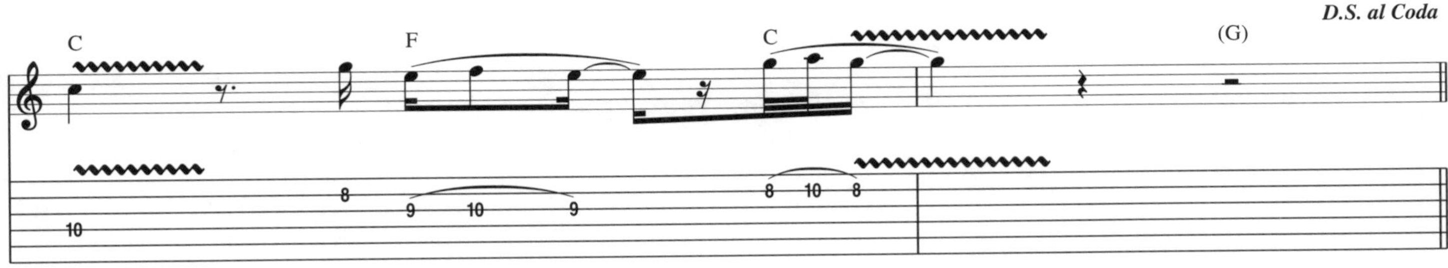
C
F
C
(G)

Coda
Outro
Gtr. 1: w/ Rhy. Fig. 1, 5 times, simile
(G)
C
C/B
Am
F
through, but while I'm gone...
No woman, no cry.
Gtr. 2
P.M.

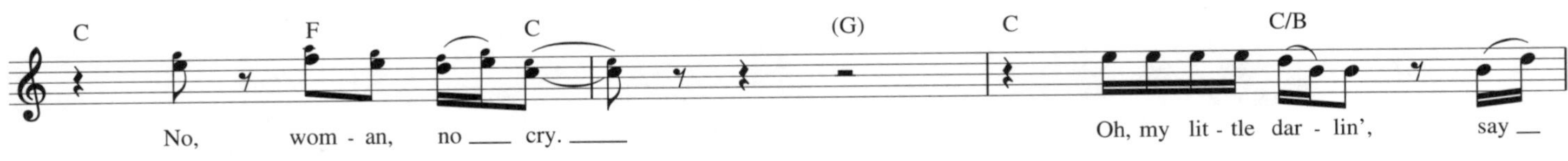
C
F
C
(G)
C
C/B
No, wom - an, no cry.
Oh, my lit - tle dar - lin', say

Am
F
C
F
C
(G)
don't shed no tears.
No, wom - an, no cry.
Eh!

C
C/B
Am
F
Lit - tle dar - lin' don't shed no tears.
C
F
C
(G)
No, wom - an, no cry.
C
C/B
Am
F
Lit - tle sis - ter, don't shed no tears.
C
F
C
(G)
No, wom - an, no cry.
C
C/B
Am
F
C
F
C
(G)
* Gtrs. 1 & 2
C
C/B
Am
F
let ring throughout
*Two gtrs. arr. for one.
C
F
C
rit.

Oye Como Va

Words and Music by Tito Puente

Am7
D9
Am7
D9
Am7
D9
Am7
D9
Am7
D9
Am7
D9
1/2
Interlude
Am7
D9
Gtrs. 1 & 2
play 3 times
Am7
D9
Gtr. 1 tacet
Gtr. 2
Am
Am(maj7)
D9sus4
D9
Am
Am(maj7)
D9sus4
D9
mp
w/ clean tone
let ring throughout

Am7
Am(maj7)
D9sus4
D9
Am
Am(maj7)
Am7
Am6
Gtrs. 1 & 2
Organ Solo
Gtr. 2: w/ Rhy. Fig. 1, 11 times, simile
Bridge
Gtrs. 1 & 2: w/ Rhy. Fig. 1, 2 times
Am
D
Am
Verse
Gtrs. 1 & 2: w/ Rhy. Fig. 1, 2 times, simile
Am7
D9
Oy - e co - mo va,
mi rit - mo.
Bue - no pa go - zar,
mu - la - ta.
Bridge
D7
Gtrs. 1 & 2
Gtr. 2
Gtr. 1
divisi
Guitar Solo
Gtr. 1: w/ Rhy. Fig. 1, 12 times, simile
Gtr. 2
w/ dist.
1/2

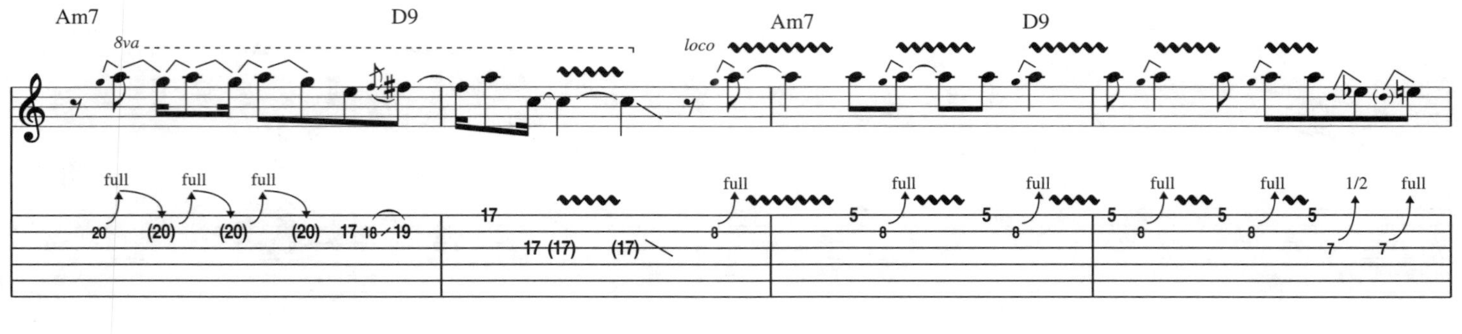
Am7
D9
8va
loco
Am7
D9
full
full
full
full
full
full
full
full
full
1/2
full

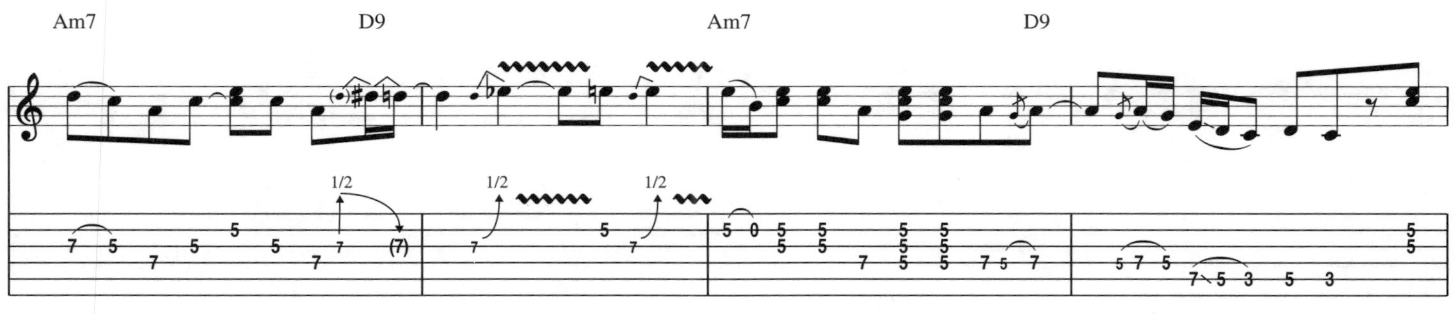
Am7
D9
Am7
D9
1/2
1/2
1/2

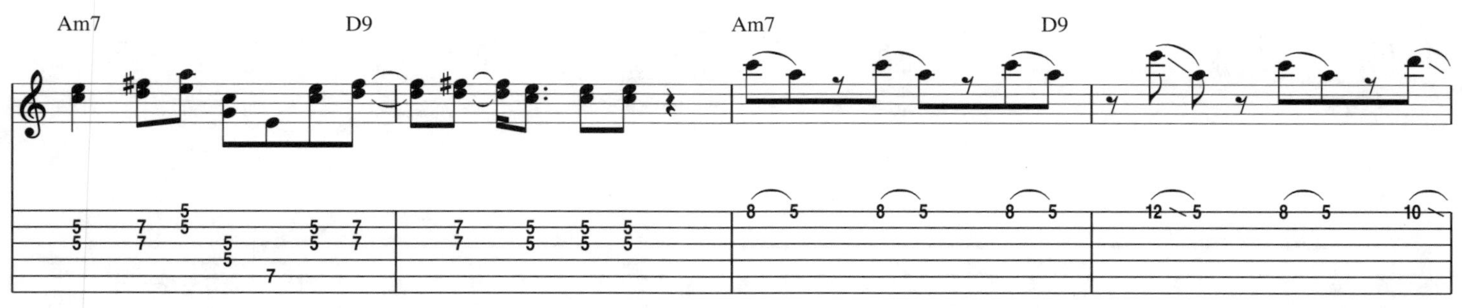
Am7
D9
Am7
D9

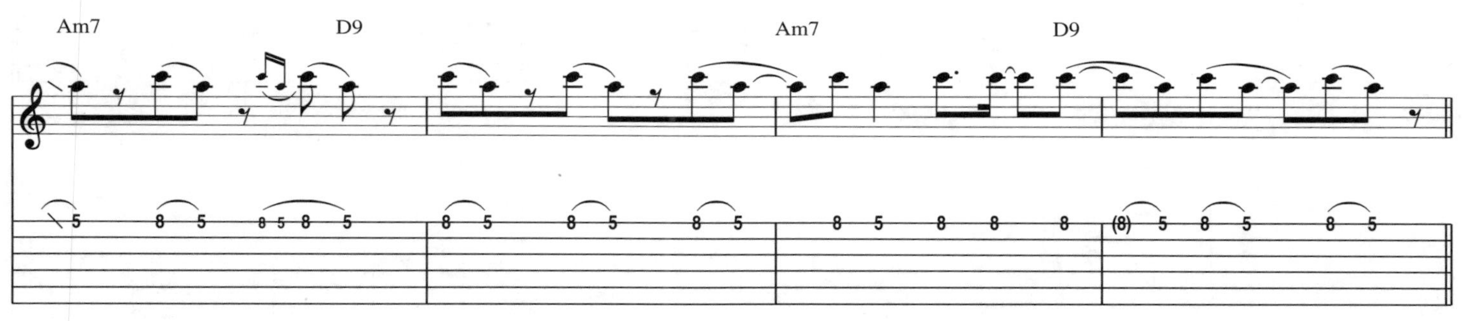
Am7
D9
Am7
D9

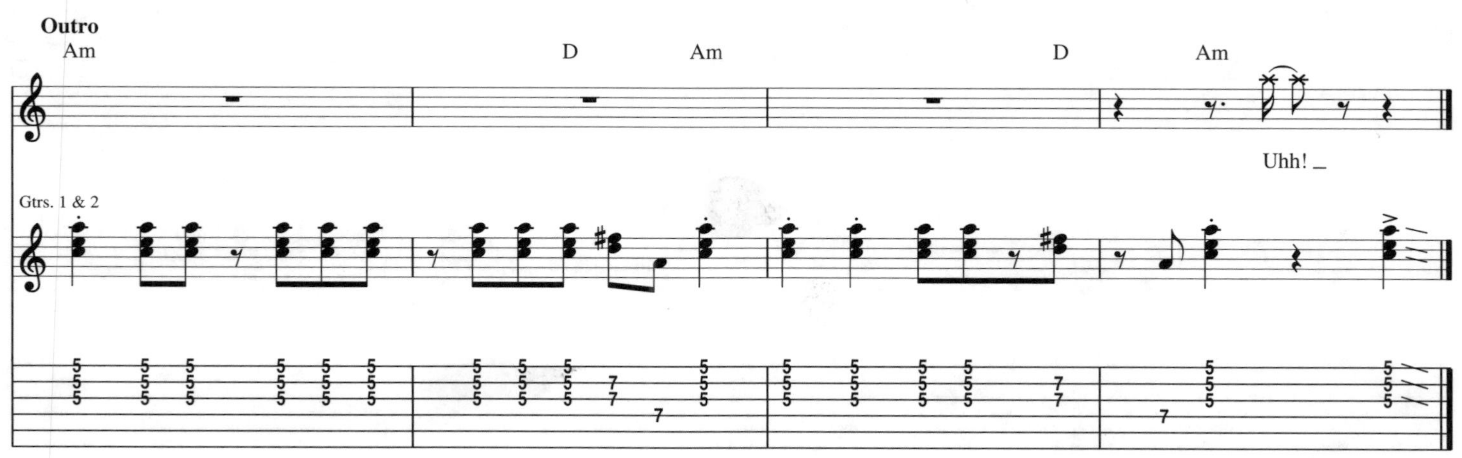
Outro
Am
D
Am
D
Am
Uhh!
Gtrs. 1 & 2

Paranoid

Words and Music by Anthony Iommi, John Osbourne, William Ward and Terence Butler

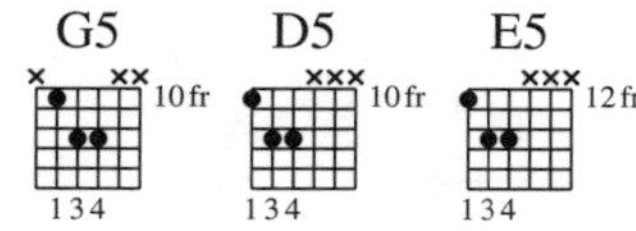

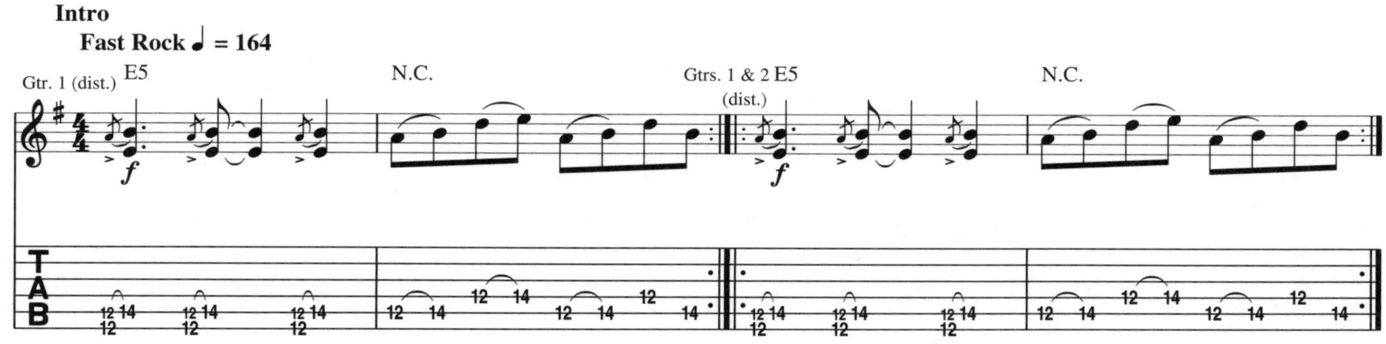

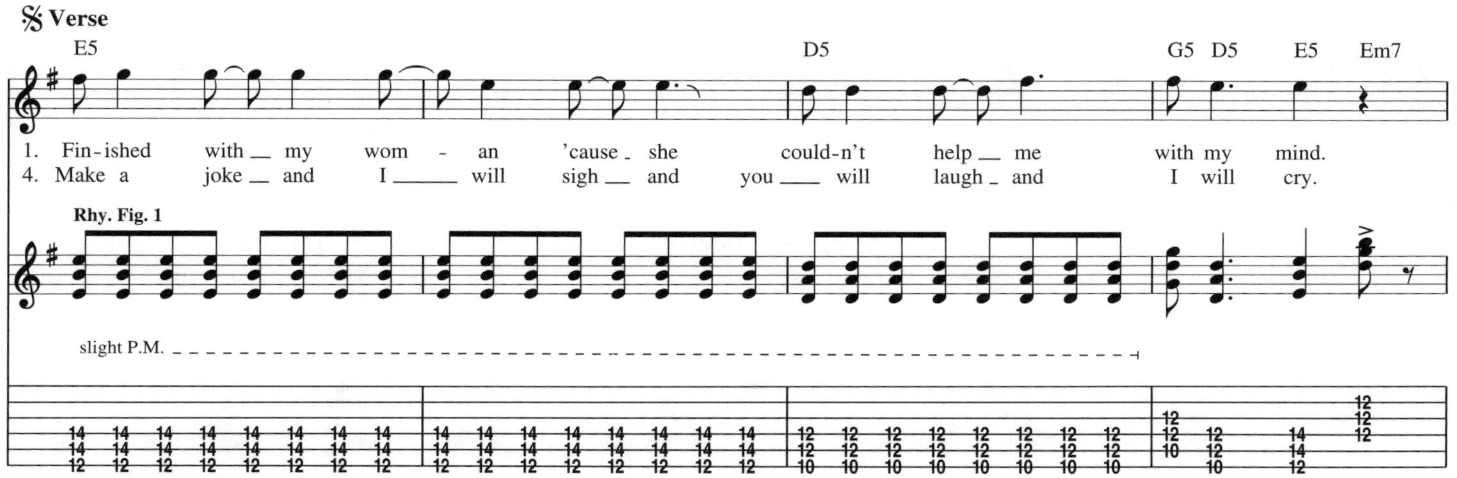

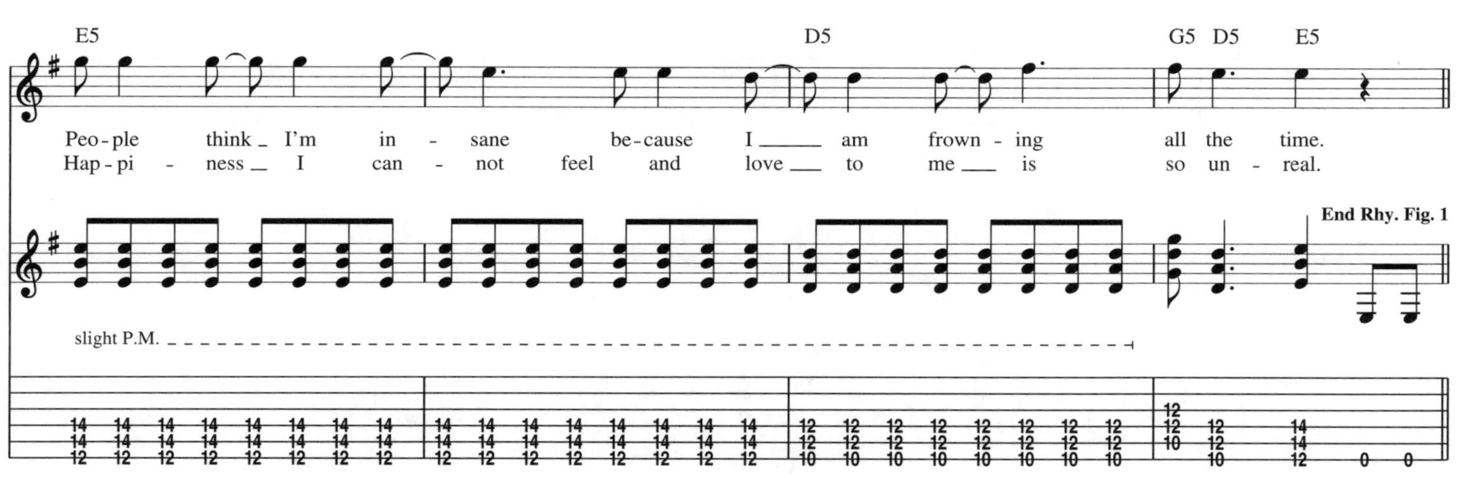

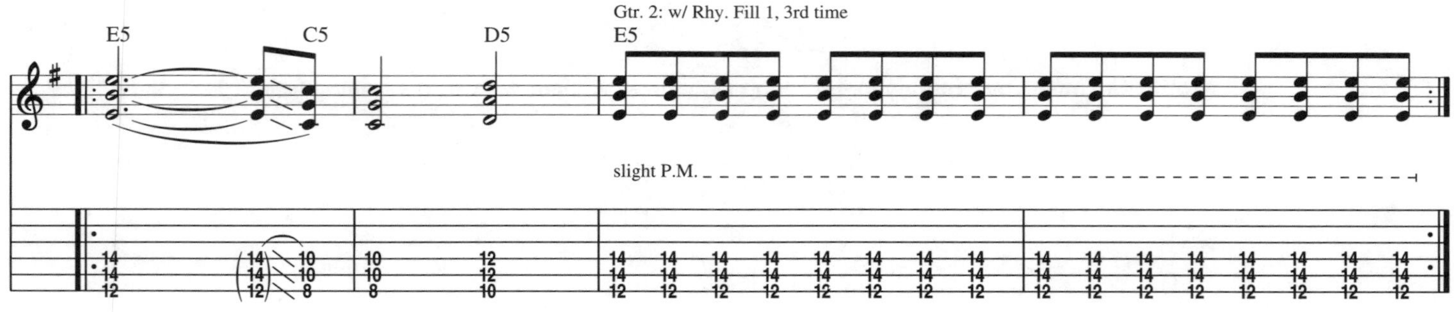

Verse

Bridge

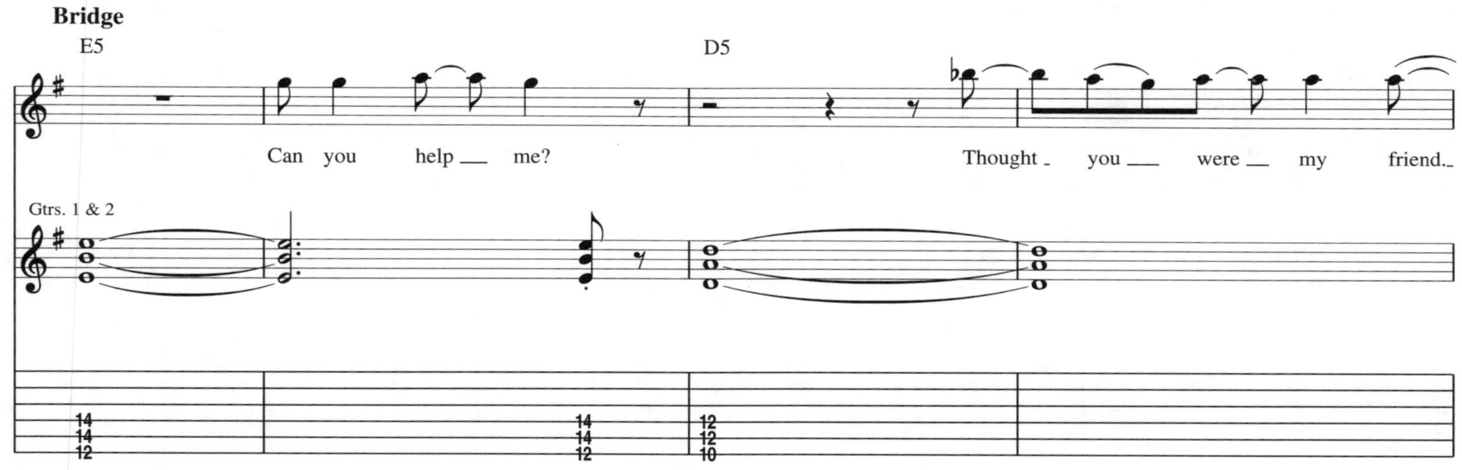

Interlude

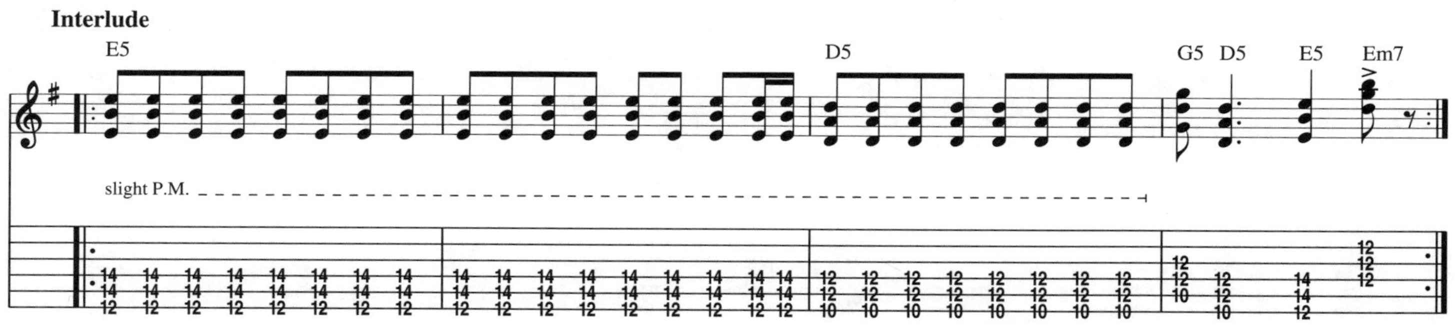

Verse

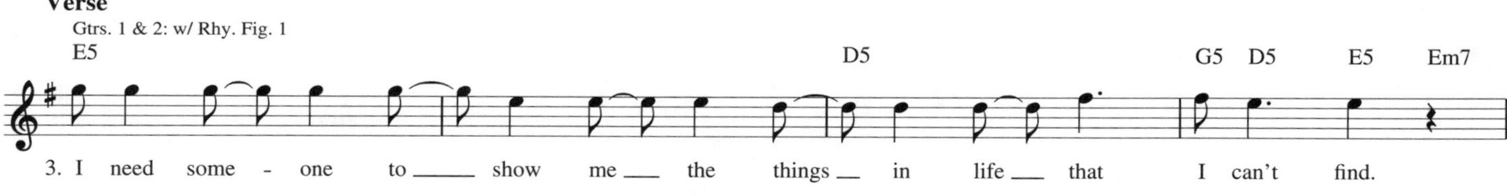

Guitar Solo

*With heavily distorted ring modulation effect in right channel.

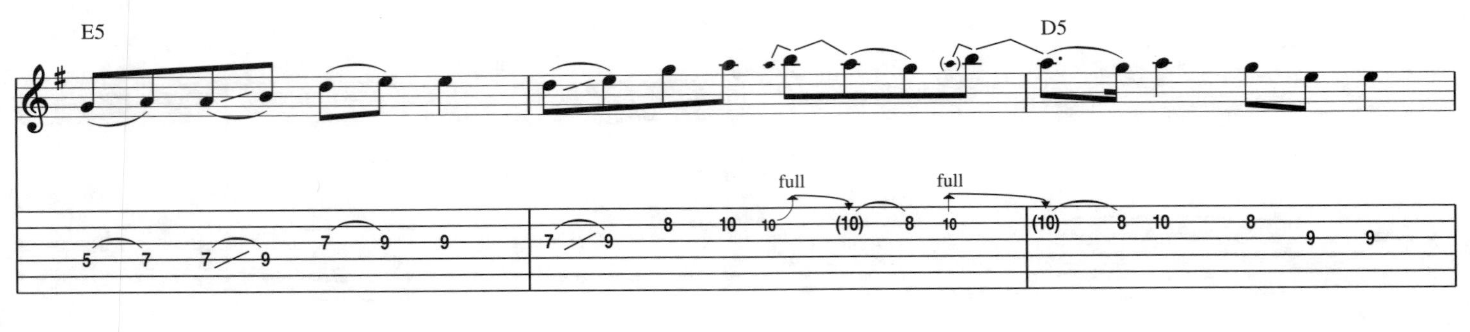
E5
D5
full
full

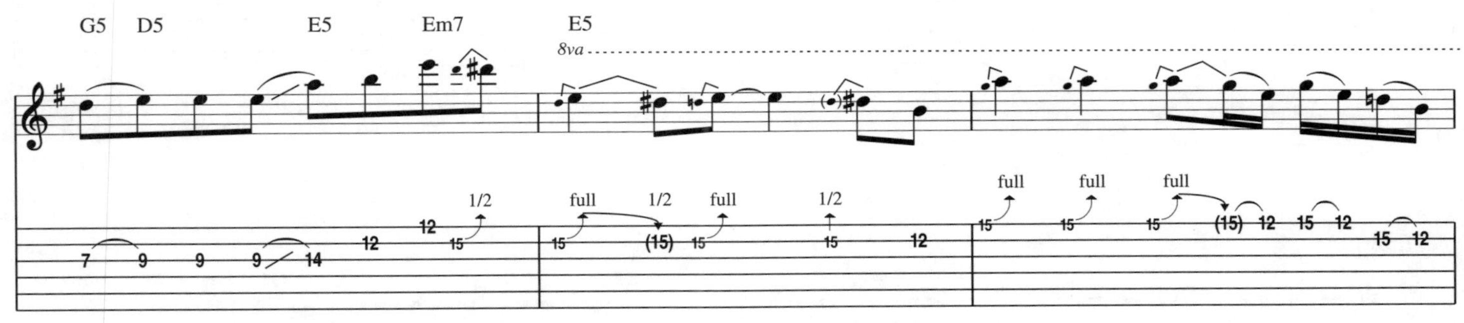
G5 D5 E5 Em7
E5
8va
1/2
full
1/2
full
1/2
full
full
full

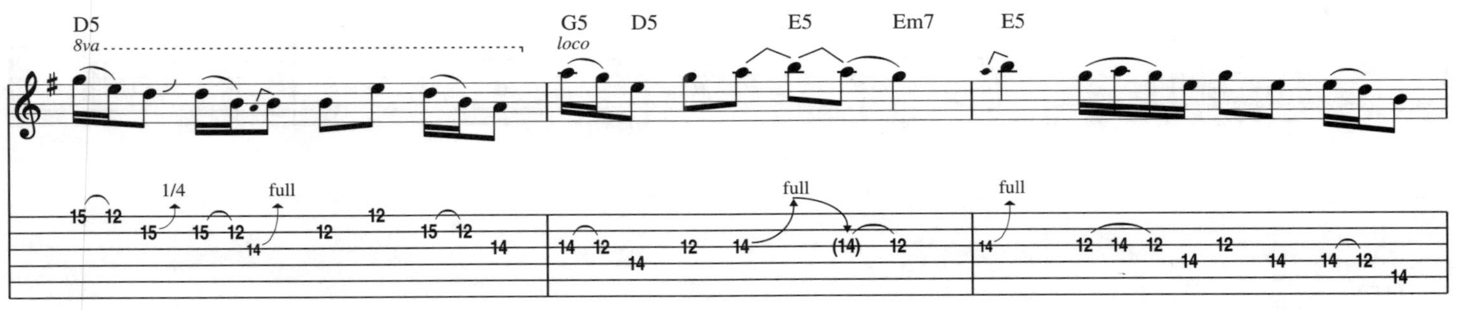
D5
8va
G5 D5 E5 Em7 E5
loco
1/4
full
full
full

Interlude
D.S. al Coda
Gtrs. 1 & 2: w/ Rhy. Fig. 1, 1st 4 meas., 2 times
D5
G5 D5 E5 Em7
8

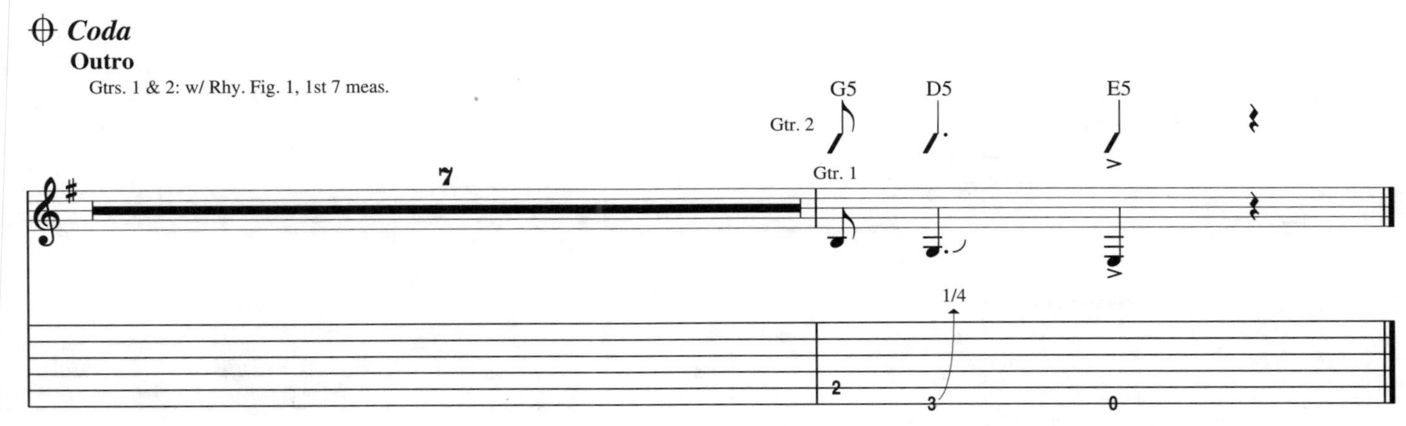
Coda
Outro
Gtrs. 1 & 2: w/ Rhy. Fig. 1, 1st 7 meas.
G5 D5 E5
Gtr. 2
Gtr. 1
7
1/4

Rock and Roll Hoochie Koo

Words and Music by Rick Derringer

Verse
A5
C5
D5
C5
1. Could-n't stop mov-in' when it first took hold.
End Riff A
Rhy. Fig. 1
End Riff A1
Rhy. Fig. 1A
let ring
1/2
N.C.
A5
C5 D5 C5
N.C.
It was a warm spring night at the old town hall.
There was a
End Rhy. Fig. 1
full
1/2
full
full
1/2
w/ bar
-1/2
-1/2

Gtr. 1: w/ Rhy. Fig. 1
A5
C5
D5
C5
N.C.
group called the Jok - ers, they were lay - in' it down.
To
Gtr. 2
w/ bar
A5
C5
D5
C5
N.C.
know I'm nev - er gon - na lose that funk - y sound.
End Rhy. Fig. 1A
w/ bar
Chorus
F5
G5
A5
N.C.
Voc. Fig. 1
F5
F6
F5
C5
G5
End Voc. Fig. 1
Rock and roll hooch - ie koo.
(Rock and roll hooch - ie koo.
Lord - y, ma - ma light my fuse.
Rhy. Fig. 2
Gtr. 1
8va
loco
Rhy. Fig. 2A
Gtr. 2
P.M.

A5
N.C.
F5
G5
Light my fuse.
Rock and roll hooch - ie koo.
8va
loco
P.M.
A5
N.C.
F5
F6
C5
G5
A5
N.C.
Drop on out an' spread the news.
Rock and roll hooch - ie koo.)
End Rhy. Fig. 2
End Rhy. Fig. 2A
1/4

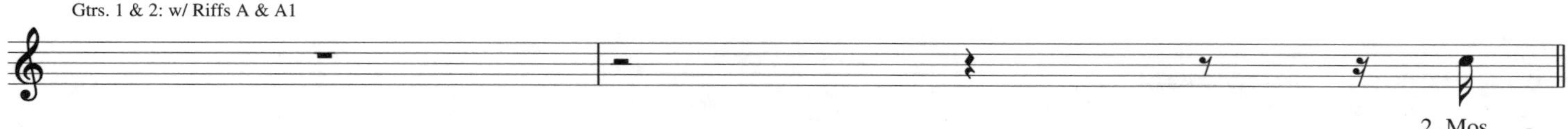
Gtrs. 1 & 2: w/ Riffs A & A1
2. Mos -

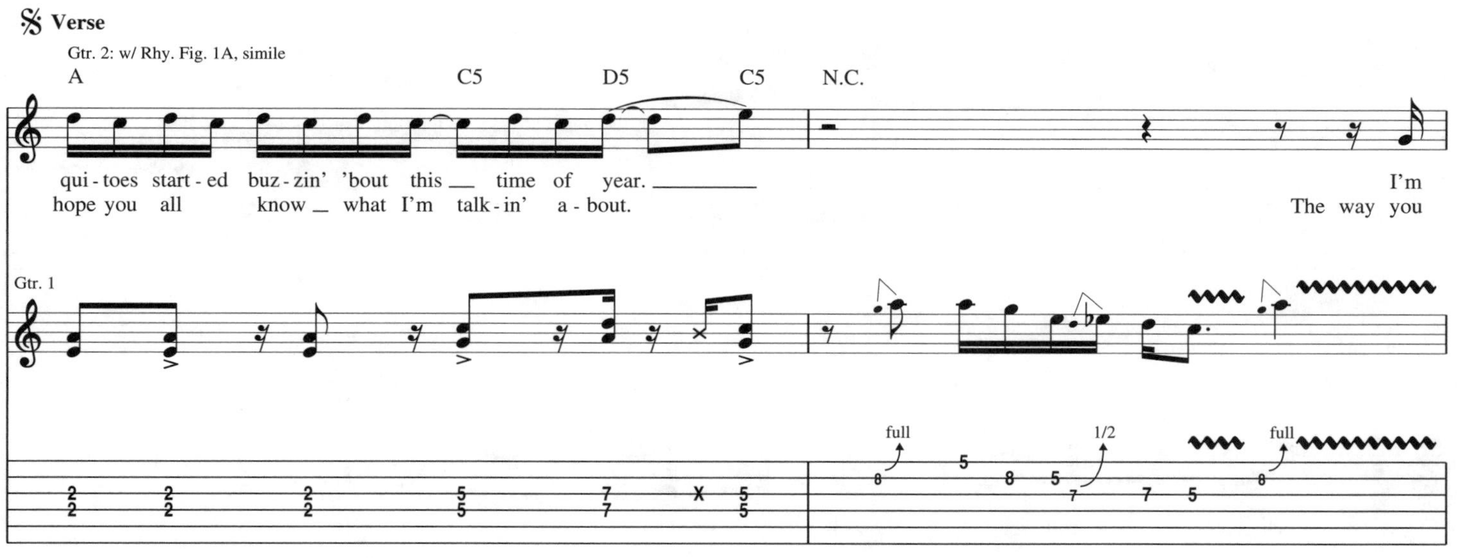
Verse
Gtr. 2: w/ Rhy. Fig. 1A, simile
A C5 D5 C5 N.C.
qui - toes start - ed buz - zin' 'bout this time of year. I'm
hope you all know what I'm talk - in' a - bout. The way you
Gtr. 1
full 1/2 full

A5 C5 D5 C5 N.C.
go - in' 'round back, said she'd meet me there. We were
wig - gle that thing real - ly knocks me out. Get - tin'
full full 1/2

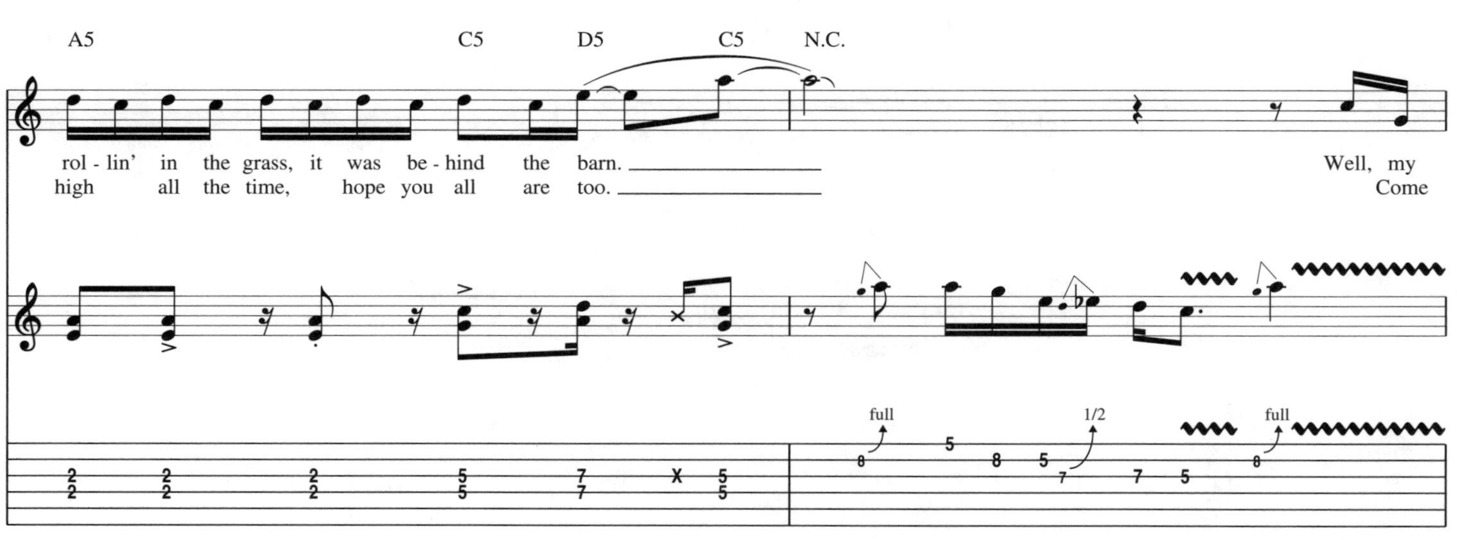
A5 C5 D5 C5 N.C.
rol - lin' in the grass, it was be - hind the barn. Well, my
high all the time, hope you all are too. Come
full 1/2 full

A5
C5
D5
C5
Gtr. 1: w/ Fill 1, 2nd time
N.C.
ears start - ed ring - in' like a fire a - larm.
on lit - tle 'cuz, I'm gon - na do it to you.
full
full
1/2
Chorus
Gtrs. 1 & 2: w/ Rhy. Figs. 2 & 2A, simile
F5
G5
Bkgd. Voc.: w/ Voc. Fig. 1
A5
N.C.
Rock and roll hooch - ie koo.
F5
C5
G5
A5
N.C.
Lord - y, ma - ma light my fuse.
F5
G5
A5
N.C.
Rock and roll hooch - ie koo.
To Coda
F5
B♭5
F5
C5
G5
A5
N.C.
Drop on out an' spread the news.
Gtrs. 1 & 2: w/ Riffs A & A1
Yeah, some-bod - y said "Keep on rock - in'."
Ow!
Fill 1
Gtr. 1
8va
full
full
1/2

Guitar Solo
Gtr. 1
Gtr. 2
Rhy. Fig. 3
End Rhy. Fig. 3
Gtr. 2: w/ Rhy. Fig. 3
Rhy. Fig. 3A
End Rhy. Fig. 3A
Gtr. 2: w/ Rhy. Fig. 3A, simile
8va
loco
A5
C5
D5

Gtr. 1
A5
C
D
let ring
full
1/4
Gtr. 2

⊕ Coda

Outro-Chorus

A5 N.C. | F G

Woo!

1., 2. Rock and roll ___ hooch - ie koo. _

3. Man, I'm tired _ of pay - in' dues. _

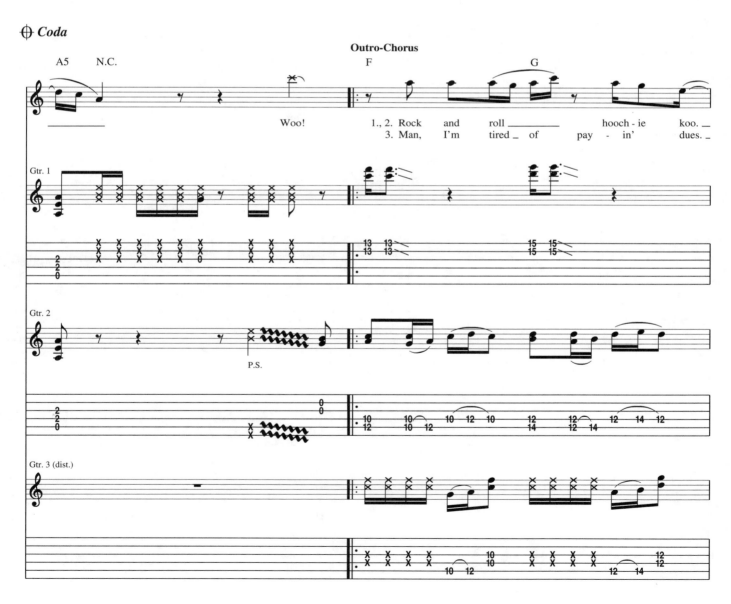

Gtr. 1

Gtr. 2

P.S.

Gtr. 3 (dist.)

Bkgd. Voc.: w/ Voc. Fig. 1
A5
F5
C5
G5
Bkgd. Voc.: w/ Voc. Fig. 1
A5
play 3 times
Lord - y ma - ma, light my fuse.
Dropped on out and spread the news.
Yeah.
Done said good - bye to all my blues.
P.M.
P.M.
P.M.
P.M.
P.M.
P.M.
Free Time
F5
G5
rit.
A5
Lord - y ma - ma, light my fuse.
Woo!
rit.
full
5:4
6:4
rit.
rit.

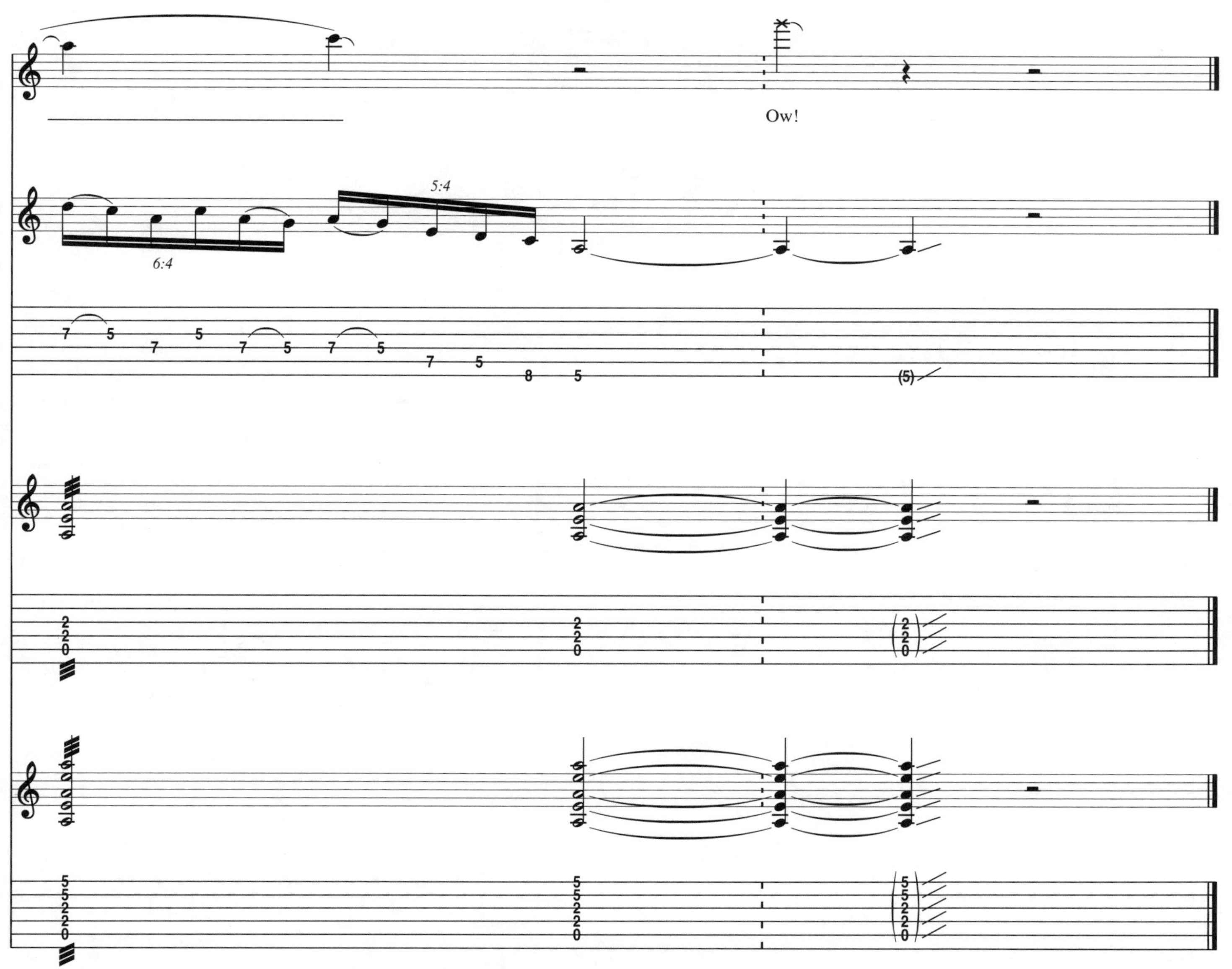
Ow!
6:4
5:4

Show Me the Way

Words and Music by Peter Frampton

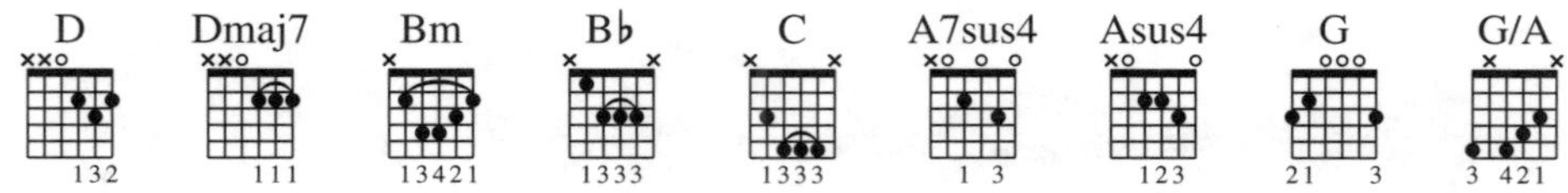

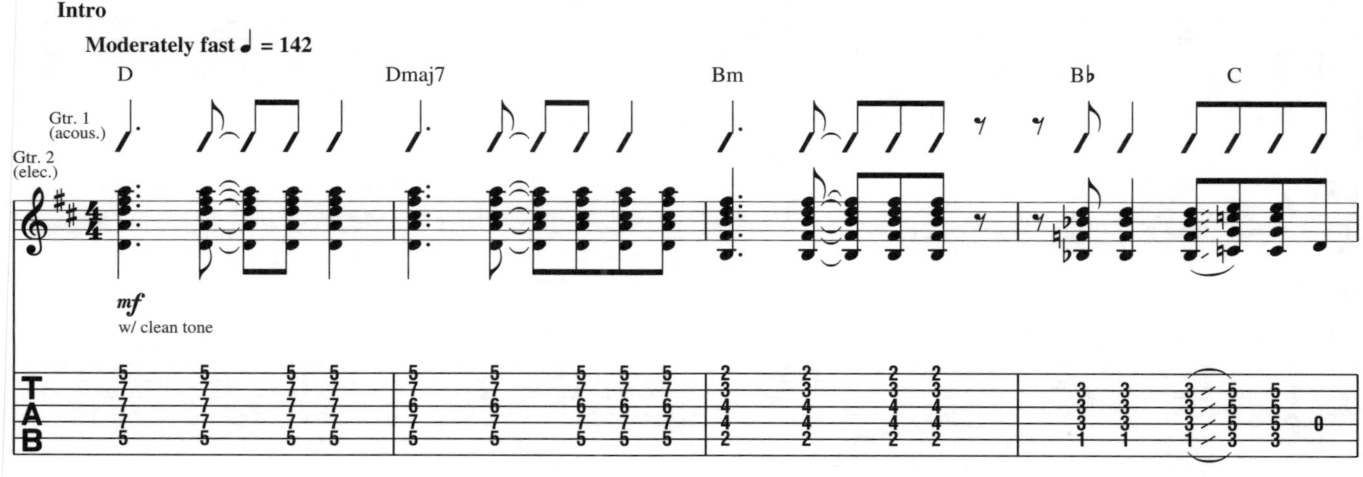

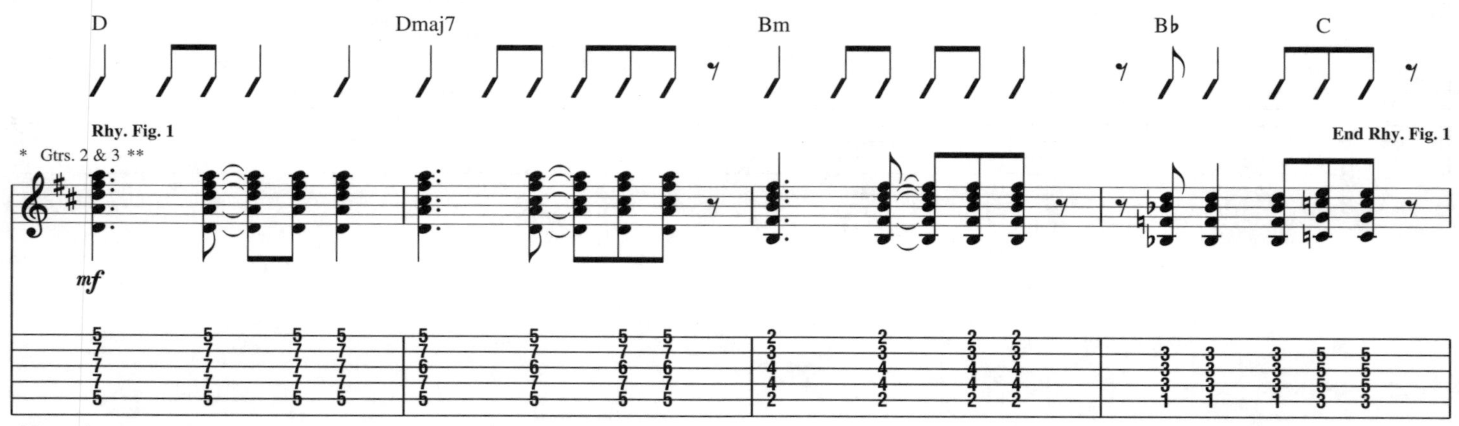

*Composite arrangement

**Gtr. 3 (elec.) w/ clean tone

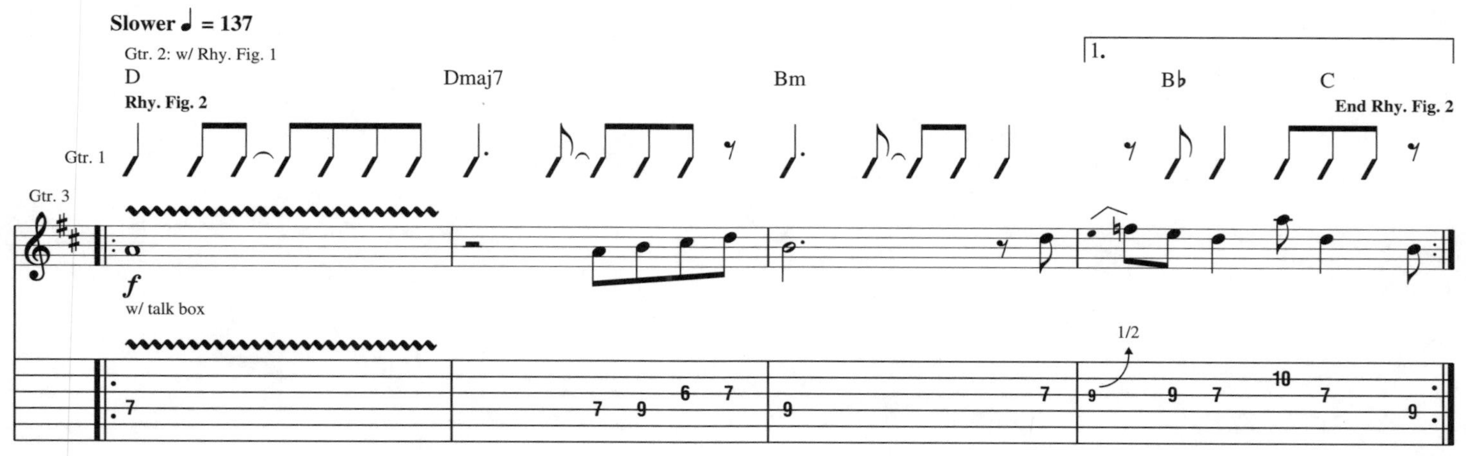

2.
Verse
B♭
C
D
Rhy. Fig. 3
Gtr. 1
1. I wonder how you're feeling, there's
I can see no reason, you
Gtrs. 2 & 3
Rhy. Fig. 3A
1/2
Dmaj7
Bm
ringing in my ears. And no one to relate
living on your nerves. when someone drops a cup
let ring
B♭
C
End Rhy. Fig. 3
to 'cept the sea.
and I submerge. I'm
End Rhy. Fig. 3A
let ring
Verse
Gtrs. 1, 2 & 3: w/ Rhy. Figs. 3 & 3A (1st 7 meas.)
D
Dmaj7
2. Who can I believe in? I'm kneeling on the floor. There
swimming in a circle, I feel I'm going down. There
wonder if I'm dreaming, I feel so unashamed. I

Bm
B♭
has to be a force, who do I phone?
has to be a fool to play my part.
can't be - lieve this is hap - pen - ing to me.
Bridge
B♭
A7sus4
Asus4
A7sus4 Asus4
A7sus4
Gtr. 1
The stars are out and shin - ing, but all I
Some - one thought of heal - ing but all I
I watch you when you're sleep - ing, oh then I
Gtrs. 2 & 3
let ring
G
G
B
G
open
3fr
Chorus
Bm
Rhy. Fig. 4
Gtr. 1
let ring
real - ly wan - na know...
real - ly wan - na know...
wan - na take your love...
Oh, won't you
Gtr. 3
Rhy. Fig. 4A
let ring
Gtr. 2
Rhy. Fig. 4A

G
End Rhy. Fig. 4
Gtr. 1
show me the way, ev - 'ry day. I want
Gtrs. 2 & 3
End Rhy. Fig. 4A
To Coda 1
To Coda 2
Bm
G
you to show me the way, yeah.
Interlude
Gtr. 2: w/ Rhy. Fig. 2
Gtr. 2: w/ Rhy. Fig. 1
D.S. al Coda 1
G/A
D
Dmaj7
Bm
B♭
C
3. Well
Gtr. 3
w/ talk box
Gtr. 2

Coda 1
G
Bm
Rhy. Fig. 5
Gtr. 1
way, oh. I want you
Gtrs. 2 & 3
Rhy. Fig. 5A
G
G/A
End Rhy. Fig. 5
Gtr. 1
day af - ter day, hey.
Gtr. 3
let ring
Gtr. 2
End Rhy. Fig. 5A

Guitar Solo
Gtrs. 1 & 2: w/ Rhy. Figs. 3 & 3A
D
Gtr. 3
Dmaj7
w/ talk box
1/2
Bm
B♭
C
P.M.
3/4
3/4
3/4
Gtrs. 1 & 2: w/ Rhy. Figs. 3 & 3A (1st 6 meas.)
D
Dmaj7
1
Bm
G
D.S.S. al Coda 2
Gtr. 1
5. An', ___ I
Gtr. 3
1
1/2
1/2
1/2
1/2
Gtr. 2

Coda 2

G

way, one more time. ___ I want

Gtrs. 1, 2 & 3: w/ Rhy. Figs. 4 & 4A

Bm G

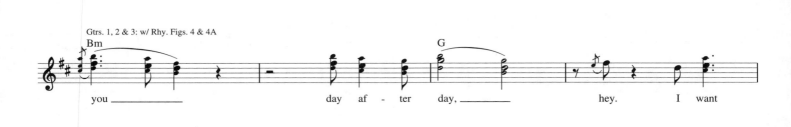

you ___ day af - ter day, ___ hey. I want

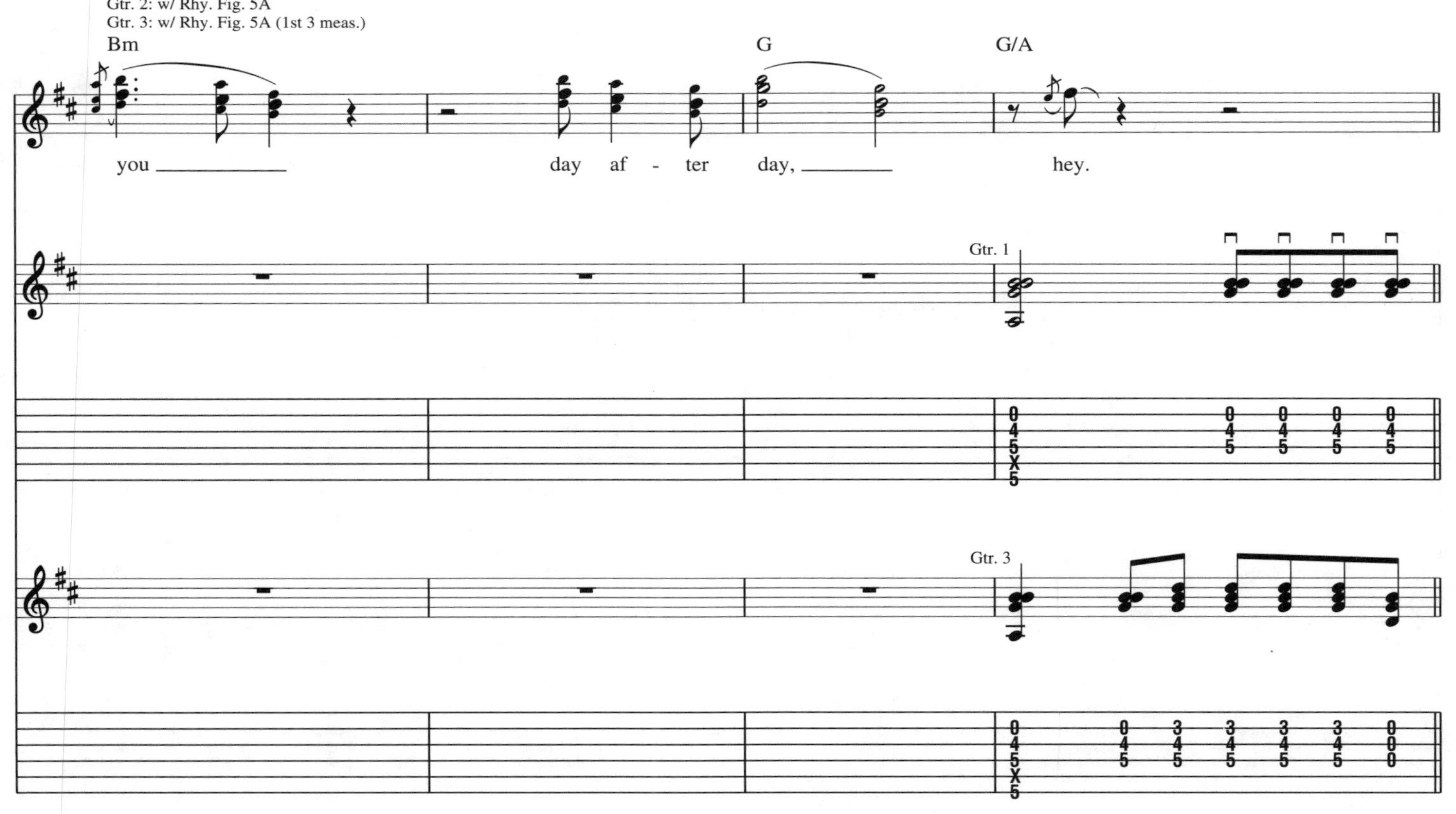

Interlude
D
Dmaj7
Bm
G
Gtr. 1
I want
Gtrs. 2 & 3
Outro-Chorus
Gtrs. 1, 2 & 3: w/ Rhy. Figs. 4 & 4A (2 times)
Bm
G
you to show me the way ev - 'ry day. I want
Bm
G
you to show me the way, night and day. I want
Gtrs. 1, 2 & 3: w/ Rhy. Figs. 5 & 5A
Bm
G
G/A
you day af - ter day, hey, hey,
D
Dmaj7
Bm
B♭
C
D
Gtr. 1
rit.
oh.
Gtrs. 2 & 3
rit.

Smoke on the Water

Words and Music by Ritchie Blackmore, Ian Gillan, Roger Glover, Jon Lord and Ian Paice

Gtr. 1: w/ Riff B, 3 times, simile

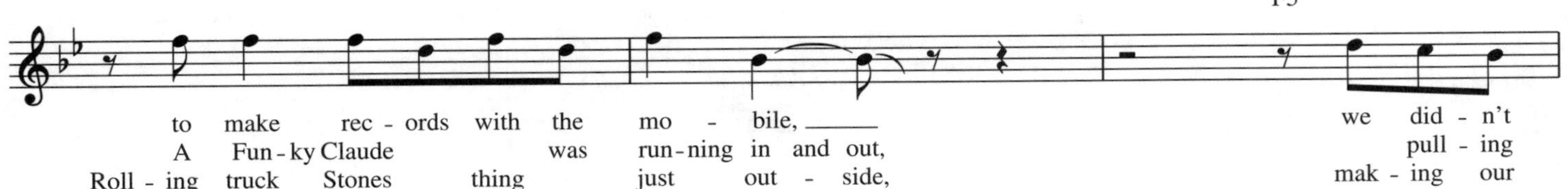

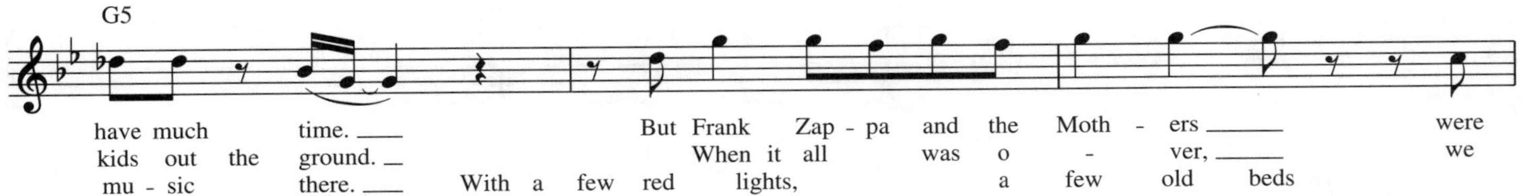

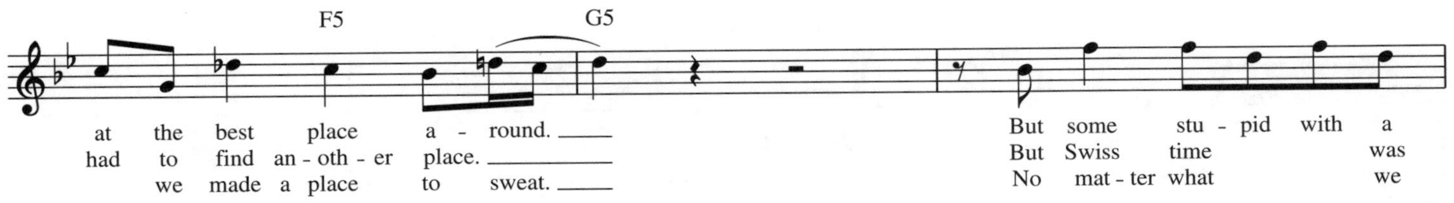

Chorus

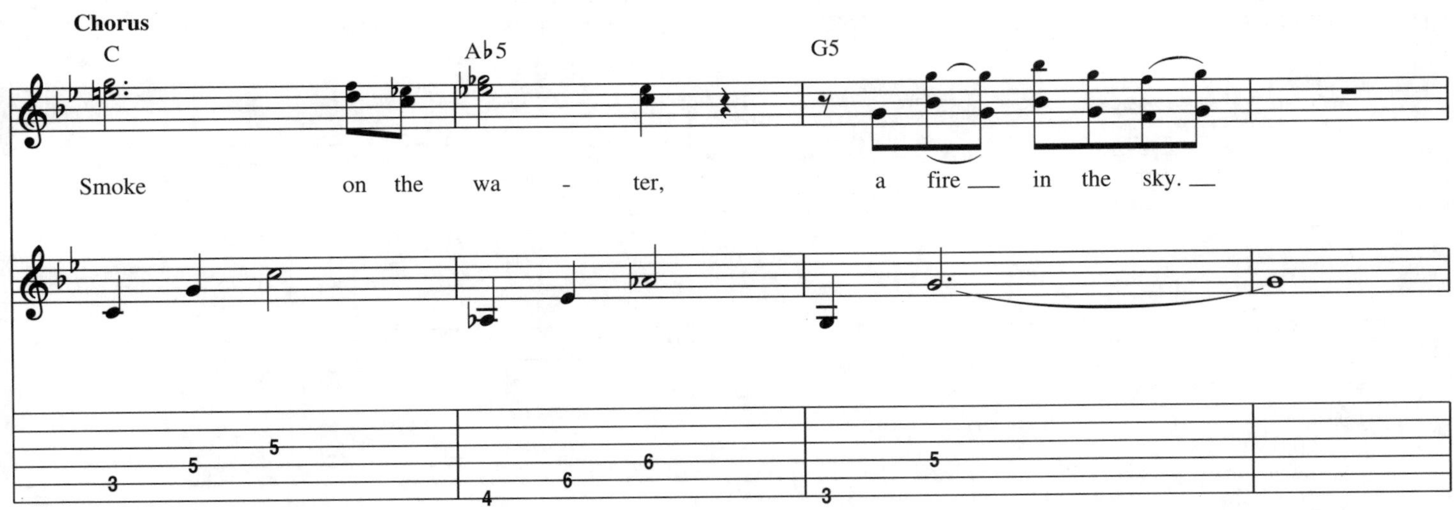

To Coda
1.
2.
Gtr. 1: w/ Riff A 1 3/4 times Gtr. 1: w/ Riff A1 Gtr. 1: w/ Riff A 1 3/4 times Gtr. 1: w/ Riff A1
C5
A♭5
N.C.(G5)
N.C.(G5)
Smoke on the wa - ter.
Gtr. 2 (dist.)
Guitar Solo
G5
C5
G5
Gtr. 2
full
1/4
1/2
full
Gtr. 1
slight P.M.
slight P.M.
C5
full
1/2
full
full
full
full
slight P.M.

G5
full
w/bar
-2 1/2
slight P.M.
C5
G5
full
1/2
full
slight P.M.
C5
G5
8va
1/2
1/2
full
slight P.M.

C5
8va
full
full
full
full
full
F5
loco
full
1/2
1/4
1/2
grad. bend
Gtr. 1: w/ Riff A, 1 3/4 times
N.C.(G5)
Gtr. 2
full
3/4
1/2
1/4
D.S. al Coda
Gtr. 2 tacet
Gtr. 1: w/ Riff A1
full

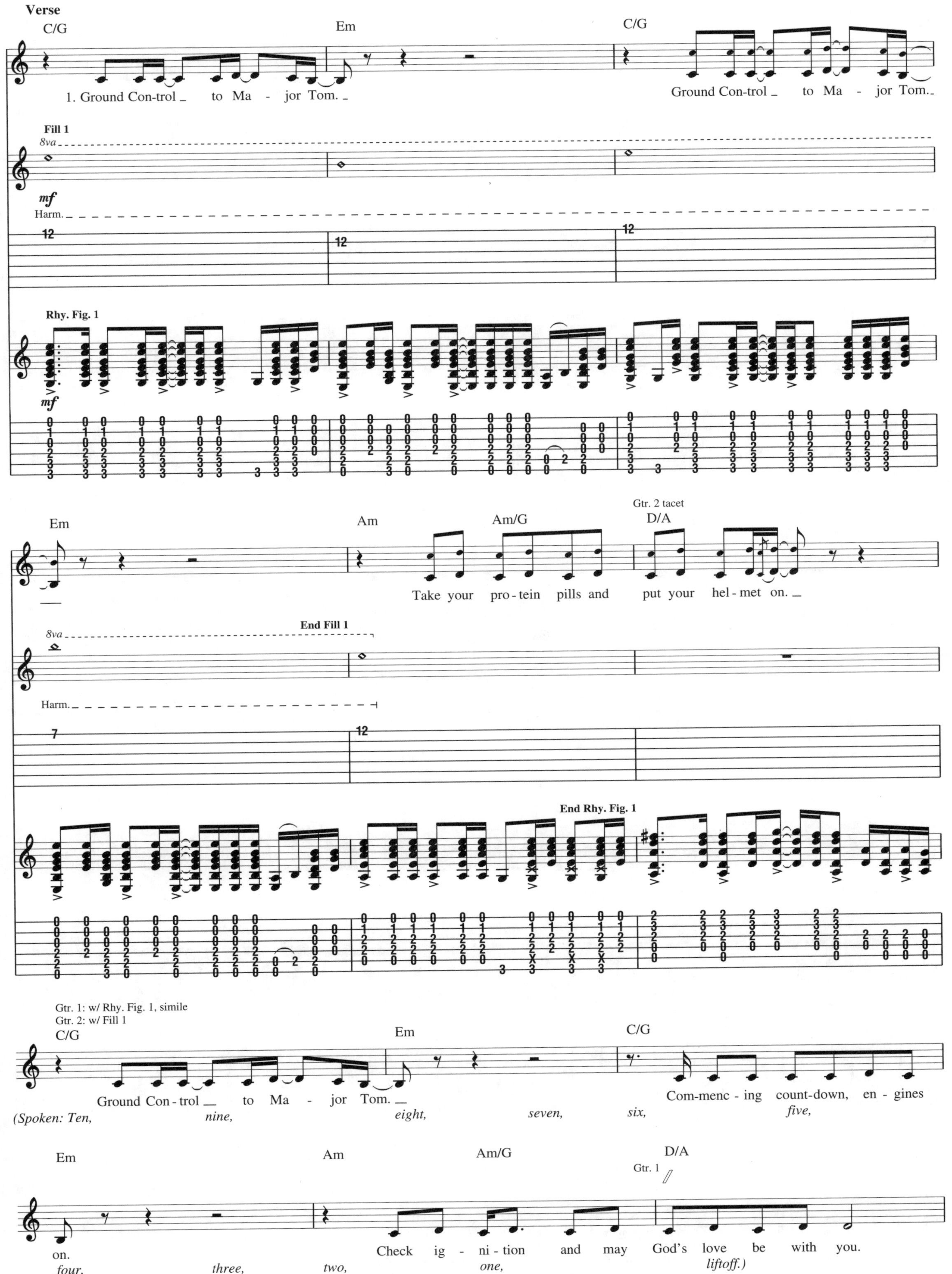

Verse
C/G
Em
C/G
1. Ground Con-trol to Ma - jor Tom.
Ground Con-trol to Ma - jor Tom.
Fill 1
8va
mf
Harm.
Rhy. Fig. 1
mf
Em
Am
Am/G
Gtr. 2 tacet
D/A
Take your pro-tein pills and put your hel-met on.
End Fill 1
End Rhy. Fig. 1
Gtr. 1: w/ Rhy. Fig. 1, simile
Gtr. 2: w/ Fill 1
Ground Con-trol to Ma - jor Tom.
Com-menc - ing count-down, en - gines
(Spoken: Ten, nine, eight, seven, six, five,
Gtr. 1
on.
Check ig - ni - tion and may God's love be with you.
four, three, two, one, liftoff.)

Gtr. 1 tacet
N.C.
Verse
C/G
Rhy. Fig. 2
Gtr. 1
(cont. in notation)
2. This is Ground Con-trol to Ma - jor Tom,
Gtr. 2
loco
8va
15ma
w/ slide
full
* Slide positioned over imaginary frets.
Gtr. 2 tacet
E7
F
Fm
C/G
you've real - ly made the grade.
And the pa - pers want to know whose shirts you wear.
Gtr. 1
F
Fm
C/G
F
Now it's time to leave the cap - sule if you dare.
End Rhy. Fig. 2
Gtr. 1: w/ Rhy. Fig. 2, simile
C/G
E7
F
This is Ma - jor Tom to Ground Con-trol, I'm stepping through the door. And I'm

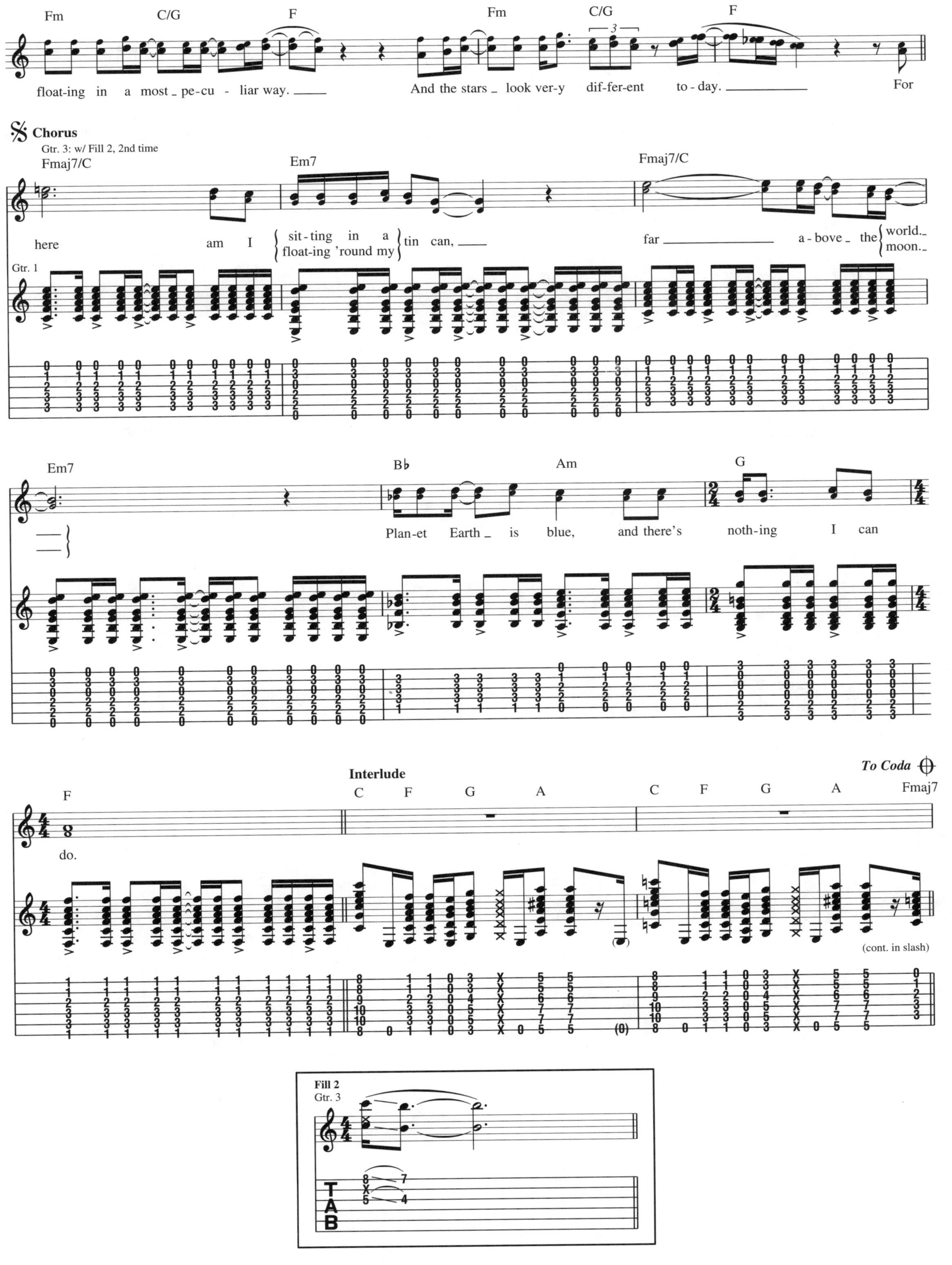
Fm
C/G
F
float-ing in a most pe-cu - liar way.
And the stars look ver-y dif-fer-ent to-day.
For
Chorus
Gtr. 3: w/ Fill 2, 2nd time
Fmaj7/C
Em7
here am I sit-ting in a floating 'round my tin can,
far a-bove the world. moon.
Gtr. 1
Bb
Am
G
Plan-et Earth is blue, and there's nothing I can
Interlude
To Coda
C F G A
Fmaj7
do.
(cont. in slash)
Fill 2
Gtr. 3
TAB

Guitar Solo
Fmaj7/C
Em7
A
Gtr. 1
Gtr. 3 (elec.)
mf w/ slight dist.
C
D
E
w/ bar
slack
Verse
Gtr. 3 tacet
Gtr. 1: w/ Rhy. Fig. 2, simile
C/G
E7
F
3. Though I'm past one hun - dred thou - sand miles,
I'm feel - ing ver - y still.
And I
Fm
C/G
F
Fm
C/G
think my space - ship knows which way to go.
Tell my wife I love her ver - y much. She knows.
F
G
E7
Am
Am/G
Gtr. 1
Ground Con - trol to Ma - jor Tom, your cir - cuit's dead, there's some - thing wrong. Can you
Gtr. 3

D.S. al Coda
D/A
C/G
G
hear me Ma - jor Tom? Can you hear me Ma - jor Tom? Can you hear me Ma - jor Tom? Can you…
Coda
Outro-Guitar Solo
Fmaj7/C
Em7
Gtr. 1
Gtr. 3
A
C
D
rake
1/4
1/4
E

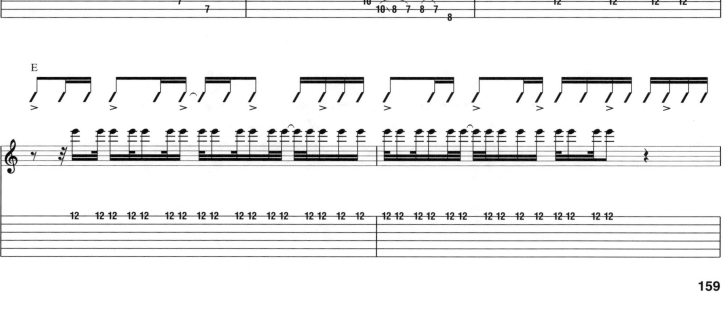

Begin Fade
* w/ slide gtr. effects, till end
8va
15ma
w/ slide
**
12 13 14 15 16 17 18 19 19 20 20 20 21
22 22.5 23 23.5 24 24 24 24.5 25 25.5 26 26.5 27
* Gtrs. picking 1st 3 strings ad lib. while moving slide up & down neck.
** Slide positioned halfway between frets.
15ma
(28) 28.5 29 29.5 30 30.5 30.5 31 31.5 32 32.5 33 33.5
34 34.5 35 35.5 36 36.5 37 37.5 38 38.5 39
Gtr. 3 cont. ad lib., simile
Gtr. 1
Fade Out
Gtr. 1 tacet
N.C.
w/ misc. slide gtr. effects, approx. 5 sec.

from the Motion Picture SATURDAY NIGHT FEVER

Stayin' Alive

Words and Music by Barry Gibb, Maurice Gibb and Robin Gibb

Gtr. 1: w/ Rhy. Fig. 3
E♭
Fm
mu - sic loud and wom - en warm, I've been kicked a - round since I was born. And now it's
Pre-Chorus
Gtrs. 1 & 2: w/ Rhy. Fig. 4 & Riff C (2 times)
B♭
Rhy. Fig. 4
End Rhy. Fig. 4
Gtr. 1
all right. It's O. - K.
1., 3. And you may look the oth - er way.
2. I'll live to see an - oth - er day.
Oh,
Gtr. 2
Riff C
End Riff C
we can try to un - der - stand the New York Time's ef - fect on man.
Chorus
Gtr. 1: w/ Rhy. Fig. 1 (5 times)
Fm
Wheth - er you're a broth - er or wheth - er you're a moth - er you're stay - in' a - live, stay - in' a - live.
Gtr. 2
Feel the cit - y break - in' and ev - 'ry - bod - y shak - in' and we're stay - in' a - live, stay - in' a - live.

2nd time, Bkgd. Voc.: w/ Voc. Fill 1
Ah, ha, ha, ha, stay-in' a-live, stay-in' a-live. Ah, ha, ha, ha,

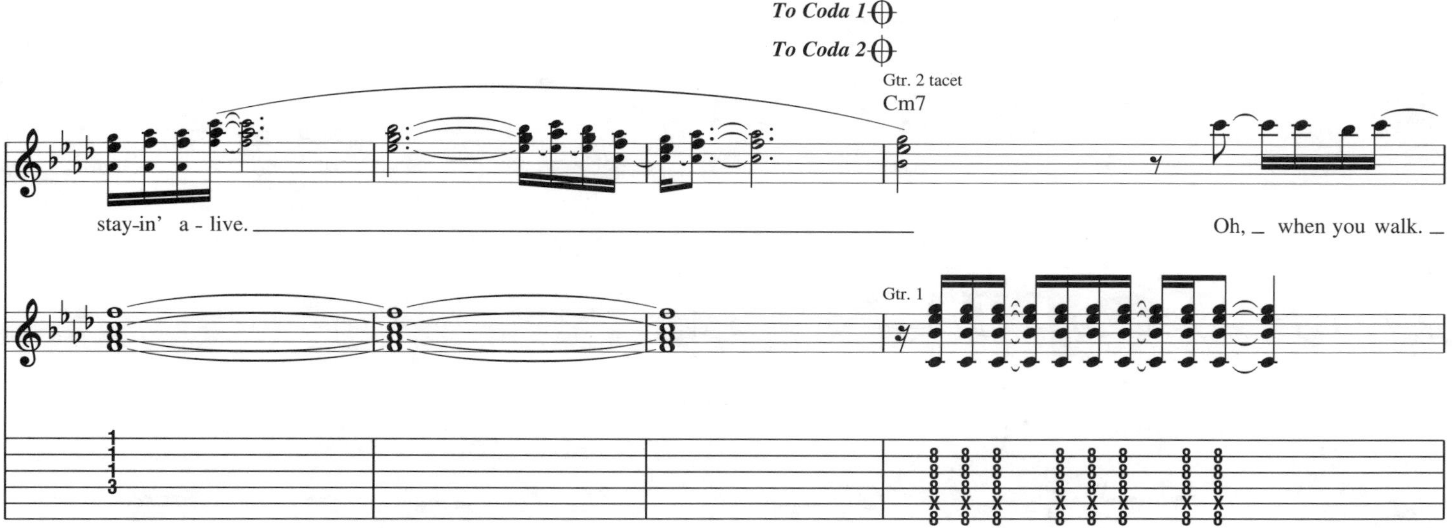
To Coda 1
To Coda 2
Gtr. 2 tacet
Cm7
stay-in' a - live.
Oh, when you walk.
Gtr. 1

Verse

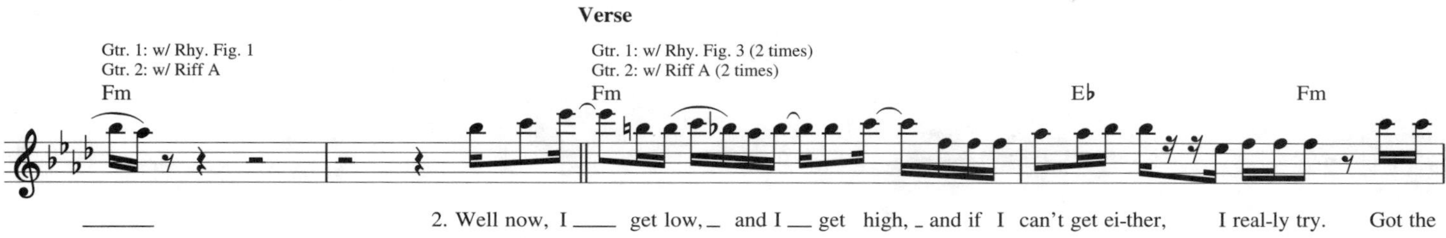
Gtr. 1: w/ Rhy. Fig. 1
Gtr. 2: w/ Riff A
Fm
Gtr. 1: w/ Rhy. Fig. 3 (2 times)
Gtr. 2: w/ Riff A (2 times)
Fm
E♭
Fm
2. Well now, I get low, and I get high, and if I can't get ei-ther, I real-ly try. Got the

D.S. al Coda 1
E♭
Fm
wings of heav - en on my shoes. I'm a danc - in' man, and I just can't lose. You know it's

Voc. Fill 1
(Oh.)

Coda 1
Gtr. 2 tacet
Cm7
Gtr. 2: w/ Riff A
N.C.
Fm
Ah.
Gtr. 1
Bridge
Gtr. 1: w/ Rhy. Fig. 2 (1 1/2 times)
Gtr. 2: w/ Riff B (1st meas.)
B♭
Gtr. 2: w/ Riff B
Life go - in' no - where.
Some - bod - y help me
Gtr. 1: w/ Rhy. Fig. 1
Gtr. 2: w/ Riff A
Fm
Some - bod - y help me, yeah.
Gtr. 1: w/ Rhy. Fig. 2 (1 1/2 times)
Gtr. 2: w/ Riff B (1st meas.)
B♭
Gtr. 2: w/ Riff B
Life go - in' no - where.
Some - bod - y help me, yeah.
D.S.S. al Coda 2
Gtr. 1: w/ Rhy. Fig. 1
Gtr. 2: w/ Riff A
Fm
I'm stay - in' a - live.
3. Well, you can tell
Coda 2
Gtr. 2 tacet
Cm7
Gtr. 2: w/ Riff A
Fm
Oh, yeah.
Gtr. 1

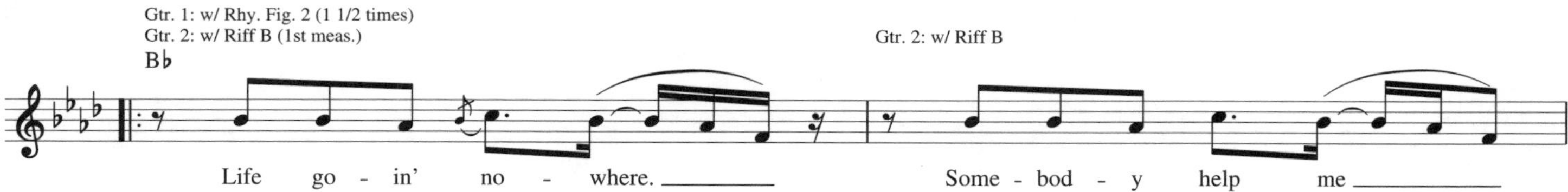

Play 4 times and fade

Gtrs. 1 & 2: w/ Rhy. Fig. 1 & Riff A (2 times)

Fm

Yeah.

(I'm stay-in' a - live.)

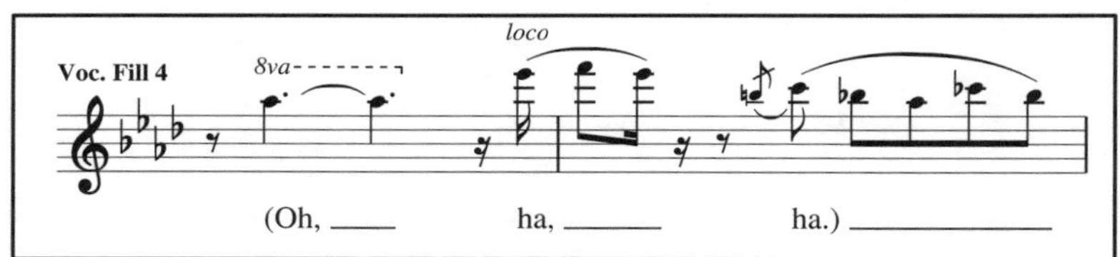

Teach Your Children

Words and Music by Graham Nash

D
Dsus2
D
A
that you can live by. And
End Rhy. Fig. 2
Gtr. 2: w/ Rhy. Fig. 2, simile
G5
so, be - come your - self be - cause the past
is just a good - bye.
Gtr. 1
let ring
full
* vol. swell
Chorus
Gtr. 2: w/ Rhy. Fig. 2, 2 1/2 times, simile
Teach your chil - dren well. Their fa - ther's
hell did slow - ly go by. And
1/2

D
Dsus2
G5
feed them on your dreams. The one they
hold bend
full
let ring
picked, the one you'll know by.
A
Don't you ev - er ask them why.
If they told you, you would
cry. So just look at them and sigh
Bm
Gtr. 1
Gtr. 2
Rhy. Fig. 3

Gtr. 2: w/ Rhy. Fig. 1, simile

G5 A D Dsus2 D G5

and know they love you.

let ring
full
hold bend
let ring
full
let ring
full
hold bend

End Rhy. Fig. 3

D Dsus2 D A

2. And

Gtr. 1

let ring
let ring
full full full full full full full full full

A
D
Dsus2
D
by. And so, please help them with your
must be free to teach your chil - dren what
full
1/2
1/2
full

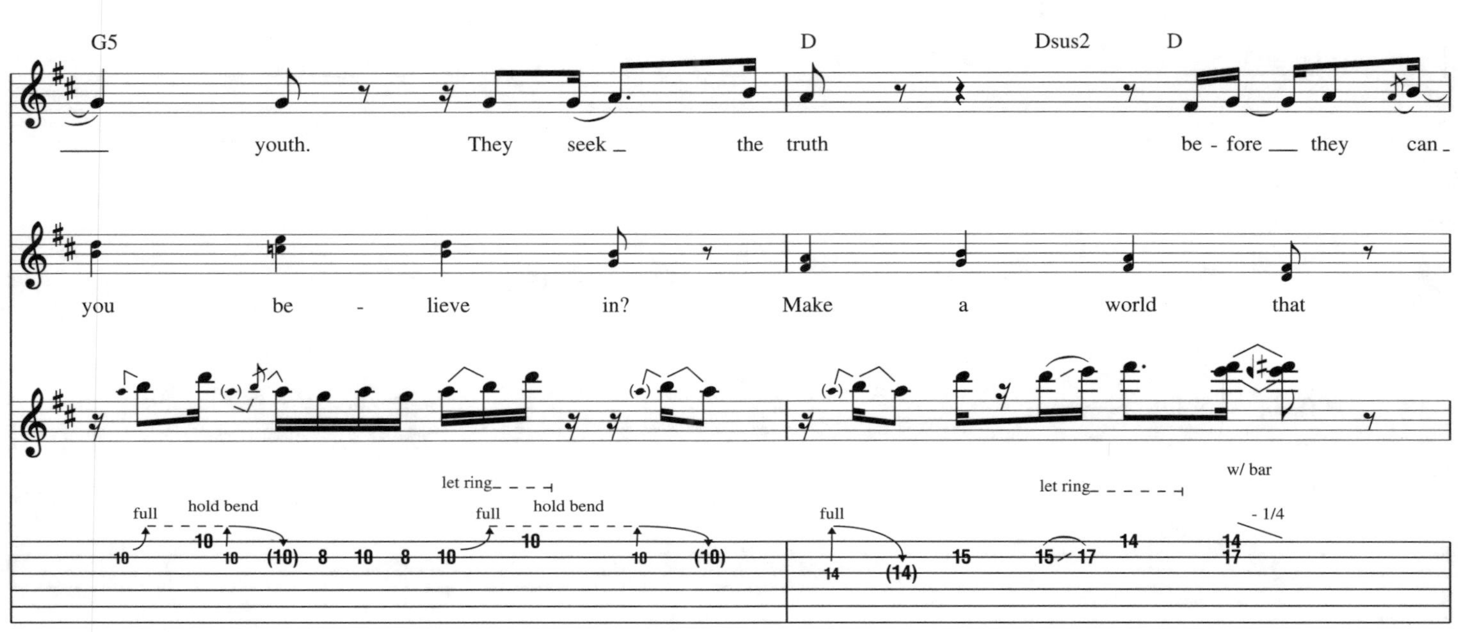
G5
D
Dsus2
D
youth. They seek the truth be - fore they can
you be - lieve in? Make a world that
let ring
let ring
w/ bar
full
hold bend
full
hold bend
full
- 1/4

Chorus

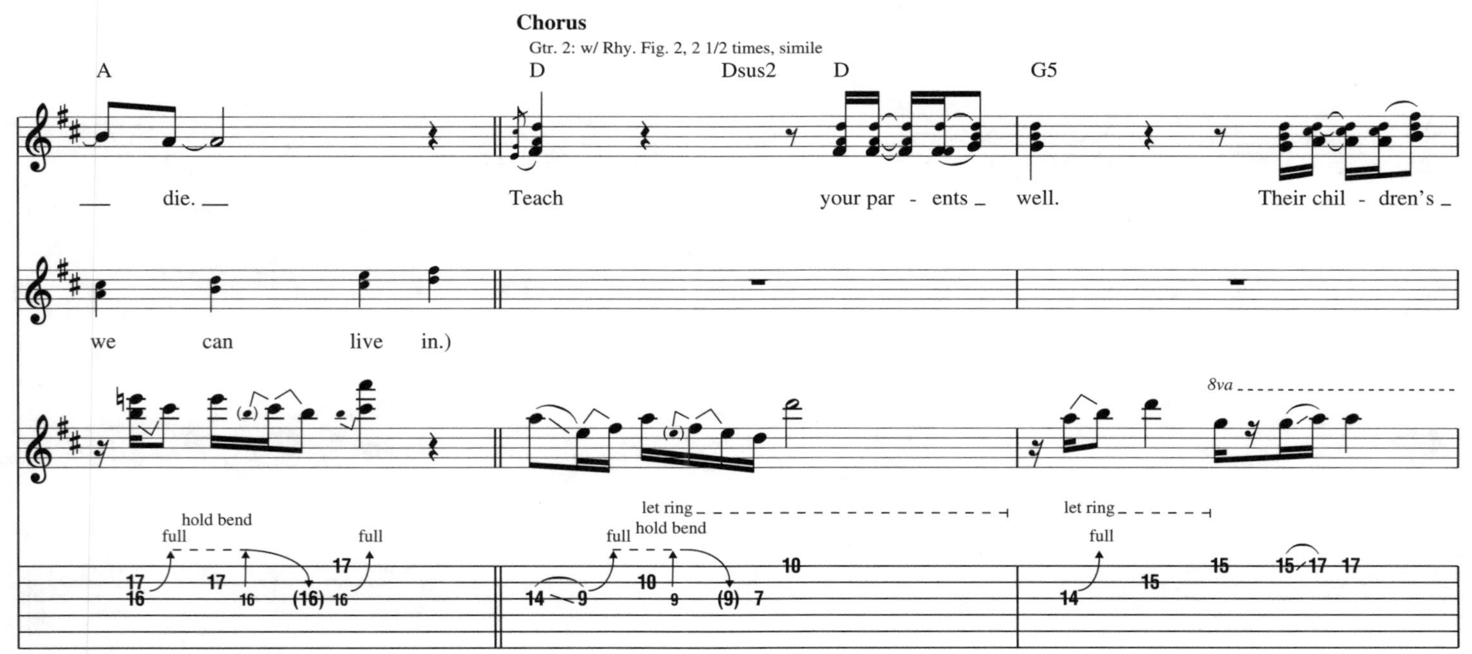
Gtr. 2: w/ Rhy. Fig. 2, 2 1/2 times, simile
A
D
Dsus2
D
G5
die. Teach your par - ents well. Their chil - dren's
we can live in.)
8va
let ring
let ring
hold bend
full
full
full
hold bend
full

D Dsus2 D A
hell will slow - ly go by. And
8va
let ring
full hold bend
1/2
D Dsus2 D G5
feed them on your dreams. The one they
loco
let ring let ring
full full full
D Dsus2 D A
picked, the one you'll know by.
full full hold bend full hold bend
D Dsus2 D G5
Don't you ev - er ask them why. If they told you, you would
let ring let ring
full full full hold bend full

Gtr. 2: w/ Rhy. Fig. 3, simile
D
Bm
G5
A
cry. So just look at them_ and sigh.
and know they
let ring
full
D
G5
love you.
8va
loco
Gtr. 1
w/ bar
- 1/2
Gtr. 2
w/ pick & fingers
w/ pick
D
A
D
A
D/A
P.M.
let ring
hold bend

Time in a Bottle

Words and Music by Jim Croce

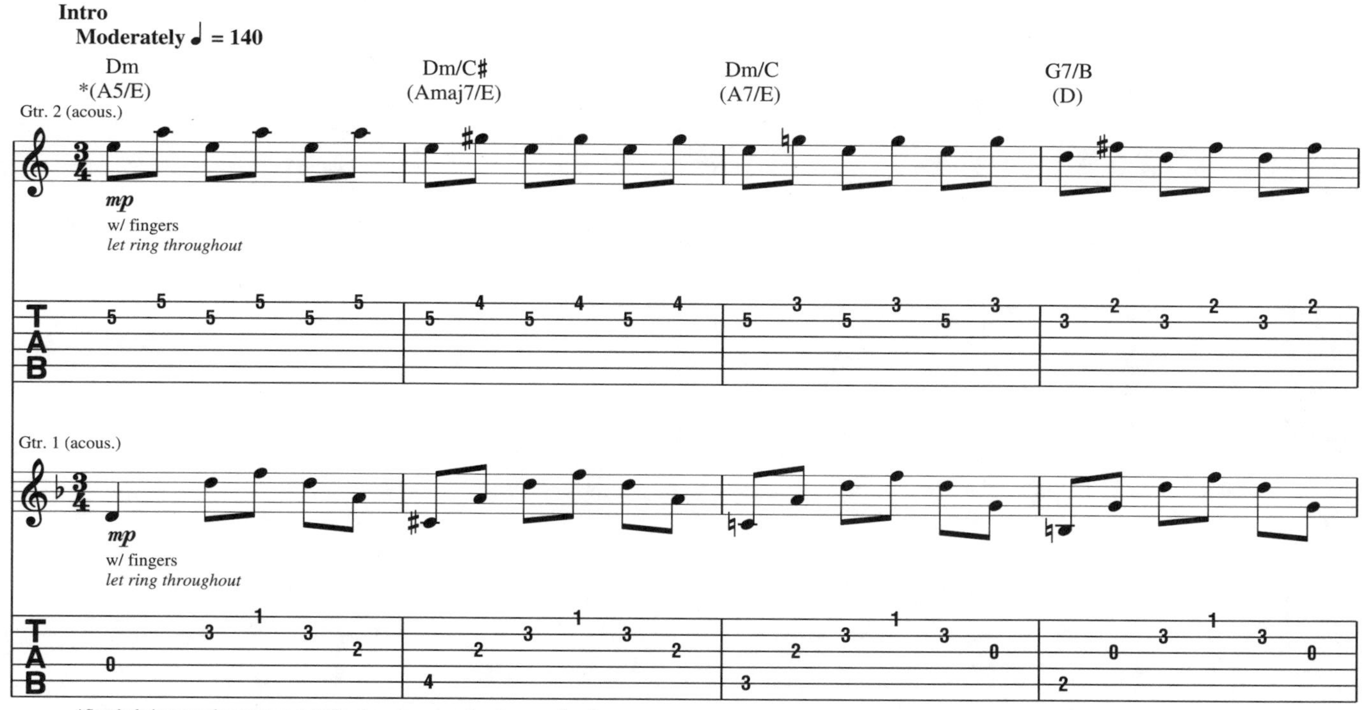

*Symbols in parentheses represent chord names respective to capoed guitar. Symbols above reflect actual sounding chord. Capoed fret is "0" in tab.

Verse

A Tempo

Dm (Am) | Dm/C# (Am/G#) | Dm/C (Am/G) | Dm/B (Am/F#)

I could save ___ time in a bot - tle, ___ the
I could make days last for - ev - er, if
I had a box just for wish - es and

Gm6/Bb (Dm6/F) | A7 (E7)

first thing ___ that I'd like to do ___ is to
words could make wish - es come true, I'd
dreams that had nev - er come true, the

2nd & 3rd times, Gtr. 2: w/ Fill 1
Dm
(Am)
Dm/C
(Am/G)
Gm6/B♭
(Dm6)
Gm6
(Dm6/F)
save ev - 'ry - day 'til e - ter - ni - ty pass - es a - way,
save ev - 'ry - day like a treas - ure and then a -
box would be emp - ty ex - cept for the mem - 'ry of how
2nd & 3rd times, Gtr. 2: w/ Fill 2
Dm/F
(Am)
Gm
(Dm)
1.
A7
(E7)
just to spend them with you.
gain, I would spend them with you.
they were an - swered by you.
2. If
Fill 1
Gtr. 2
Fill 2
Gtr. 2

2.
A7
(E7)
Bridge
D
(A)
But there nev - er seems to
Riff A1
Riff A
D/C♯
(A/G♯)
D/B
(A/F♯)
D/A
(A/E)
be e - nough time to do the things you want to do once you
G6
(D6/F♯)
Dadd9/F♯
(Aadd9/E)
Em7
(Bm7)
A
(E)
find them.
I've
End Riff A1
End Riff A

Gtrs. 1 & 2: w/ Riffs A & A1
D
(A)
D/C#
(A/G#)
Bm7
(A/F#)
looked a - round e - nough to know that you're the one I

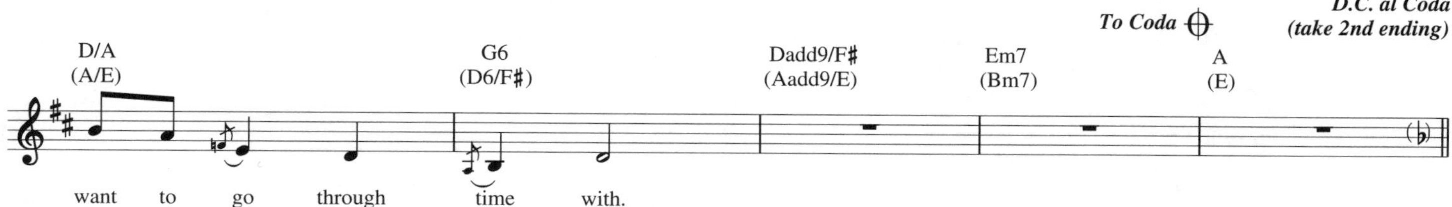
To Coda
D.C. al Coda
(take 2nd ending)
D/A
(A/E)
G6
(D6/F#)
Dadd9/F#
(Aadd9/E)
Em7
(Bm7)
A
(E)
want to go through time with.

Coda
Outro
A
(E)
Dm(add9)
Am(add9)
Gtr. 2
Harm.
Gtr. 1
Harm.

Harm.
Harm.
Harm.
Harm.

Walk This Way

Words and Music by Steven Tyler and Joe Perry

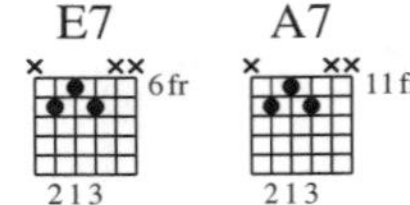

Intro

Moderate Rock ♩ = 120

(drums) 2

N.C.(E5)

Gtr. 1 (dist.)

f

let ring

Gtr. 3: w/ Rhy. Fill 1

A5

Verse

N.C.(C7)

1. Back - stroke lov - er al - ways hid - in' 'neath the cov - ers, "Gon - na talk to you," my dad - dy say, said, "You
3. School girl skin - ny with a class - y kind - a sas - sy lit - tle skirt's climb - in' way up her knee, there was

Gtrs. 1 & 2 (dist.)

Rhy. Fig. 1

End Rhy. Fig. 1

f

P.M.

Rhy. Fill 1

Gtr. 3 (dist.)

f

ain't seen noth-in' till you're down on a muf-fin and you're sure to be a-chang-in' your ways." I met a
three young la-dies in the school gym lock-er when I no-ticed they was look-in' at me. I was a
P.M.
Gtr. 3: w/ Rhy. Fill 2, 2nd time
cheer - lead - er, was a real young bleed-er all the times I could rem - i - nisce, 'cause the
high school los-er, nev-er made it with a la-dy 'til the boys told me some-thin' I missed, then my
Rhy. Fig. 2
P.M.
A5
best things in lov-in' with a sis-ter and a cou-sin on-ly start-ed with a lit-tle kiss, a-like this!
next door neigh-bor with a daugh-ter had a fav-or so I gave her just a lit-tle kiss a-like this!
End Rhy. Fig. 2
P.M.
f
Rhy. Fill 2
Gtr. 3
T
A
B

Interlude

Gtr. 1: w/ Riff A, 2nd time

N.C.(E5)

Gtr. 1

Gtr. 2 *divisi*

P.M.

Gtr. 3: w/ Rhy. Fill 1

Gtrs. 1 & 2

A5

P.M.

Verse

Gtrs. 1 & 2: w/ Rhy. Fig. 1, 3 times, simile

N.C.(C7)

2., 4. See - saw swing-in' with the boys in the school and your feet fly - in' up in the air, I sing,

"Hey did - dle did - dle" with your kit - ty in the mid - dle of the swing like you did - n't care. So I

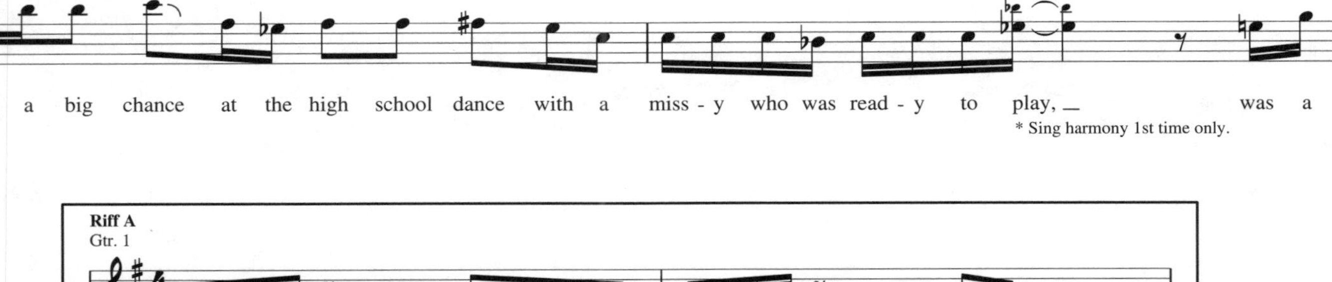

To Coda
me she was fool-in' 'cause she knew what she was do-in'
and I know'd love was here to stay when she told me to...
when she told me how to walk this way. She told me to...
Gtrs. 1 & 2
P.M.
Chorus
C7
F7
C7
(Walk this way, talk this way, walk this way,
Gtr. 1
Gtr. 2
Guitar Solo
Gtrs. 1 & 2: w/ Rhy. Fig. 2
N.C.(C7)
F7
walk this way.)
Uh, just gim-me a kiss.
Gtr. 3
1/2
full

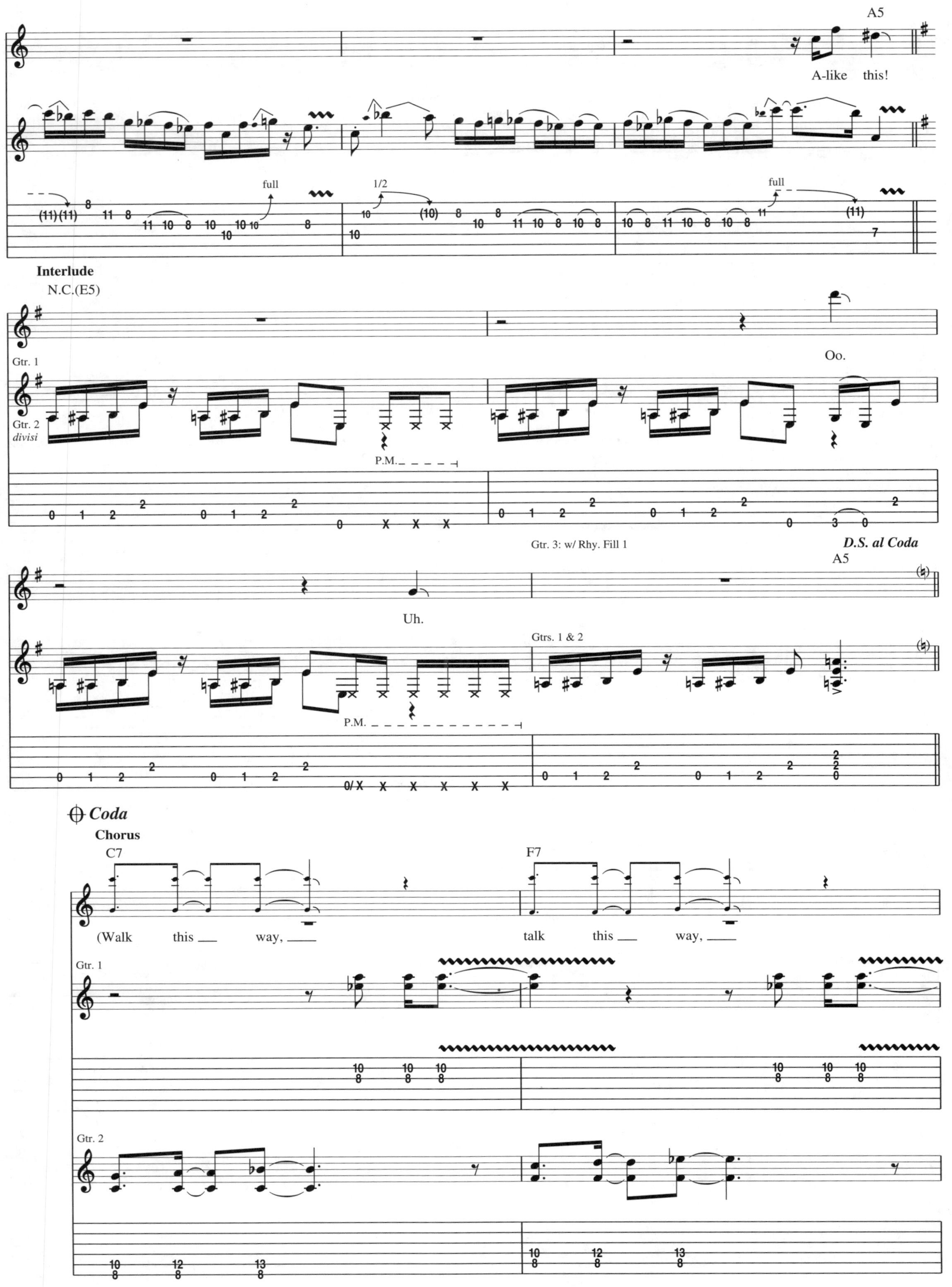
A5
A-like this!
full
1/2
full
Interlude
N.C.(E5)
Gtr. 1
Gtr. 2
divisi
Oo.
P.M.
Gtr. 3: w/ Rhy. Fill 1
D.S. al Coda
A5
Uh.
Gtrs. 1 & 2
P.M.
Coda
Chorus
C7
F7
(Walk this way, talk this way,
Gtr. 1
Gtr. 2

C7
talk this _ way, _
F7
walk this _ way, _
C7
talk this _ way, _
10
8
F7
talk this _ way, _
C7
walk this _ way, _
F7
talk this _ way. _)
Uh, just gim-me a kiss._

Guitar Solo
Gtrs. 1 & 2: w/ Rhy. Fig. 2
N.C.(C7)
Gtr. 3
1/2
A5
Like this!
Guitar Solo
Gtrs. 1 & 2: w/ Riff B, till fade
Gtr. 3 N.C.(E5)
A5
N.C.(E5)
w/ bar
full
1 1/2
-1/2
Riff B
Gtrs. 1 & 2

Gtr. 4
(dist.)
E7
A7
mf
8va
loco
full
1/2

E7
A7
full
Begin Fade
1/2
1/4
let ring
Fade Out

Wheel in the Sky

Words and Music by Robert Fleischman, Neal Schon and Diane Valory

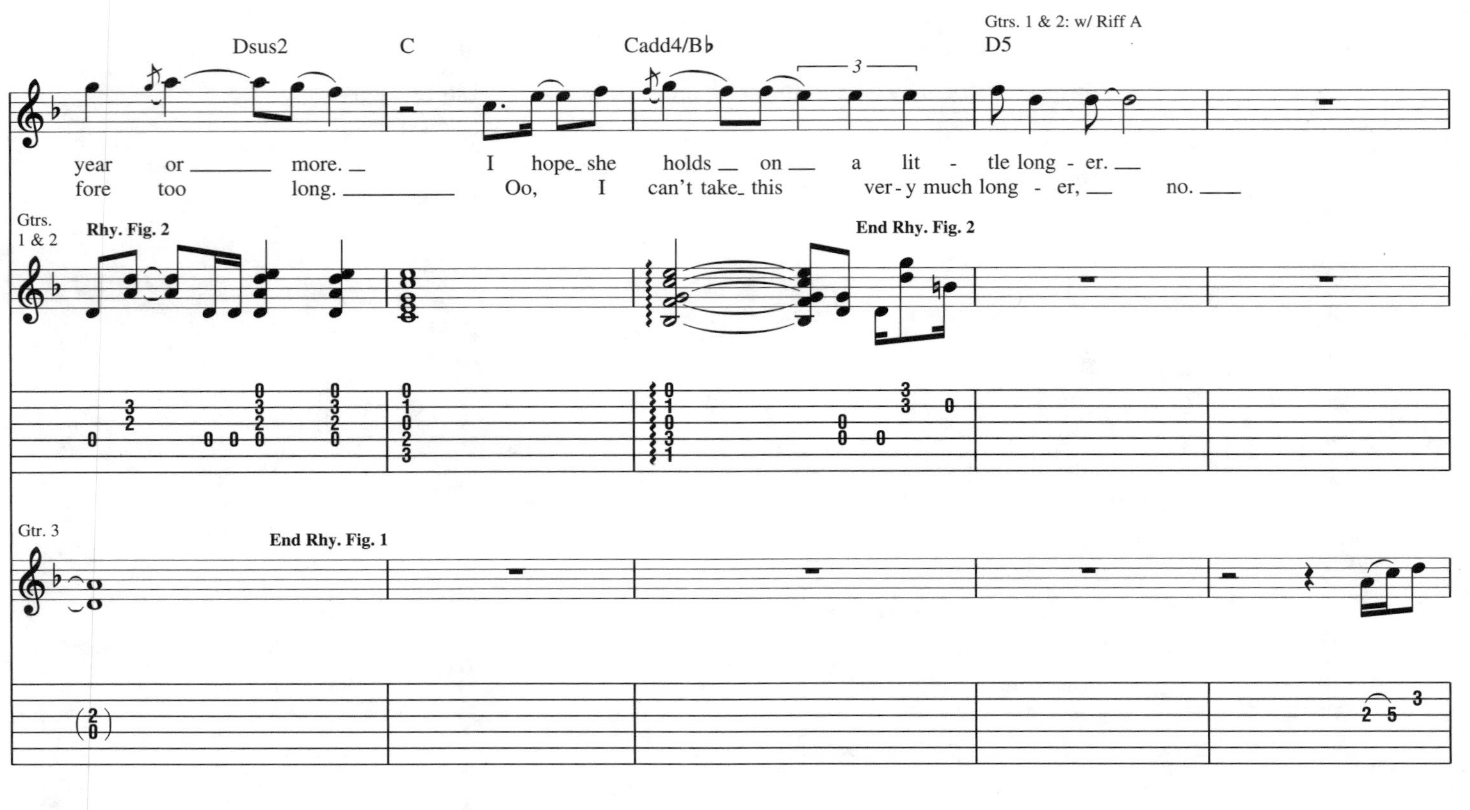
Gtrs. 1 & 2: w/ Riff A
Dsus2
C
Cadd4/B♭
D5
year or more. I hope she holds on a lit - tle long - er.
fore too long. Oo, I can't take this ver - y much long - er, no.
Gtrs. 1 & 2
Rhy. Fig. 2
End Rhy. Fig. 2
Gtr. 3
End Rhy. Fig. 1

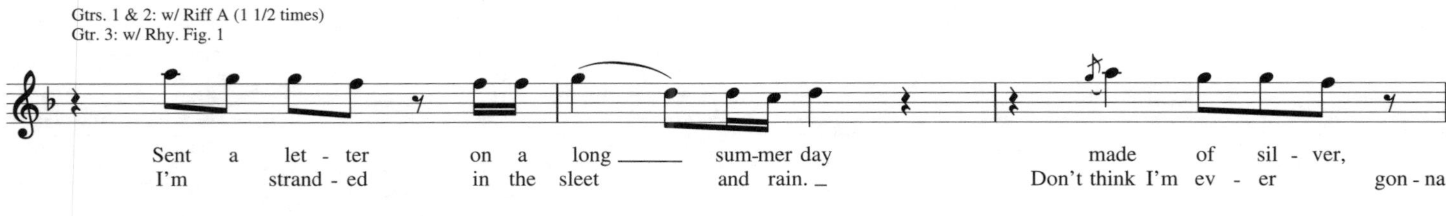
Gtrs. 1 & 2: w/ Riff A (1 1/2 times)
Gtr. 3: w/ Rhy. Fig. 1
Sent a let - ter on a long sum-mer day made of sil - ver,
I'm strand - ed in the sleet and rain. Don't think I'm ev - er gon - na

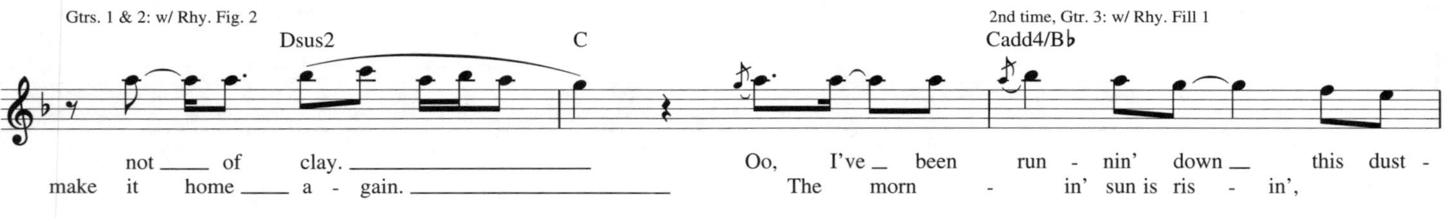
Gtrs. 1 & 2: w/ Rhy. Fig. 2
Dsus2
C
2nd time, Gtr. 3: w/ Rhy. Fill 1
Cadd4/B♭
not of clay. Oo, I've been run - nin' down this dust -
make it home a - gain. The morn - in' sun is ris - in',

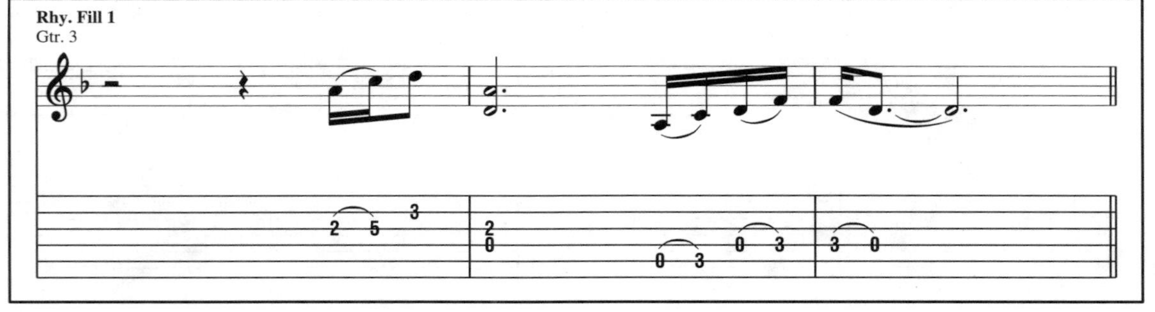
Rhy. Fill 1
Gtr. 3

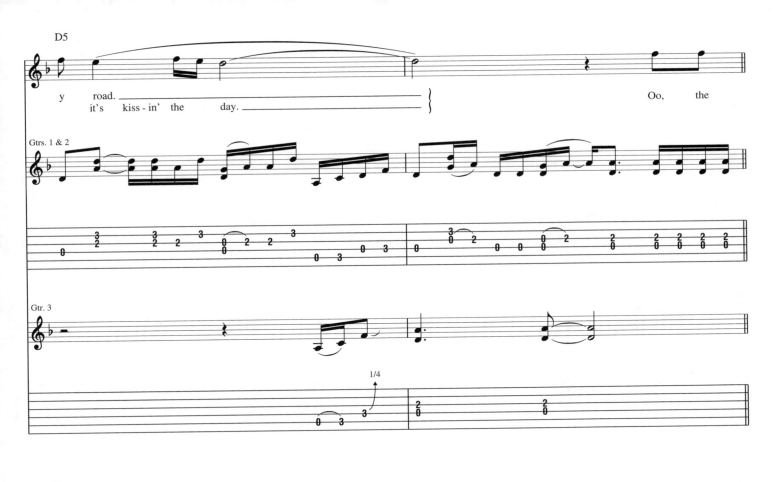

D5

y road.
it's kiss - in' the day.
Oo, the

Gtrs. 1 & 2

Gtr. 3

1/4

Chorus

* Doubled throughout

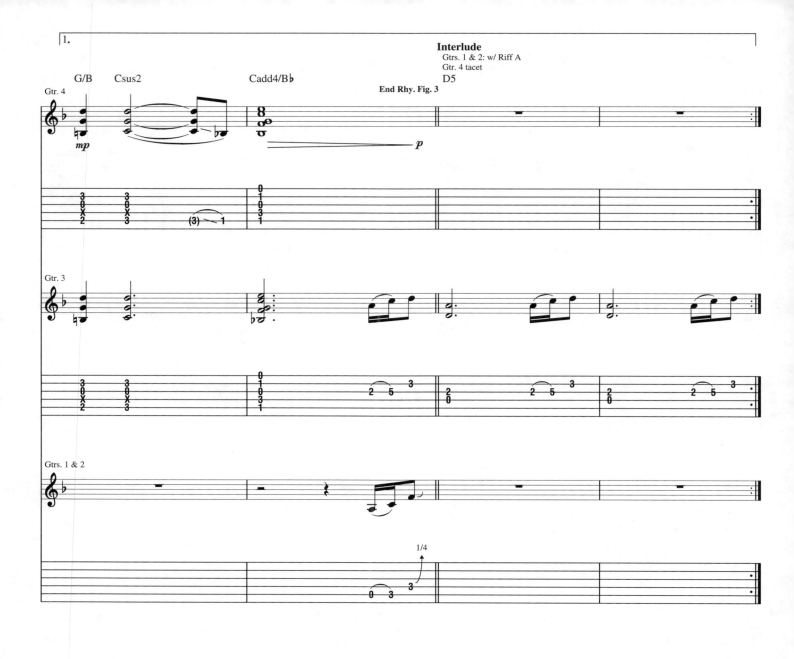

1.

Interlude

Gtrs. 1 & 2: w/ Riff A
Gtr. 4 tacet

G/B Csus2 Cadd4/B♭ D5

End Rhy. Fig. 3

Gtr. 4

mp

p

Gtr. 3

Gtrs. 1 & 2

1/4

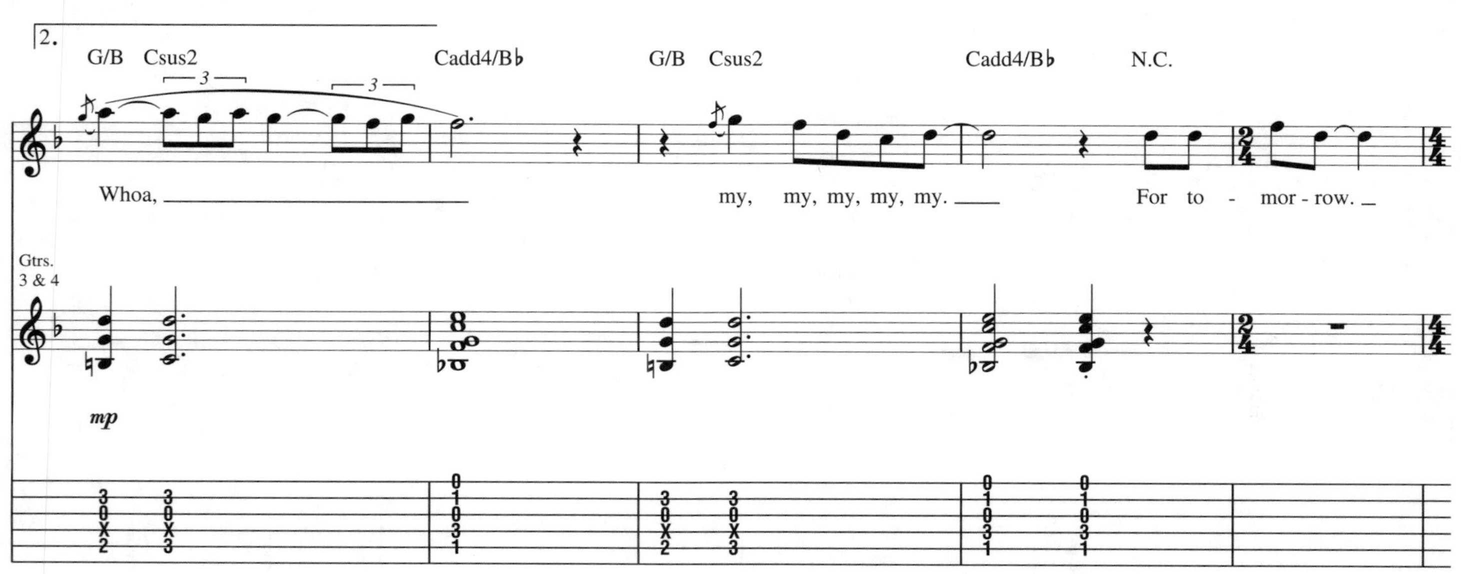

Guitar Solo

Gtr. 5 (elec.)
D5
D5
f w/ dist.
Gtr. 3
Gtr. 4 *divisi*
f
pp
Gtrs. 1 & 2
Rhy. Fig. 4

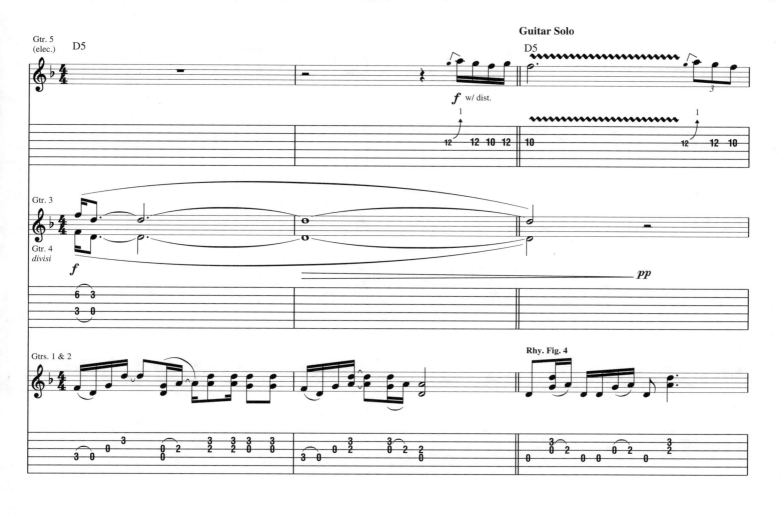

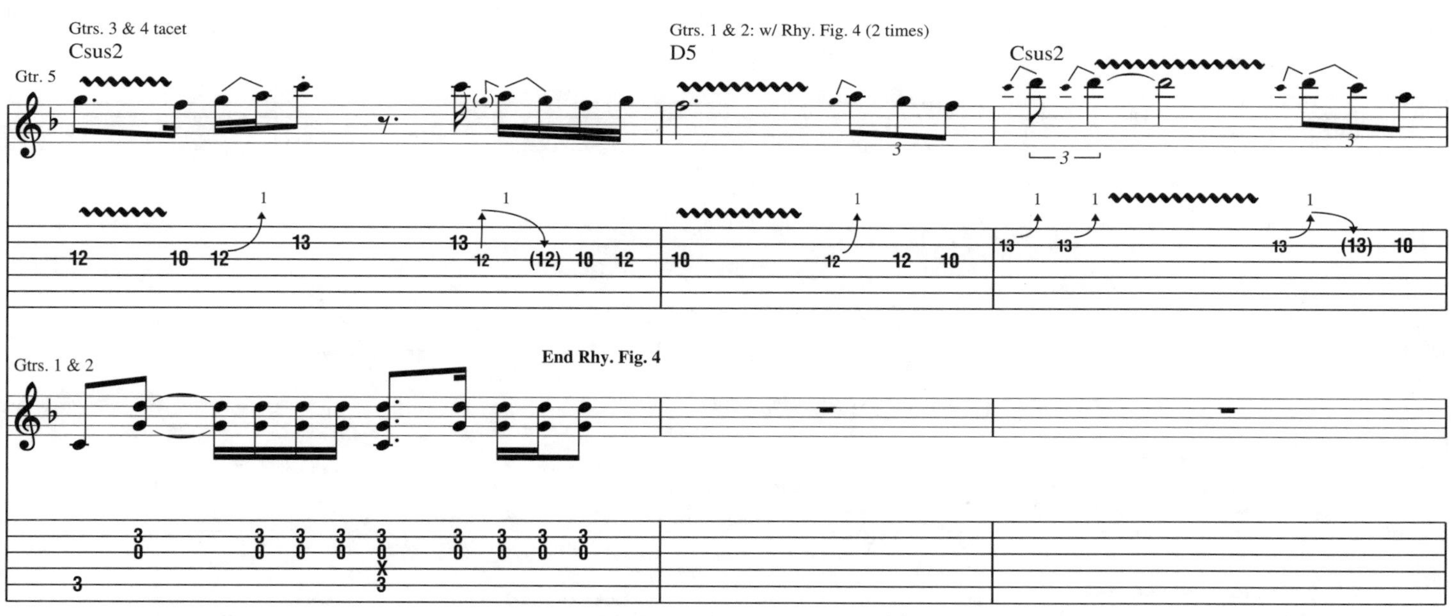

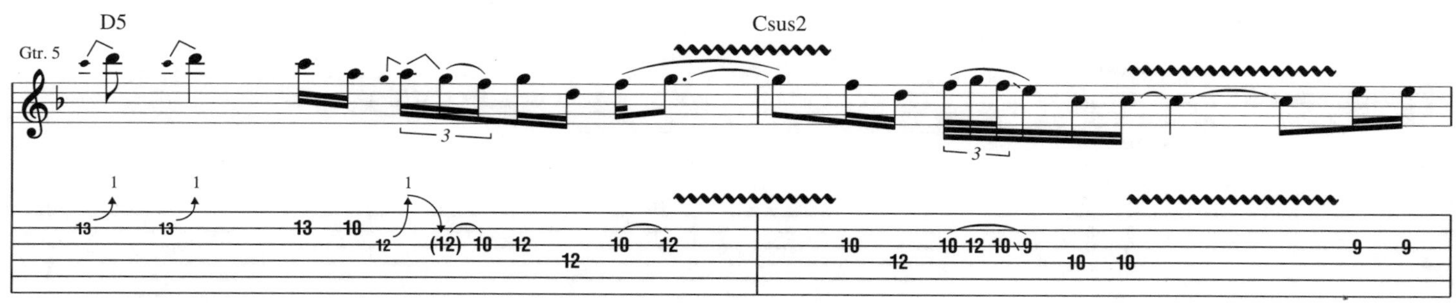

Gtr. 5
B♭6
Csus2
D5
Gtrs. 1 & 2
8va
loco
Chorus
Gtrs. 1 & 2 tacet
Gtr. 4: w/ Rhy. Fig. 3
G/B
F
C5
Oh, the wheel in the sky _ keeps on turn - in.' ___ Oo, I don't know _ where I'll be to -
mf

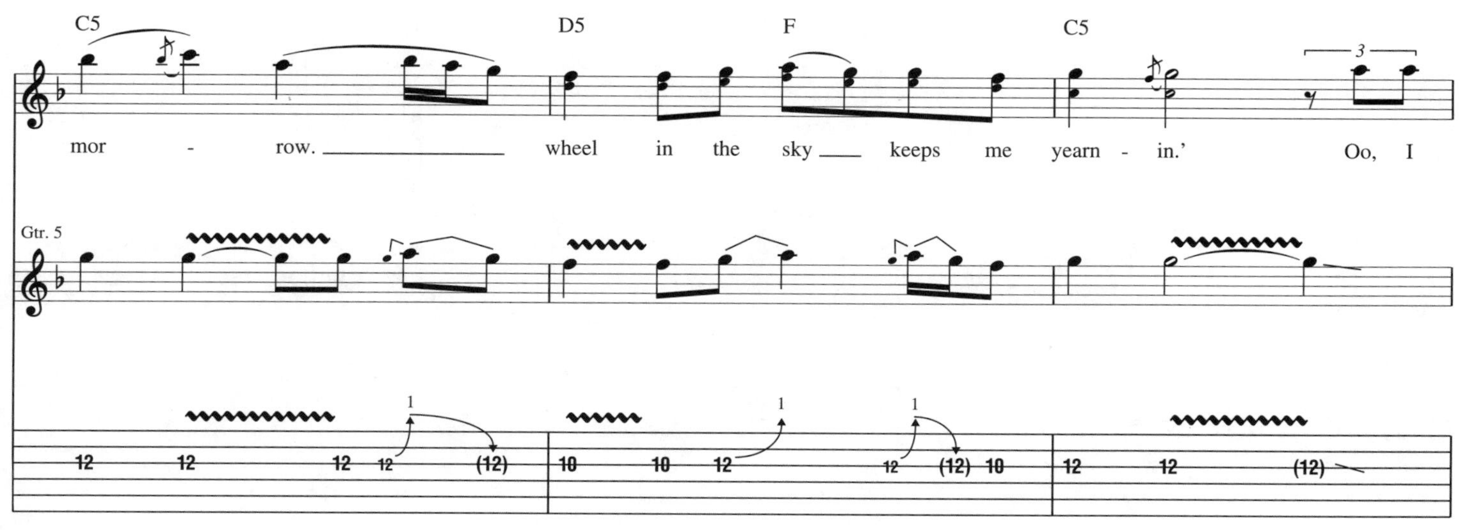

G/B Csus2 Cadd4/B♭ D5

don't know, I don't know.

Gtr. 5

f

Gtr. 3

Gtrs. 1 & 2

Outro-Chorus
Gtrs. 1 & 2 tacet
Gtr. 4: w/ Rhy. Fig. 3 (1st 4 meas., 4 times)
D5
F
C5
Oh, the wheel in the sky keeps on turn - in.' Oo, I
pp
Gtr. 3 tacet
D5
F
C5
D5
F
don't know where I'll be to - mor - row. Wheel in the sky keeps on
Gtr. 5
C5
D5
F
C5
turn - in.' Oo, I don't know I don't know, I don't know.
8va

D5 F C5
Wheel in the sky keeps on turn - in'.
8va
D5 F C5
Don't know where I'll be to - mor - row. Oo, the
8va
D5 F C5 D5 F
wheel in the sky keeps turn - in'. Wheel in the sky keeps on
loco
8va
Begin fade
Repeat and fade
C5 B♭
turn - in'.
Gtr. 5
8va
loco
Gtr. 4

You Ain't Seen Nothin' Yet

Words and Music by Randy Bachman

Gtrs. 3 & 4 tacet
G D A G D A
She took my heart a - way.
'Cause I found out for sure.
She said I've had it com - ing to me.
She took me to her doc - tor.

G D A G D
But I want-ed it that way.
And he told me I was cured.
I think that
He said that

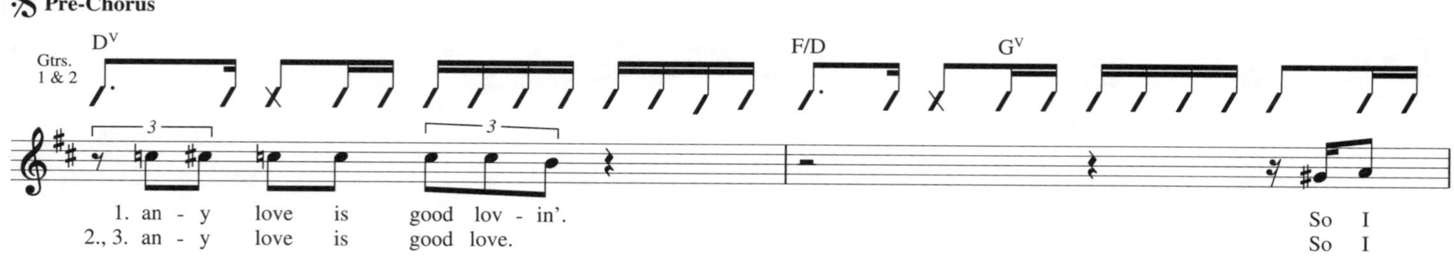

Pre-Chorus
Gtrs. 1 & 2
D F/D G
1. an - y love is good lov - in'.
2., 3. an - y love is good love.
So I
So I

A C#m7 E/F# F#m7 E/F# F#m7
took what I could get. Mmm. Ooh. Ooh.
took what I could get. Yes I took what I could get. And then she

Bm7
Gtr. 3: w/Fill 1
A/B Bm7 A/B Bm7
She looked at me with big brown eyes.
looked at me with her big brown eyes.
And said you

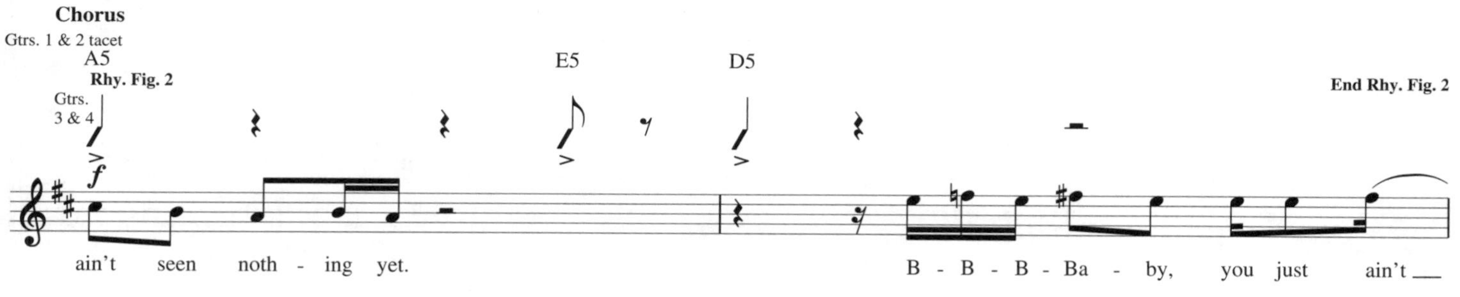

Chorus
Gtrs. 1 & 2 tacet
A5 E5 D5
Rhy. Fig. 2
Gtrs. 3 & 4
End Rhy. Fig. 2
ain't seen noth - ing yet.
B - B - B - Ba - by, you just ain't

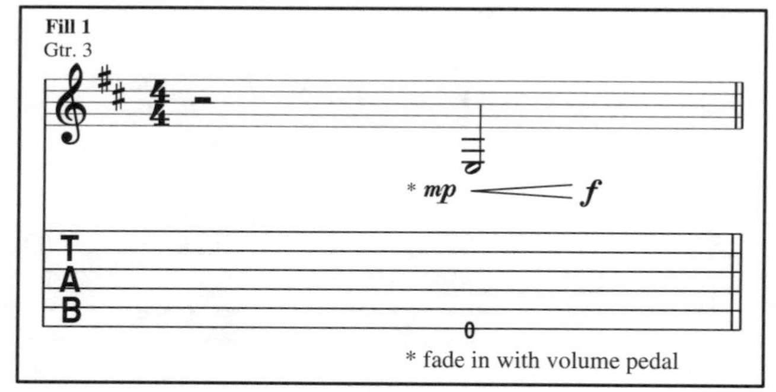

Fill 1
Gtr. 3
* mp f
T
A
B
0
* fade in with volume pedal

Gtrs. 3 & 4: w/Rhy. Fig. 2, 3 times

A5 E5 D5

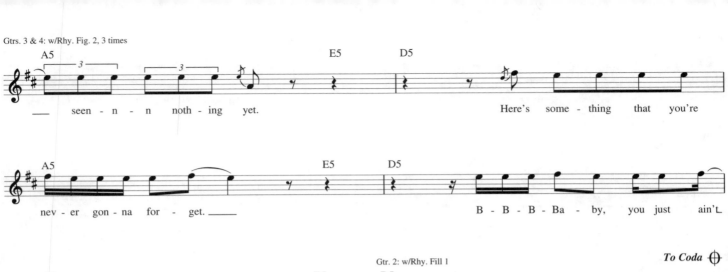

___ seen - n - n noth - ing yet. Here's some - thing that you're

A5 E5 D5

nev - er gon - na for - get. ___ B - B - B - Ba - by, you just ain't

Gtr. 2: w/Rhy. Fill 1

To Coda 𝄌

A5 E5 D5

___ seen - n - n noth - ing yet. Noth - ing yet, you ain't been a - round.
(2. *Spoken:* You need educating.)

1. **Interlude**

Gtrs. 1 & 2: w/Rhy. Figs. 1 & 1A, 2 times

Gtrs. 3 & 4

A G D A G D

mf

2. Guitar Solo
Gtrs. 1 & 2: w/Rhy. Figs. 1 & 1A, 4 times
A G D A G D
Spoken: Got-ta go to school.
Gtrs. 3 & 4
slight vib.
A G D A G D
slight vib.
A G D A G D
8va
full
A G D A G D
D.S. al Coda
8va
full
Coda
Outro
Gtrs. 3 & 4: w/Rhy. Fig. 2, 8 times
A^VII E D^V
Rhy. Fig. 3
End Rhy. Fig. 3
Gtrs. 1 & 2
Ain't seen noth-ing yet. Spoken: That's what she told me. She said I need-ed
Gtr. 5
loco
mf

Gtrs. 1 & 2: w/Rhy. Fig. 3, 7 times
A E D A E
ed - u - cat - ing. Go to school. I know I ain't seen noth-ing yet.
D A E D
I know I ain't seen noth-ing yet. Ooh, ooh, ooh.
slight vib.
A E D
Spoken: You got some-thing wait - ing for me when I get home.
slight vib.
A E D A E
It bet-ter be good. I've been eve - ry - where.
8va
slight vib.
D A E D
Fade Out
But I ain't seen noth - ing yet.
8va
slight vib.
slight vib.

You Really Got Me

Words and Music by Ray Davies

B5
so I can't sleep at night.
Girl, you real - ly
(Girl,
15ma
loco
15ma
loco
P.M.
P.H.
P.H.
P.M.
1/2
full
1/2
1/2
pitch: F♯ G F♯ F♯ G♯ B C C♯ F♯ G G♯ G♮ A
D5 D♯5
got me now, you got me so I don't know where I'm go - in', yeah.
Oh
oh
E5 D5 E5 D5 E5 D5 E5 D5 E5 D5 E5 D5
yeah, you real - ly got me now, you got me so I can't sleep at night!
yeah.
You
f
P.M.
P.M.
E D E D E D E
Oh!
Oh!
real - ly got me. You real - ly got me. You real - ly got me.)
1/2
1 1/2

Verse
D5
A5
2. Please, don't ev - er let me be, I on - ly
P.S.
let ring
slight P.M.
P.M.
wan - na be by your side.
Please, don't ev - er
15ma
loco
rake
P.H.
1 1/2
full
pitch: G♯ B G♯
let me be, I on - ly wan - na be by your side, ah!
6:4
7:4
*Continue trill while tapping & sliding above with pick hand.
**Tap 1st & 2nd stgs.
B5
D5 D♯5
Girl, you rea - ly got me now, you got me so I don't know what I'm do - in', yeah. Oh
(Girl, oh

E5 D5 E5 D5 E D E D E D E D E D E D
yeah, you real - ly got me now, got me so I can't sleep at night! Ah!
yeah. You real - ly got me. You
f
E E D E D5
Oh! Oh, no, no, ah!
real - ly got me. You real - ly got me.)
Harm.
P.S.
w/ flanger
full
*Harmonic found between second & third frets.
Guitar Solo
A G A G A G A G
full
A G A C D G
hold bend
*Vib. w/ tap hand.
A G A G A G A G
full
1 1/2

A G A F G A G A G
semi-harm.
1 1/2
1 1/2
2 1/2
full
grad. bend
full
A G A G A G A G A
dim.
1 1/2
ff
P.S.
flanger off
*Flick toggle switch between on & off pickup selection to create specified rhythm. Rhythm shown is only for the "on" position sound.
Interlude
Gtr. 1 tacet
N.C.
Ah. Ah. Ah. Ah. Ah.
(Ah, ah, ah, ah. Ah, ah. Chu, chu, chu, chu, chu, ch, ch.)
Verse
w/ ad lib vocal effects
N.C.
3. Girl, you real - ly got me now, you got me so I don't know what I'm do - in'.
Ah. Girl, you real - ly got me now, you got me so I can't sleep at night!
mf
P.H.
ff
P.S.
B5 A5 B5 A5 B5 A5 B5 A5 B5 A5 B5 A5
Girl, you real - ly got me now, you got me so I don't know where I'm go - in',
(Girl,
P.S.

B5 A5 B5 D5 D#5 E5 D5 E5 D5 E D E D
yeah. Oh yeah, you real - ly got me now, got me
oh yeah.
E D E D E D E D E D E D
so I can't sleep at night!
You real - ly got me. You real - ly got me. You
Oh!
Harm.
1 1/2
Free-Time
E D E E7#9 N.C.
rit.
Oh! Oh! Oh!
real - ly got me!)
grad. bend
full
1 1/2
3
6:4
E5
5:4
7:8
rit.
fdbk.
1 1/2
pitch: F#
A

You've Got a Friend

Words and Music by Carole King

*Symbols in parentheses represent chord names respective to capoed guitar. Symbols above reflect actual sounding chord. Capoed fret is "0" in TAB.

Bm7 (Am7) E7sus4 (D7sus4) A (G) Asus4 (Gsus4) A (G)

noth-ing, whoa, noth-ing is go - ing __ right, __

G♯m7 (F♯m7) C♯7 (B7) C♯7sus4 (B7sus4) C♯7 (B7) F♯m (Em) C♯7 (B7) F♯m7 (Em7)

close your eyes __ and think of me, and soon I will __ be there __ to

Bm7
(Am7)

C♯m7
(Bm7)

E7sus4
(D7sus4)

bright-en up e - ven your dark - est night. _ You just call_

3

| 2 4 | 3 2 | 4 | X | 2 4 | 3 2 | 4 2 | 4 |

| 6 | 5 4 | 6 | 5 4 | 6 | 6 |

| 0 | 2 4 | 2 4 | 2 3 | 4 | 2 3 |

| 5 7 | 5 | 10 | 9 | 7 | 10 7 | 10 |

Chorus

A
(G)

Amaj7
(Gmaj7)

Dmaj7
(Cmaj7)

Bm7
(Am7)

E7sus4
(D7sus4)

_____ out my ___ name, _ and you know wher-ev - er I am, ___ I'll come run -

A
(G)
Amaj7
(Gmaj7)
E7sus4
(D7sus4)

- ning, oh _ yeah, babe, _ to see you a - gain. __

A
(G)
Amaj7
(Gmaj7)
D
(C)
F#m7
(Em7)

Win-ter, spring, sum-mer or fall, __ now, all you got to do _ is __ call, __ and I'll

3

Dmaj7 (Cmaj7) C#m7 (Bm7) D/E (C/D) E7sus4 (D7sus4) A (G) D (C)

be there, yeah, yeah, yeah. You've got a friend.

Verse

A (G) G#m7 (F#m7) C#7sus4 (B7sus4) C#7 (B7) F#m (Em)

Gtr. 2 tacet

C#7 (B7) C#7/G# (B7/F#) C#7 (B7)

2. If the sky above you should turn

F#m (Em) C#7 (B7) F#m (Em) F#m7 (Em7) Bm7 (Am7) E7sus4 (D7sus4)
dark and full of clouds, and that old North wind should be-gin to blow,
Gtr. 1
A (G) Asus4 (Gsus4) A (G) G#m7 (F#m7) C#7 (B7) C#7sus4 (B7sus4) C#7 (B7)
keep your head to-geth-er and
Gtr. 2
Gtr. 1
F#m7 (Em) C#7 (B7) F#m (Em) F#m7 (Em7) Bm7 (Am7) C#m7 (Bm7)
call my name out loud, now. Soon I'll be knock-in' up-on your door.

E7sus4 (D7sus4) E (D)

Chorus

Amaj7 (Gmaj7)

You just call __ out my name __ and you know __

Dmaj7 (Cmaj7) Bm7 (Am7) E7sus4 (D7sus4) A (G) Asus4 (Gsus4) A (G)

wher-ev - er I am, __ I'll come run - ning, __ oh yes I will, to see you a - gain. __

E7sus4 (D7sus4)
A (G)
Amaj7 (Gmaj7)
Win-ter, spring, sum-mer or fall, yeah,
Dmaj7 (Cmaj7)
F♯m7 (Em7)
Dmaj7 (Cmaj7)
C♯m7 (Bm7)
Bm7 (Am7)
D/E (C/D)
E7sus4 (D7sus4)
all you got to do is call, and I'll be there, yeah, yeah, yeah. Hey, ain't
Bridge
Gtr. 2 tacet
D/G (C/F)
G (F)
D (C)
A (G)
Asus4 (Gsus4)
Amaj7 (Gmaj7)
it good to know that you've got a friend when peo-ple can be so cold? They'll
Gtr. 1

D (C) Gmaj7 (Fmaj7) F#m7 (Em7) B7 (A7) B9 (A9) B7 (A7)

hurt you and de - sert you. Well, they'll take your soul if you let them, oh yeah, but don't

Gtr. 2

6

Gtr. 1

Chorus

E7sus4 (D7sus4) E7 (D7) Amaj7 (Gmaj7)

you let them. You just call out my name, and you

(Call out my name, and you

Dmaj7 (Cmaj7) Bm7 (Am7) E7sus4 (D7sus4) A (G) Asus4 (Gsus4) A (G)

know wher-ev - er I am, I'll come run - ning to see you a - gain.
know wher-ev - er I am, I'll come run - ning.)

E7sus4 (D7sus4) A (G) Amaj7 (Gmaj7)

Oh, babe, don't you know 'bout win-ter, spring, sum-mer or fall, hey, now

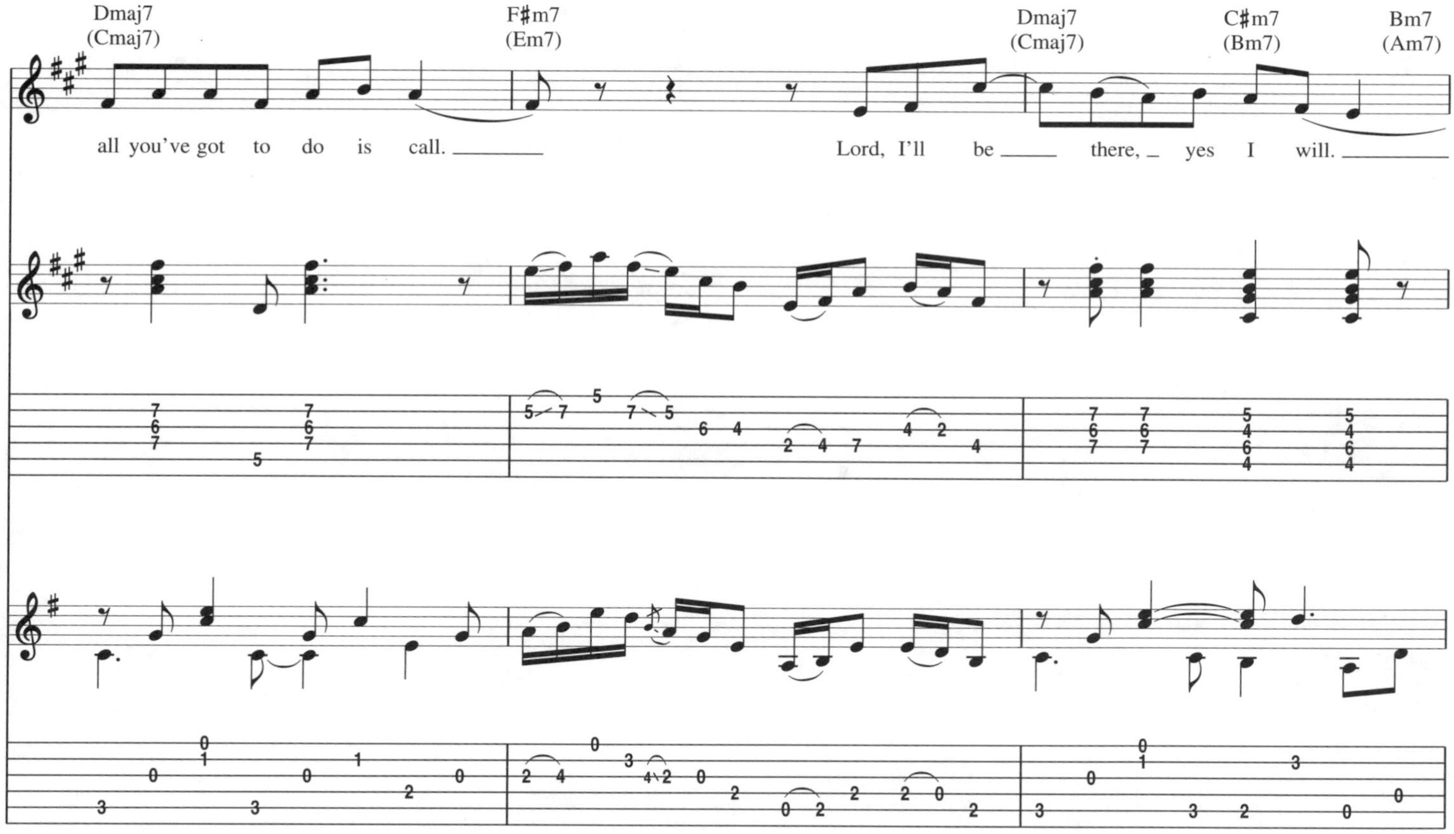

Dmaj7 (Cmaj7) F#m7 (Em7) Dmaj7 (Cmaj7) C#m7 (Bm7) Bm7 (Am7)

all you've got to do is call. Lord, I'll be there, yes I will.

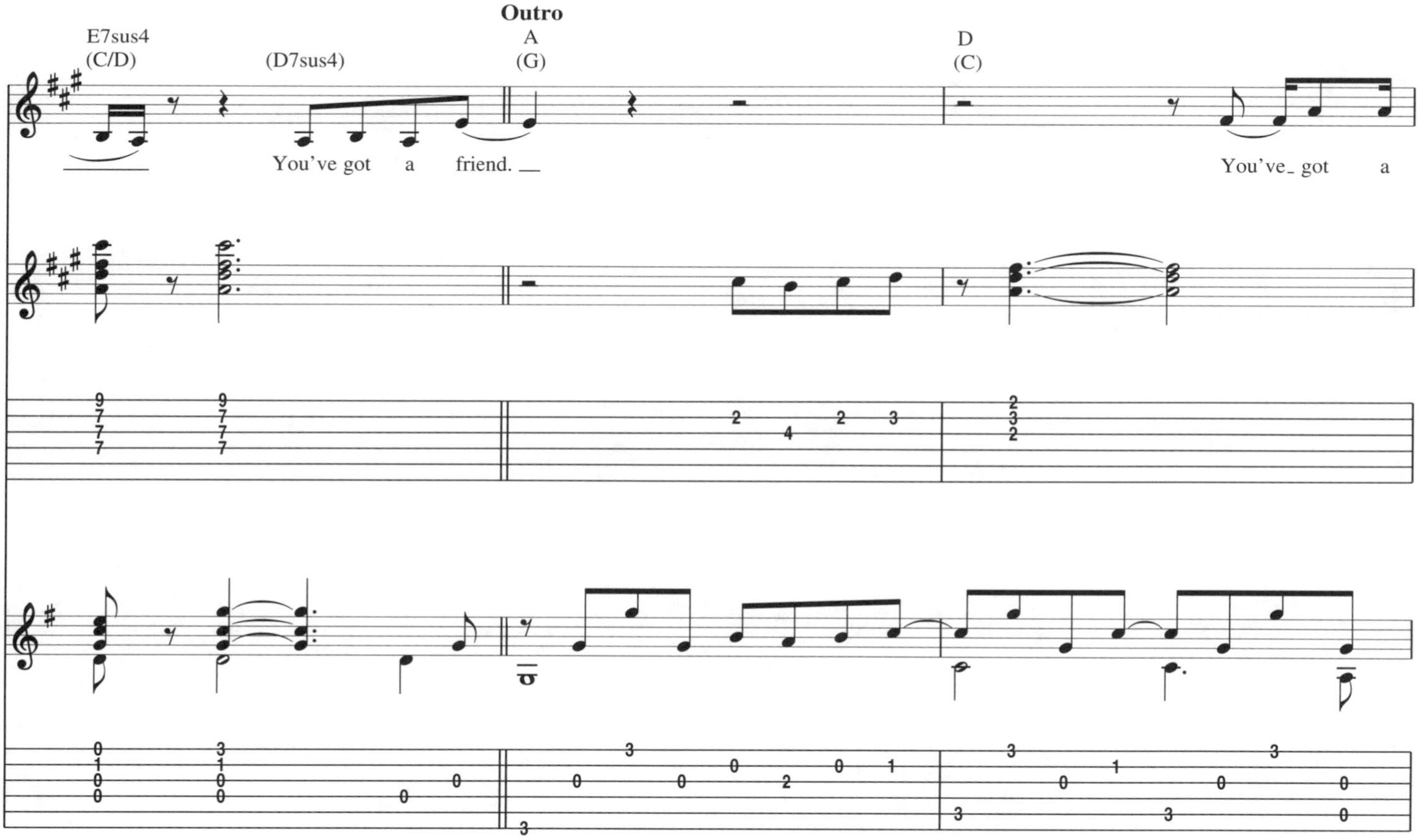

Outro

E7sus4 (C/D) (D7sus4) A (G) D (C)

You've got a friend. You've got a

A
(G)

D
(C)

A
(G)

D
(C)

friend, yeah. Ain't it good to know you've got a friend? Ain't it good to know you've got a friend?

8va

loco

8va

Harm.

Harm.

A
(G)

D
(C)

A
(G)

Oh, yeah, yeah. You've got a friend.

loco

8va

loco

Harm.

Guitar Notation Legend

Guitar Music can be notated three different ways: on a *musical staff*, in *tablature*, and in *rhythm slashes*.

RHYTHM SLASHES are written above the staff. Strum chords in the rhythm indicated. Use the chord diagrams found at the top of the first page of the transcription for the appropriate chord voicings. Round noteheads indicate single notes.

THE MUSICAL STAFF shows pitches and rhythms and is divided by bar lines into measures. Pitches are named after the first seven letters of the alphabet.

TABLATURE graphically represents the guitar fingerboard. Each horizontal line represents a a string, and each number represents a fret.

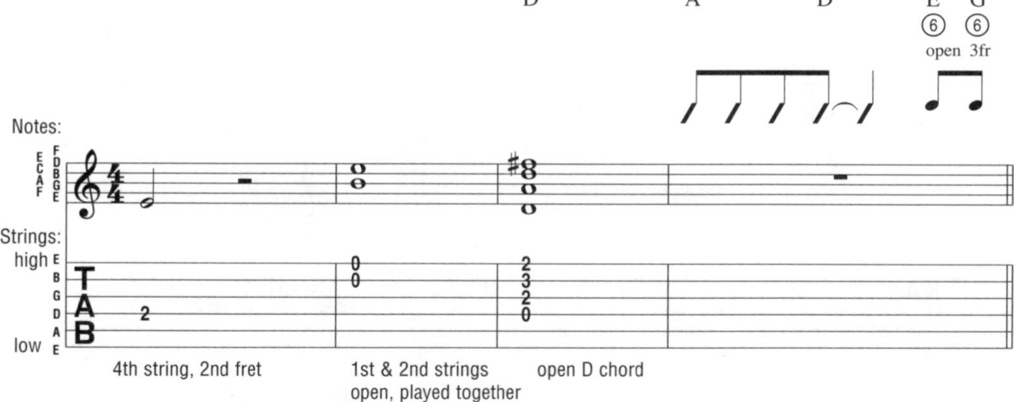

Definitions for Special Guitar Notation

HALF-STEP BEND: Strike the note and bend up 1/2 step.

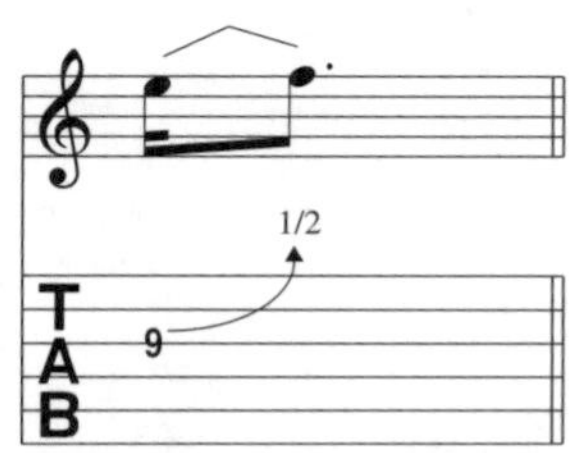

WHOLE-STEP BEND: Strike the note and bend up one step.

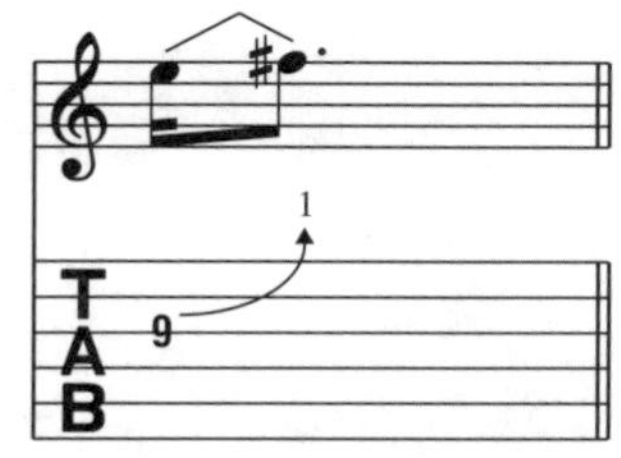

GRACE NOTE BEND: Strike the note and immediately bend up as indicated.

SLIGHT (MICROTONE) BEND: Strike the note and bend up 1/4 step.

BEND AND RELEASE: Strike the note and bend up as indicated, then release back to the original note. Only the first note is struck.

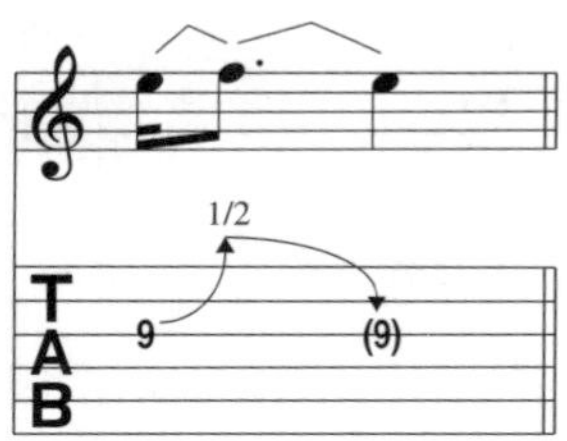

PRE-BEND: Bend the note as indicated, then strike it.

PRE-BEND AND RELEASE: Bend the note as indicated. Strike it and release the bend back to the original note.

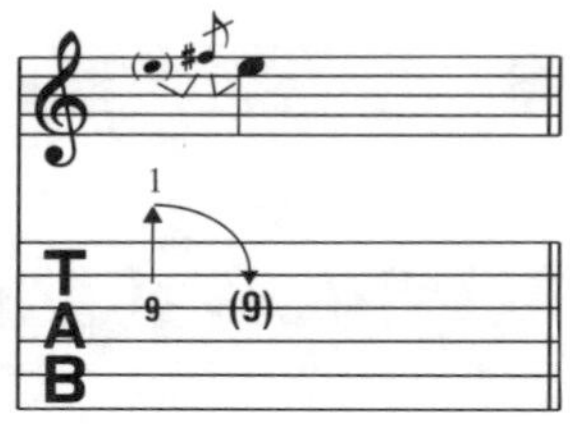

UNISON BEND: Strike the two notes simultaneously and bend the lower note up to the pitch of the higher.

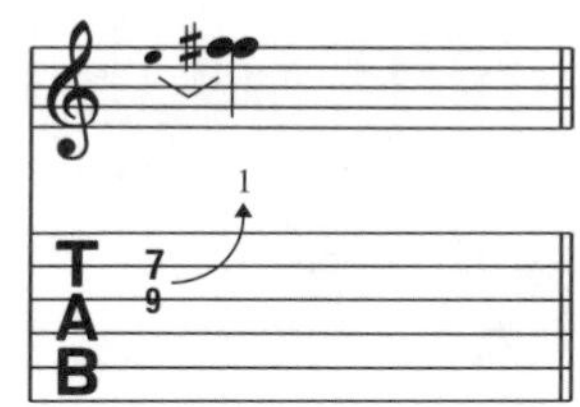

VIBRATO: The string is vibrated by rapidly bending and releasing the note with the fretting hand.

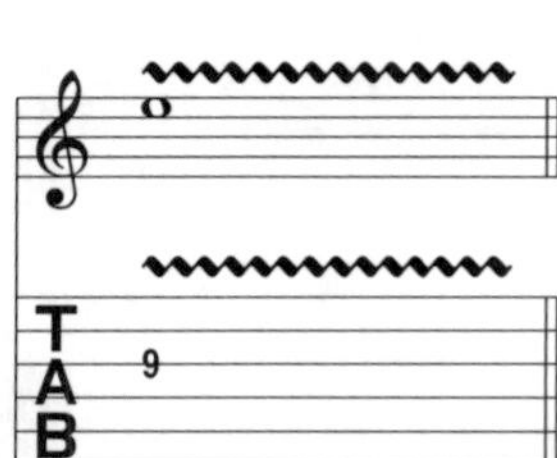

WIDE VIBRATO: The pitch is varied to a greater degree by vibrating with the fretting hand.

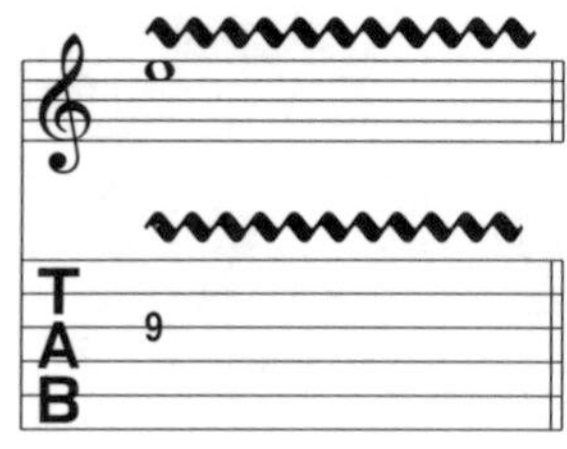

HAMMER-ON: Strike the first (lower) note with one finger, then sound the higher note (on the same string) with another finger by fretting it without picking.

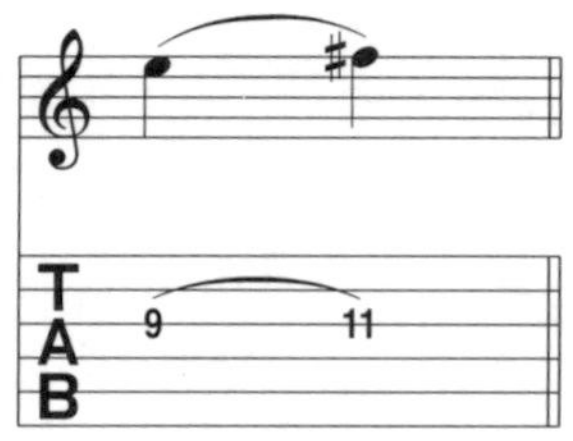

PULL-OFF: Place both fingers on the notes to be sounded. Strike the first note and without picking, pull the finger off to sound the second (lower) note.

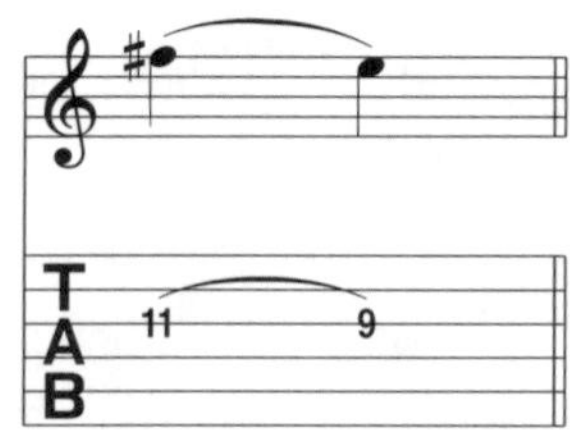

LEGATO SLIDE: Strike the first note and then slide the same fret-hand finger up or down to the second note. The second note is not struck.

SHIFT SLIDE: Same as legato slide, except the second note is struck.

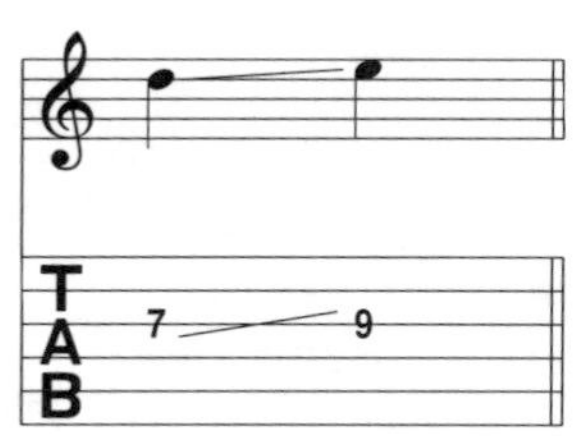

TRILL: Very rapidly alternate between the notes indicated by continuously hammering on and pulling off.

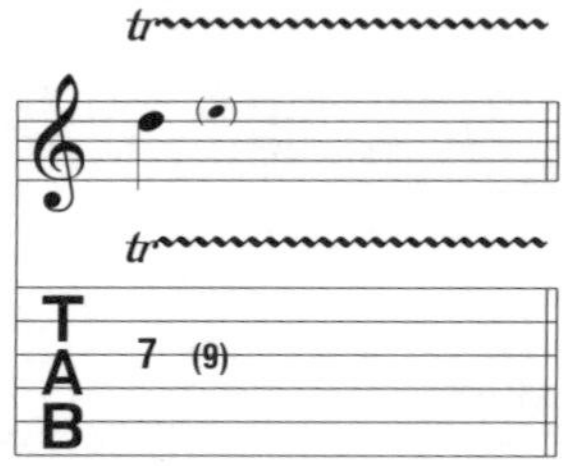

TAPPING: Hammer ("tap") the fret indicated with the pick-hand index or middle finger and pull off to the note fretted by the fret hand.

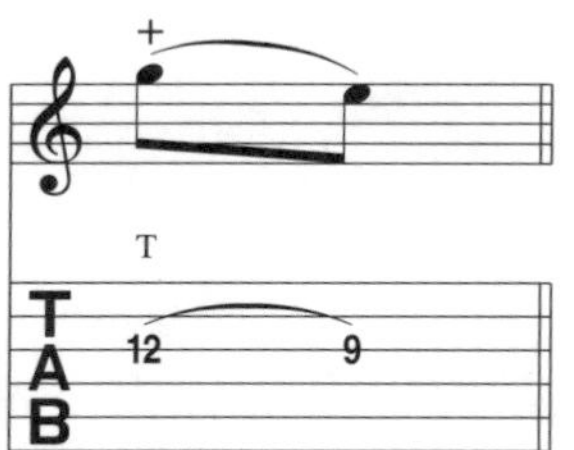

NATURAL HARMONIC: Strike the note while the fret-hand lightly touches the string directly over the fret indicated.

PINCH HARMONIC: The note is fretted normally and a harmonic is produced by adding the edge of the thumb or the tip of the index finger of the pick hand to the normal pick attack.

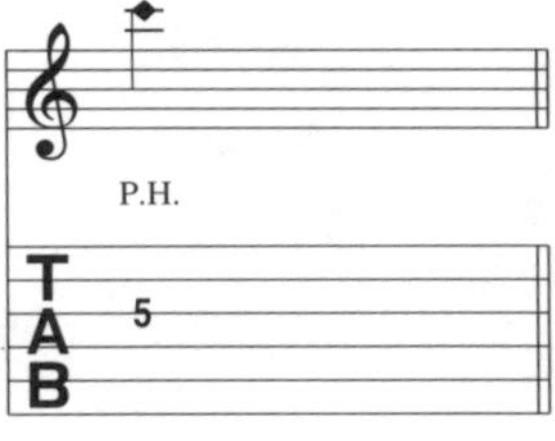

HARP HARMONIC: The note is fretted normally and a harmonic is produced by gently resting the pick hand's index finger directly above the indicated fret (in parentheses) while the pick hand's thumb or pick assists by plucking the appropriate string.

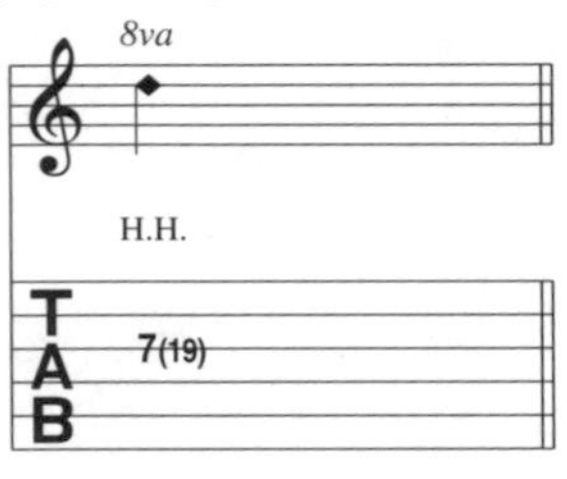

PICK SCRAPE: The edge of the pick is rubbed down (or up) the string, producing a scratchy sound.

MUFFLED STRINGS: A percussive sound is produced by laying the fret hand across the string(s) without depressing, and striking them with the pick hand.

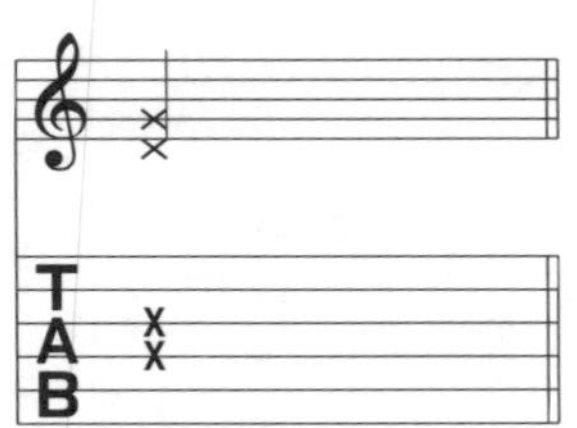

PALM MUTING: The note is partially muted by the pick hand lightly touching the string(s) just before the bridge.

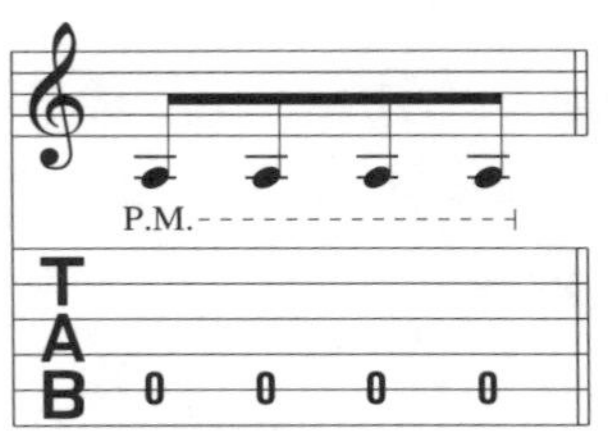

RAKE: Drag the pick across the strings indicated with a single motion.

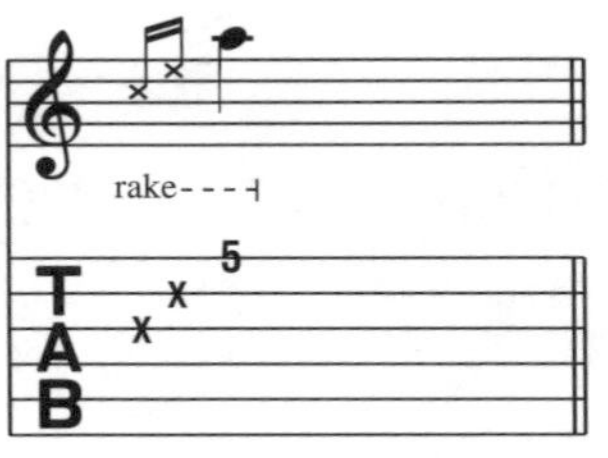

TREMOLO PICKING: The note is picked as rapidly and continuously as possible.

ARPEGGIATE: Play the notes of the chord indicated by quickly rolling them from bottom to top.

VIBRATO BAR DIVE AND RETURN: The pitch of the note or chord is dropped a specified number of steps (in rhythm) then returned to the original pitch.

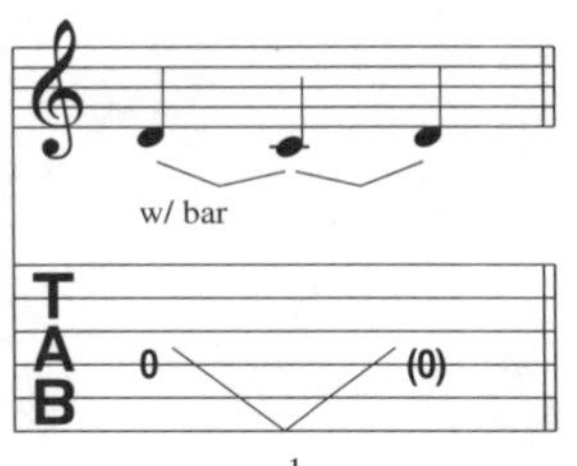

VIBRATO BAR SCOOP: Depress the bar just before striking the note, then quickly release the bar.

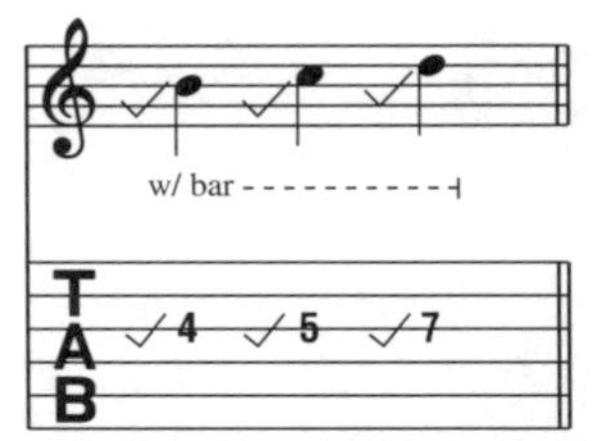

VIBRATO BAR DIP: Strike the note and then immediately drop a specified number of steps, then release back to the original pitch.

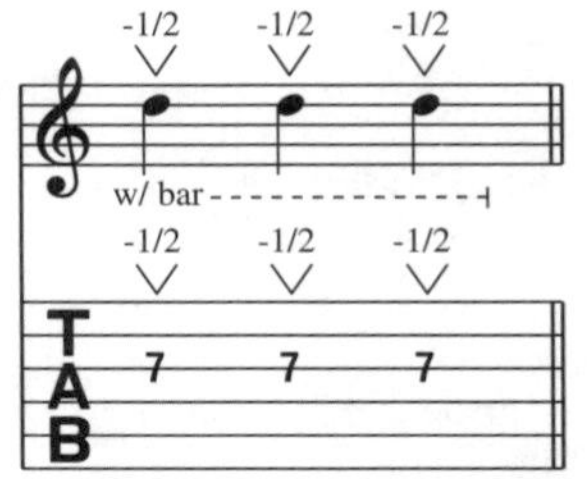

Additional Musical Definitions

(accent)	• Accentuate note (play it louder)	
(accent)	• Accentuate note with great intensity	
(staccato)	• Play the note short	
⊓	• Downstroke	
V	• Upstroke	
D.S. al Coda	• Go back to the sign (𝄋), then play until the measure marked "***To Coda,***" then skip to the section labelled "**Coda.**"	
D.C. al Fine	• Go back to the beginning of the song and play until the measure marked "***Fine***" (end).	

Rhy. Fig. • Label used to recall a recurring accompaniment pattern (usually chordal).

Riff • Label used to recall composed, melodic lines (usually single notes) which recur.

Fill • Label used to identify a brief melodic figure which is to be inserted into the arrangement.

Rhy. Fill • A chordal version of a Fill.

tacet • Instrument is silent (drops out).

• Repeat measures between signs.

• When a repeated section has different endings, play the first ending only the first time and the second ending only the second time.

NOTE: Tablature numbers in parentheses mean:
1. The note is being sustained over a system (note in standard notation is tied), or
2. The note is sustained, but a new articulation (such as a hammer-on, pull-off, slide or vibrato begins), or
3. The note is a barely audible "ghost" note (note in standard notation is also in parentheses).

THE DECADE SERIES

These collections, especially for guitarists, feature the top tunes that shaped a decade, transcribed note-for-note.

The 1950s

35 pivotal songs from the early rock years: All Shook Up • Be-Bop-a-Lula • Bo Diddley • Boppin' the Blues • Cannonball • Donna • Foggy Mountain Breakdown • Get Rhythm • Guitar Boogie Shuffle • Heartbreak Hotel • Hound Dog • I'm Lookin' for Someone to Love • I'm Movin' On • I'm Your Hoochie Coochie Man • Lonesome Town • Matchbox • Moonlight in Vermont • My Babe • Poor Little Fool • Put Your Cat Clothes On • Race With the Devil • Rebel 'Rouser • Reconsider Baby • Rock Around the Clock • Rocket '88 • Rockin' Robin • Sleepwalk • Slippin' and Slidin' • Susie-Q • Sweet Little Angel • Tequila • (They Call It) Stormy Monday (Stormy Monday Blues) • Wake Up Little Susie • The World Is Waiting for the Sunrise • Yankee Doodle Dixie

_______**00690543 Guitar Recorded Versions $14.95**

The 1960s

30 songs that defined the '60s: Badge • Blackbird • Fun, Fun, Fun • Gloria • Good Lovin' • Green Onions • Happy Together • Hello Mary Lou • Hey Joe • Hush • I Can See for Miles • I Feel Fine • I Get Around • In the Midnight Hour • Jingo (Jin-Go-Lo-Ba) • Let's Live for Today • Louie, Louie • My Girl • Oh, Pretty Woman • On the Road Again • The Promised Land • Somebody to Love • Soul Man • Suite: Judy Blue Eyes • Susie-Q • Time Is on My Side • (So) Tired of Waiting for You • Train Kept A-Rollin' • Walk Don't Run • Wild Thing

_______**00690542 Guitar Recorded Versions $14.95**

The 1970s

30 top songs from the '70s: Barracuda • Best of My Love • Blue Collar Man (Long Nights) • Breakdown • Burning Love • Dust in the Wind • Evil Woman • Freeway Jam • Godzilla • Happy • Landslide • Lay Down Sally • Let It Be • Maggie May • No Woman No Cry • Oye Como Va • Paranoid • Rock and Roll Hoochie Koo • Show Me the Way • Smoke on the Water • So Into You • Space Oddity • Stayin' Alive • Teach Your Children • Time in a Bottle • Walk This Way • Wheel in the Sky • You Ain't Seen Nothin' Yet • You Really Got Me • You've Got a Friend

_______**00690541 Guitar Recorded Versions $15.95**

The 1980s

30 songs that best represent the decade: Caught Up in You • Down Boys • 867-5309/Jenny • Every Breath You Take • Eye of the Tiger • Fight for Your Right (To Party) • Heart and Soul • Hit Me With Your Best Shot • I Love Rock 'N Roll • In and Out of Love • La Bamba • Land of Confusion • Love Struck Baby • (Bang Your Head) Metal Health • Money for Nothing • Mony, Mony • Rag Doll • Refugee • R.O.C.K. in the U.S.A. (A Salute to '60s Rock) • Rock Me • Rock You Like a Hurricane • Running on Faith • Seventeen • Start Me Up • Summer of '69 • Sweet Child O' Mine • Wait • What I Like About You • Working for the Weekend • You May Be Right

_______**00690540 Guitar Recorded Versions $15.95**

The 1990s

30 essential '90s classics: All I Wanna Do • Are You Gonna Go My Way • Barely Breathing • Blue on Black • Boot Scootin' Boogie • Building a Mystery • Bulls on Parade • Come Out and Play • Cryin' • (Everything I Do) I Do It for You • Fields of Gold • Free As a Bird • Friends in Low Places • Give Me One Reason • Hold My Hand • I Can't Dance • I'm the Only One • The Impression That I Get • Iris • Jump, Jive an' Wail • More Than Words • Santa Monica • Semi-Charmed Life • Silent Lucidity • Smells Like Teen Spirit • Smooth • Tears in Heaven • Two Princes • Under the Bridge • Wonderwall

_______**00690539 Guitar Recorded Versions $15.95**

FOR MORE INFORMATION, SEE YOUR LOCAL MUSIC DEALER,
OR WRITE TO:

7777 W. BLUEMOUND RD. P.O. BOX 13819 MILWAUKEE, WI 53213

Prices, contents and availability subject to change without notice.

www.halleonard.com

RECORDED VERSIONS

The Best Note-For-Note Transcriptions Available

RECORDED VERSIONS GUITAR ®

ALL BOOKS INCLUDE TABLATURE

00690016 Will Ackerman Collection $19.95
00690146 Aerosmith – Toys in the Attic $19.95
00694865 Alice In Chains – Dirt $19.95
00694932 Allman Brothers Band – Volume 1 ......$24.95
00694933 Allman Brothers Band – Volume 2 ......$24.95
00694934 Allman Brothers Band – Volume 3 ......$24.95
00694877 Chet Atkins – Guitars For All Seasons $19.95
00690418 Best of Audio Adrenaline $17.95
00694918 Randy Bachman Collection $22.95
00690366 Bad Company Original Anthology - Bk 1 ..$19.95
00690367 Bad Company Original Anthology - Bk 2 ..$19.95
00694880 Beatles – Abbey Road $19.95
00694863 Beatles – Sgt. Pepper's Lonely Hearts Club Band ..$19.95
00690383 Beatles – Yellow Submarine $19.95
00690174 Beck – Mellow Gold $17.95
00690346 Beck – Mutations $19.95
00690175 Beck – Odelay $17.95
00694884 The Best of George Benson $19.95
00692385 Chuck Berry $19.95
00692200 Black Sabbath – We Sold Our Soul For Rock 'N' Roll $19.95
00690115 Blind Melon – Soup $19.95
00690305 Blink 182 – Dude Ranch $19.95
00690028 Blue Oyster Cult – Cult Classics $19.95
00690219 Blur $19.95
00690168 Roy Buchanon Collection $19.95
00690364 Cake – Songbook $19.95
00690337 Jerry Cantrell – Boggy Depot $19.95
00690293 Best of Steven Curtis Chapman $19.95
00690043 Cheap Trick – Best Of $19.95
00690171 Chicago – Definitive Guitar Collection $22.95
00690415 Clapton Chronicles – Best of Eric Clapton .$17.95
00690393 Eric Clapton – Selections from Blues $19.95
00660139 Eric Clapton – Journeyman $19.95
00694869 Eric Clapton – Live Acoustic $19.95
00694896 John Mayall/Eric Clapton – Bluesbreakers $19.95
00690162 Best of the Clash $19.95
00690166 Albert Collins – The Alligator Years $16.95
00694940 Counting Crows – August & Everything After $19.95
00690197 Counting Crows – Recovering the Satellites .$19.95
00694840 Cream – Disraeli Gears $19.95
00690401 Creed – Human Clay $19.95
00690352 Creed – My Own Prison $19.95
00690184 dc Talk – Jesus Freak $19.95
00690333 dc Talk – Supernatural $19.95
00660186 Alex De Grassi Guitar Collection $19.95
00690289 Best of Deep Purple $17.95
00694831 Derek And The Dominos – Layla & Other Assorted Love Songs $19.95
00690322 Ani Di Franco – Little Plastic Castle $19.95
00690187 Dire Straits – Brothers In Arms $19.95
00690191 Dire Straits – Money For Nothing $24.95
00695382 The Very Best of Dire Straits – Sultans of Swing $19.95
00660178 Willie Dixon – Master Blues Composer ...$24.95
00690250 Best of Duane Eddy $16.95
00690349 Eve 6 ....$19.95
00313164 Eve 6 – Horrorscope $19.95
00690323 Fastball – All the Pain Money Can Buy $19.95
00690089 Foo Fighters $19.95
00690235 Foo Fighters – The Colour and the Shape .$19.95
00690394 Foo Fighters – There Is Nothing Left to Lose $19.95
00690222 G3 Live – Satriani, Vai, Johnson $22.95
00694807 Danny Gatton – 88 Elmira St $19.95
00690438 Genesis Guitar Anthology $19.95
00690127 Goo Goo Dolls – A Boy Named Goo $19.95
00690338 Goo Goo Dolls – Dizzy Up the Girl $19.95
00690117 John Gorka Collection $19.95
00690114 Buddy Guy Collection Vol. A-J $22.95
00690193 Buddy Guy Collection Vol. L-Y $22.95
00694798 George Harrison Anthology $19.95
00690068 Return Of The Hellecasters $19.95
00692930 Jimi Hendrix – Are You Experienced? $24.95
00692931 Jimi Hendrix – Axis: Bold As Love $22.95
00692932 Jimi Hendrix – Electric Ladyland $24.95
00690218 Jimi Hendrix – First Rays of the New Rising Sun $27.95
00690038 Gary Hoey – Best Of $19.95
00660029 Buddy Holly $19.95
00660169 John Lee Hooker – A Blues Legend $19.95
00690054 Hootie & The Blowfish – Cracked Rear View $19.95
00694905 Howlin' Wolf $19.95
00690136 Indigo Girls – 1200 Curfews $22.95
00694938 Elmore James – Master Electric Slide Guitar $19.95
00690167 Skip James Blues Guitar Collection $16.95
00694833 Billy Joel For Guitar $19.95
00694912 Eric Johnson – Ah Via Musicom $19.95
00690169 Eric Johnson – Venus Isle $22.95
00694799 Robert Johnson – At The Crossroads $19.95
00693185 Judas Priest – Vintage Hits $19.95
00690277 Best of Kansas $19.95
00690073 B. B. King – 1950-1957 ....$24.95
00690098 B. B. King – 1958-1967 ....$24.95
00690444 B.B. King and Eric Clapton – Riding with the King $19.95
00690134 Freddie King Collection $17.95
00690157 Kiss – Alive $19.95
00690163 Mark Knopfler/Chet Atkins – Neck and Neck $19.95
00690296 Patty Larkin Songbook $17.95
00690018 Living Colour – Best Of $19.95
00694845 Yngwie Malmsteen – Fire And Ice $19.95
00694956 Bob Marley – Legend $19.95
00690283 Best of Sarah McLachlan $19.95
00690382 Sarah McLachlan – Mirrorball $19.95
00690354 Sarah McLachlan – Surfacing $19.95
00690442 Matchbox 20 – Mad Season $19.95
00690239 Matchbox 20 – Yourself or Someone Like You .$19.95
00690244 Megadeath – Cryptic Writings $19.95
00690236 Mighty Mighty Bosstones – Let's Face It ...$19.95
00690040 Steve Miller Band Greatest Hits $19.95
00694802 Gary Moore – Still Got The Blues $19.95
00694958 Mountain, Best Of $19.95
00690448 MxPx – The Ever Passing Moment $19.95
00694913 Nirvana – In Utero $19.95
00694883 Nirvana – Nevermind $19.95
00690026 Nirvana – Acoustic In New York $19.95
00690121 Oasis – (What's The Story) Morning Glory .$19.95
00690204 Offspring, The – Ixnay on the Hombre $17.95
00690203 Offspring, The – Smash $17.95
00694830 Ozzy Osbourne – No More Tears $19.95
00694855 Pearl Jam – Ten $19.95
00690053 Liz Phair – Whip Smart $19.95
00690176 Phish – Billy Breathes $22.95
00690424 Phish – Farmhouse $19.95
00690331 Phish – The Story of Ghost $19.95
00690428 Pink Floyd – Dark Side of the Moon $19.95
00693800 Pink Floyd – Early Classics $19.95
00690456 P.O.D. – The Fundamental Elements of Southtown $19.95
00694967 Police – Message In A Box Boxed Set $70.00
00694974 Queen – A Night At The Opera $19.95
00690395 Rage Against The Machine – The Battle of Los Angeles $1
00690145 Rage Against The Machine – Evil Empire . .$1
00690179 Rancid – And Out Come the Wolves $2
00690055 Red Hot Chili Peppers – Bloodsugarsexmagik $1
00690379 Red Hot Chili Peppers – Californication ..$1
00690090 Red Hot Chili Peppers – One Hot Minute .$2
00694937 Jimmy Reed – Master Bluesman $1
00694899 R.E.M. – Automatic For The People $1
00690260 Jimmie Rodgers Guitar Collection $1
00690014 Rolling Stones – Exile On Main Street ...$2
00690186 Rolling Stones – Rock & Roll Circus $1
00690135 Otis Rush Collection $1
00690031 Santana's Greatest Hits $1
00690150 Son Seals – Bad Axe Blues $1
00690128 Seven Mary Three – American Standards .$1
00120105 Kenny Wayne Shepherd – Ledbetter Heights $1
00120123 Kenny Wayne Shepherd – Trouble Is $1
00690196 Silverchair – Freak Show $1
00690130 Silverchair – Frogstomp $1
00690041 Smithereens – Best Of $1
00690385 Sonicflood $1
00694885 Spin Doctors – Pocket Full Of Kryptonite .$1
00694921 Steppenwolf, The Best Of $2
00694957 Rod Stewart – Acoustic Live $2
00690021 Sting – Fields Of Gold $1
00690242 Suede – Coming Up $1
00694824 Best Of James Taylor $1
00690238 Third Eye Blind $1
00690403 Third Eye Blind – Blue $1
00690267 311 ....$1
00690030 Toad The Wet Sprocket $1
00690228 Tonic – Lemon Parade $1
00690295 Tool – Aenima $1
00690039 Steve Vai – Alien Love Secrets $2
00690172 Steve Vai – Fire Garden $2
00690023 Jimmie Vaughan – Strange Pleasures $1
00690370 Stevie Ray Vaughan and Double Trouble – The Real Deal: Greatest Hits Volume 2 ...$2
00690455 Stevie Ray Vaughan – Blues at Sunrise $1
00660136 Stevie Ray Vaughan – In Step $1
00690417 Stevie Ray Vaughan – Live at Carnegie Hall $1
00694835 Stevie Ray Vaughan – The Sky Is Crying ..$1
00694776 Vaughan Brothers – Family Style $1
00120026 Joe Walsh – Look What I Did... ....$2
00694789 Muddy Waters – Deep Blues $2
00690071 Weezer $1
00690286 Weezer – Pinkerton $1
00690447 Who, The – Best of $2
00694970 Who, The – Definitive Collection A-E $2
00694971 Who, The – Definitive Collection F-Li $2
00694972 Who, The – Definitive Collection Lo-R $2
00694973 Who, The – Definitive Collection S-Y $2
00690319 Stevie Wonder Hits $1

Prices and availability subject to change without notice. Some products may not be available outside the U.S.A.

FOR A COMPLETE LIST OF GUITAR RECORDED VERSIONS TITLES, SEE YOUR LOCAL MUSIC DEALER, OR WRITE TO:

HAL•LEONARD CORPORATION

7777 W. BLUEMOUND RD. P.O. BOX 13819 MILWAUKEE, WI 53213

Visit Hal Leonard online at **www.halleonard.com** 04

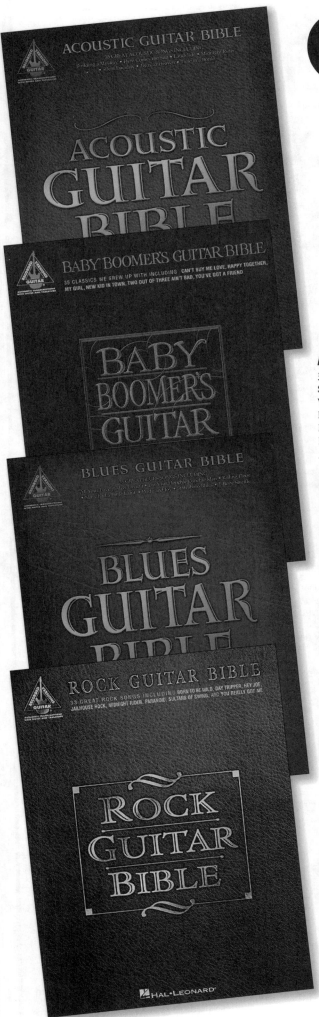

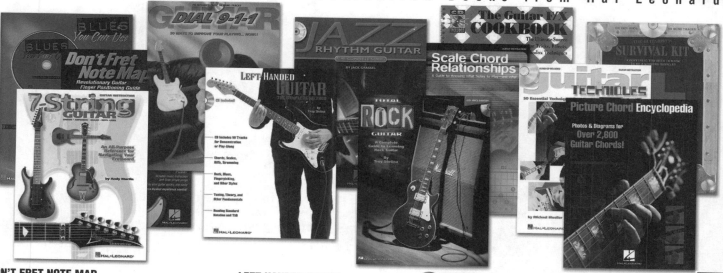